IMAGES
of America

HISTORIC OAKWOOD CEMETERY

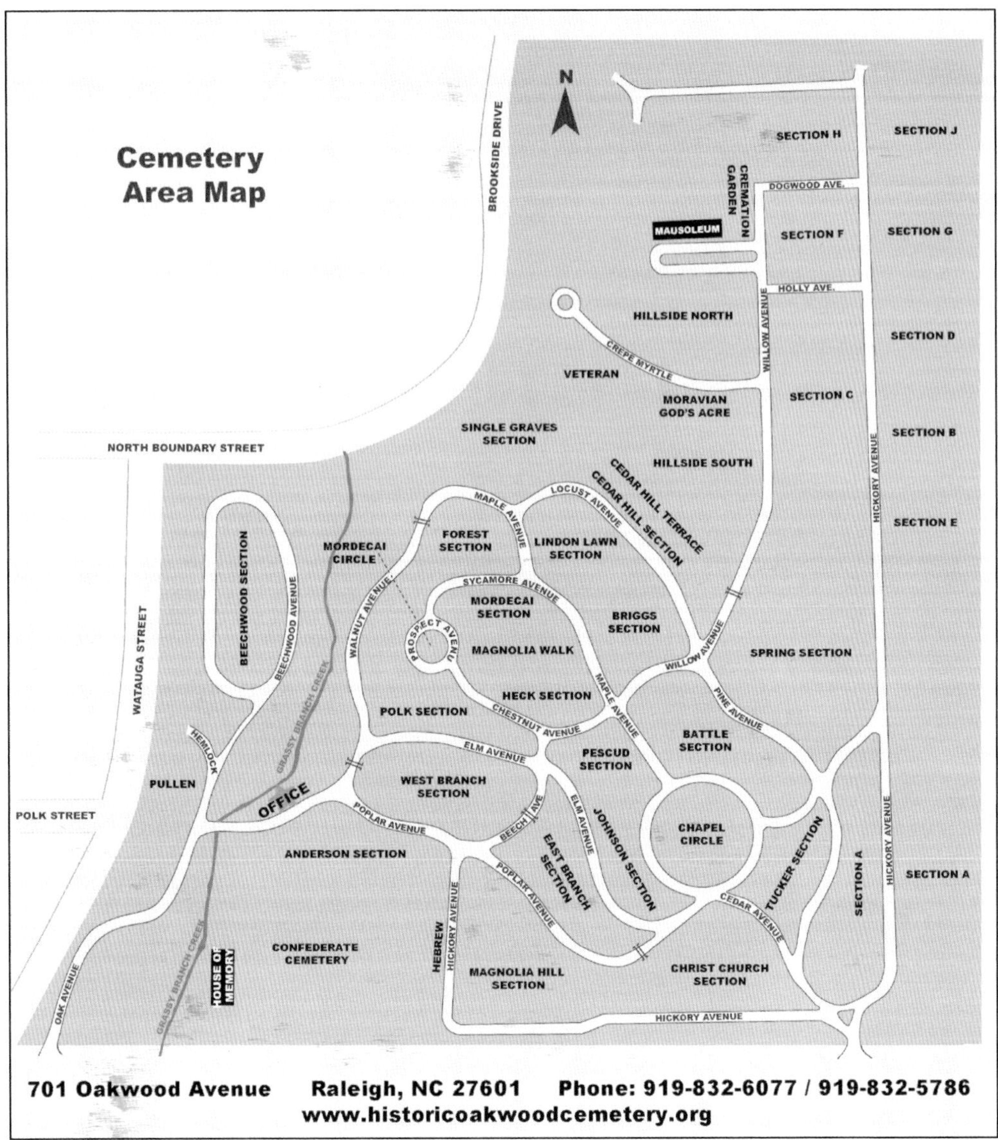

This current map of Oakwood Cemetery shows the street and section plan. Locations of interments mentioned in the book may be found in the index, listed by cemetery section. (Historic Oakwood Cemetery archives.)

On the Cover: The Historic Oakwood Second Line Band is pictured at the cemetery's main gate. (Ian F.G. Dunn.)

IMAGES
of America

Historic Oakwood Cemetery

Bruce Miller and Robin Simonton

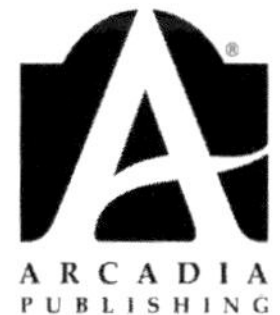

ISBN 978-1-4671-2658-8

Published by Arcadia Publishing
Charleston, South Carolina

Printed in the United States of America

Library of Congress Control Number: 2017942082

For all general information, please contact Arcadia Publishing:
Telephone 843-853-2070
Fax 843-853-0044
E-mail sales@arcadiapublishing.com
For customer service and orders:
Toll-Free 1-888-313-2665

Visit us on the Internet at www.arcadiapublishing.com

To those who, for the past century and a half, have cherished and preserved this very special place.

Contents

Acknowledgments		6
Introduction		7
1.	Breaking Ground	9
2.	Oakwood Cemetery, "Sleeping Place among the Oaks"	21
3.	Men and Women at Arms	33
4.	Politicos	47
5.	Company Men and Women	61
6.	Academics	67
7.	Great Romances	79
8.	Their Stories	89
9.	Symbols in Stone	107
10.	A Cemetery Full of Life	119
Index		126

Acknowledgments

Contributors who made this book possible include cemetery office volunteers Charlene Stell and Jorja Frazier, whose hours spent proofing and editing the text saved the authors major embarrassment; grounds superintendent Sam Smith and foreman Charles Batts; Kim Anderson, Karl Larson, and Ian Dunn of the Audio Visual Materials Unit, Special Collections Section, State Archives of North Carolina, who suggested and searched for many of the historical images in this book; the research staff of the State Library of North Carolina; the trustees of the Raleigh Cemetery Association; and individual families who provided photographs and information on many family members whose stories are included here.

A special thank-you goes to volunteer photographer in residence Michael Palko, who patiently walked the rows and braved the weather to supplement historical cemetery photographs with contemporary tombstone images.

Key to photograph credits:
Adolph Oettinger Goodwin's 1916 *Who's Who in Raleigh* (Goodwin)
Historic Oakwood Cemetery archives (HOC)
Michael Palko (Palko)
North Carolina Collection Photographic Archives, Louis Round Wilson Special Collections Library, University of North Carolina at Chapel Hill (NCCUNCLCH)
State Archives of North Carolina (SANC)
Valvano/Charles photograph, page 72—Athletics, Media Relations Records, UA 015.010, item #ua015_010-004-bx0092-002-001, Special Collections Research Center, NCSU Libraries (NCSU)

Other credits are as noted with individual photographs.

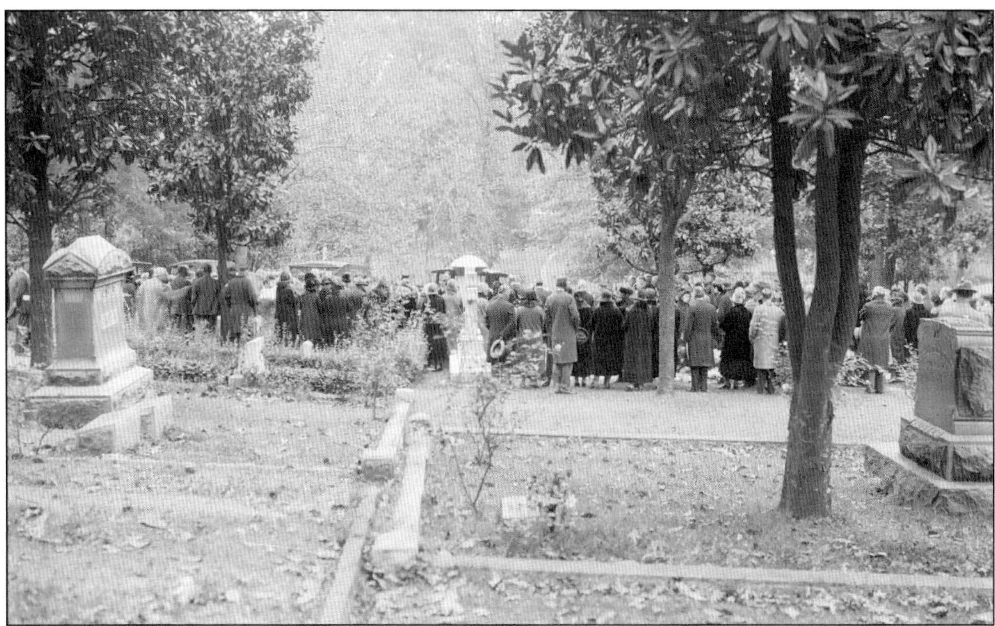

Mourners are pictured at Oakwood Cemetery in the 1920s. (SANC.)

INTRODUCTION

British prime minister William Ewart Gladstone is said to have observed, "Show me the manner in which a nation or community cares for its dead and I will measure with mathematical exactness the tender mercies of its people."

With that as his criterion, Gladstone would have been impressed by the "tender mercies" of the people of Raleigh, North Carolina's capital founded in the geographic center of the state in 1792. Six years later, the North Carolina General Assembly meeting in the new statehouse called for a small, public cemetery to be laid out on the eastern edge of the city. As the only formal burial ground in Raleigh for over 60 years, this City Cemetery holds the remains of many of the capital's earliest residents, many of them important to both city and state. Not on a river and geographically isolated in its early years, Raleigh grew slowly—only 5,000 residents lived here when William Tecumseh Sherman's Union army occupied the city in April 1865. City Cemetery fully met the needs of that thin populace, white and black. (It was not until after the Civil War that separate cemeteries for African Americans were established—one south of town named Mount Hope, and the other in Oberlin, a nearby village settled by newly emancipated slaves.) The coming of the Civil War, however, would challenge those "tender mercies," for while some 35 Confederate soldiers lie in City Cemetery, that was but a fraction of those needing burial space during and after that bloody conflict.

Raleigh was a "hospital town" during the war: three hospitals nursed thousands of wounded Confederate soldiers. Alas, many could not be saved, and perhaps 500 of these were interred in a small cemetery to the east of town, not in City Cemetery. When the Union army occupied Raleigh, it took control of not only the hospitals but also that outlying cemetery and began burying its dead among Confederate remains. Raleigh citizens thought that an affront to the honor of their own dead; in response, women of the city organized a Ladies Memorial Association (LMA), obtained land for a new cemetery, and moved the remains of Southern soldiers there in 1867. That original site confiscated by occupiers would become Raleigh National Cemetery, one of the early ones founded during and after the Civil War for Federal dead—but not for Confederates. As a result of such "tender mercies," now tinged with patriotism by both sides, many Civil War remains will be forever divided in separate burial grounds: Union-Confederate, Blue-Gray, North-South.

The new Confederate Cemetery prompted what soon would become Oakwood Cemetery—a story told in this book—and through the years Oakwood Cemetery came to reflect the postwar development of the capital city. That Raleigh would be a political town was a given, but what of its economic, social, and cultural life? The city grew more quickly after the war than before as it became a major center for so-called King Cotton and a marginal market for tobacco. Textile factories, major financial institutions, railroad lines, four colleges, and a university (the future North Carolina State) were in place by 1900—all of them together providing a sound foundation for growth in the 20th century. The city became a magnet for men and women from rural Carolina and the region at large; even many northerners saw opportunity in a reconstructed Southland. As newcomers and their families prospered and increased, so did Oakwood, which grew not only physically but also in the eyes of ever more city residents as *the* place to be remembered. That remains true today.

The city evolved with the times, and the cemetery evolved with the city. Today, Raleigh, with its burgeoning population, high-tech industry, Centennial Campus at North Carolina State, and the nearby Research Triangle Park, is known for its vitality, and Oakwood is known as a "cemetery full of life," a repository of Raleigh history, and also a place attuned to the present. Prime Minister Gladstone would be pleased, and we hope you, too, will enjoy Oakwood's tales.

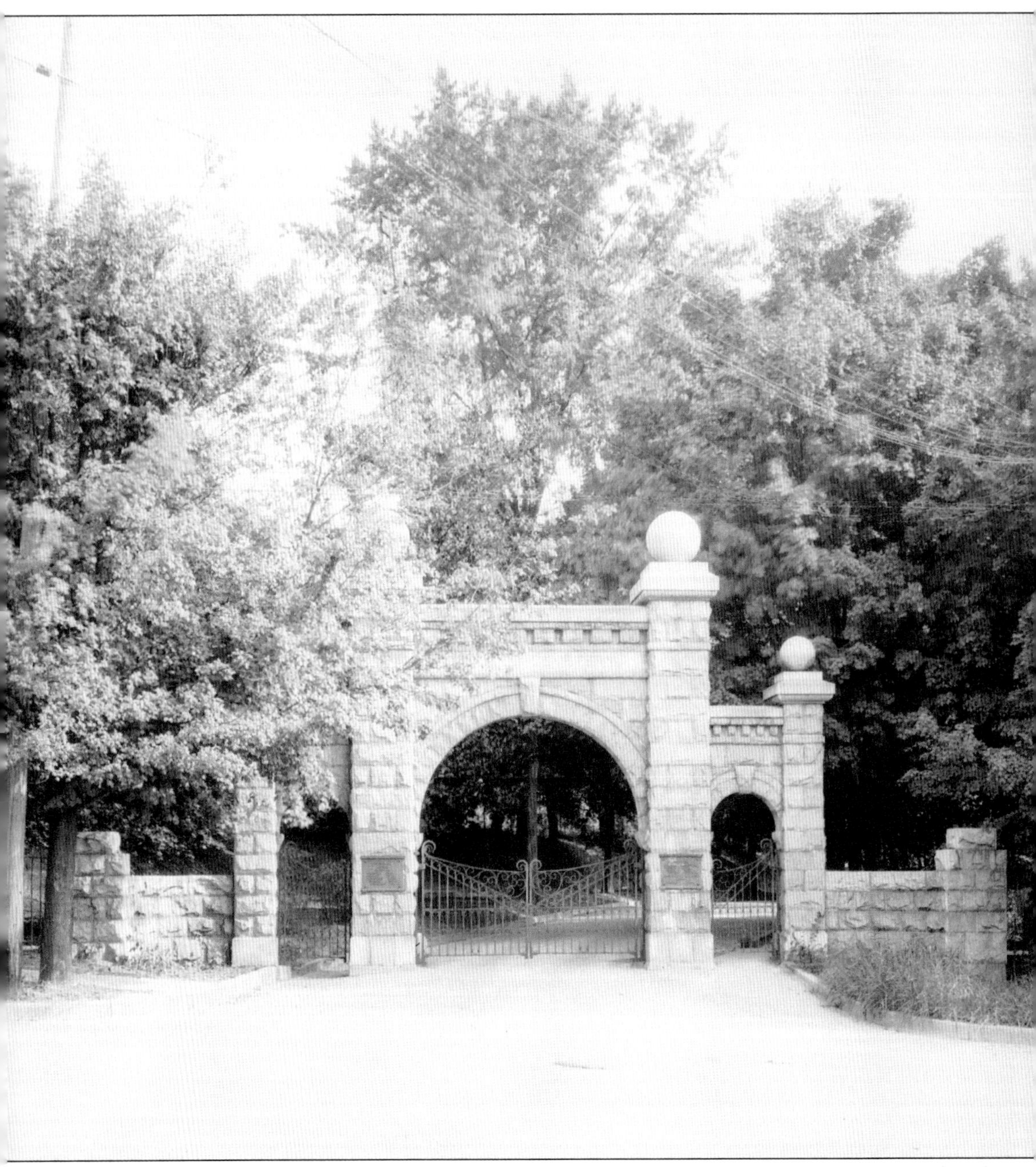

Oakwood's main gate, erected in 1910, has become the symbol of the cemetery, used as an official logo today. Onetime Oakwood District resident Harry Prescott Swartz Keller rests in the Beechwood Section of the cemetery, not far beyond the gate he designed. (SANC.)

One

Breaking Ground

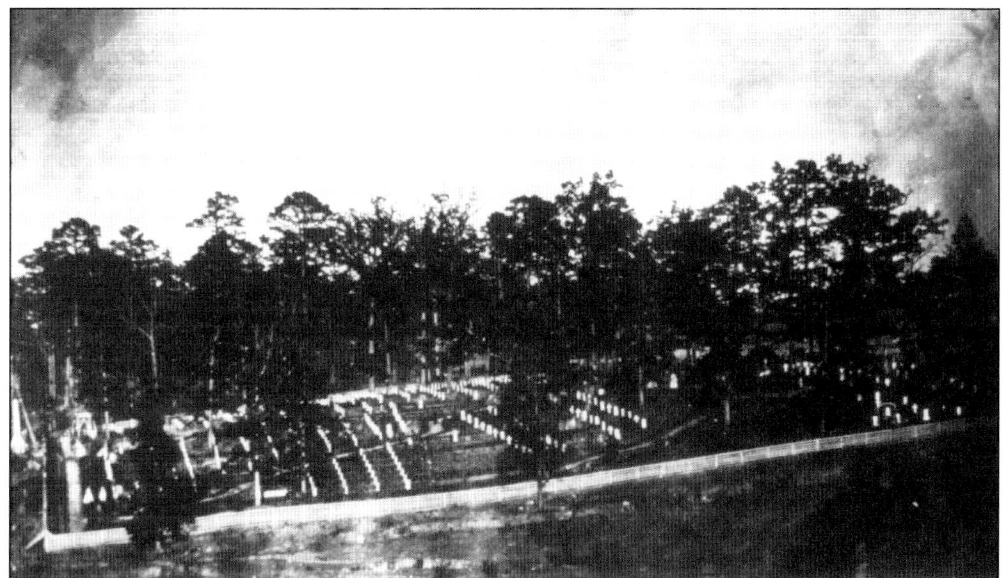

This Confederate Cemetery was the precursor to the larger Oakwood Cemetery. Over the years, the Confederate Cemetery expanded from the original 500 interments in 1867 to nearly 1,400 by the 1930s, when all burials except for grave transfers came to an end. The markers themselves evolved from wooden ones (seen in this c. 1868 photograph) to small, numbered stone blocks to pointed Confederate tombstones issued by the federal government. (SANC.)

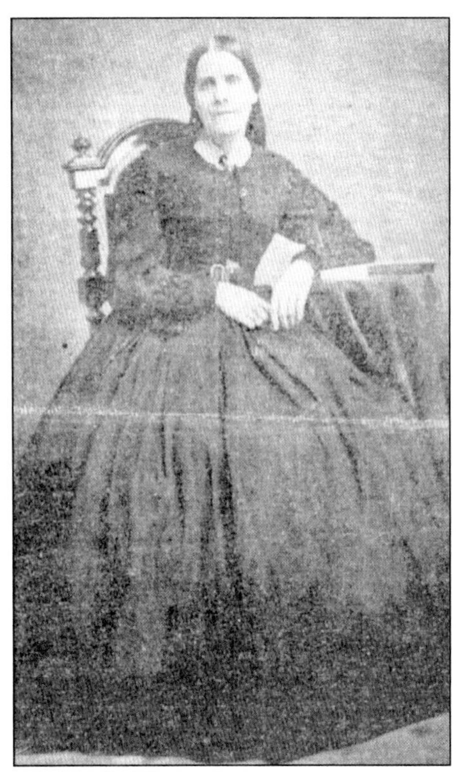

Sophia Arms Partridge (1817–1881) was a New York–born Raleigh schoolmistress who had her students, mostly girls, make bandages for soldiers in the city's military hospitals. In 1866, she suggested a Ladies Memorial Association (LMA) for "the re-interment and future care of our young braves," this in response to the confiscation of a cemetery and hospitals for Confederate soldiers by the Union army of occupation. After the dedication of the cemetery on Confederate Memorial Day, May 10, 1867, the LMA watched over the "young braves" for some three decades, until replaced by the United Daughters of the Confederacy (UDC) around the turn of the 20th century. (Left, SANC; below, Palko.)

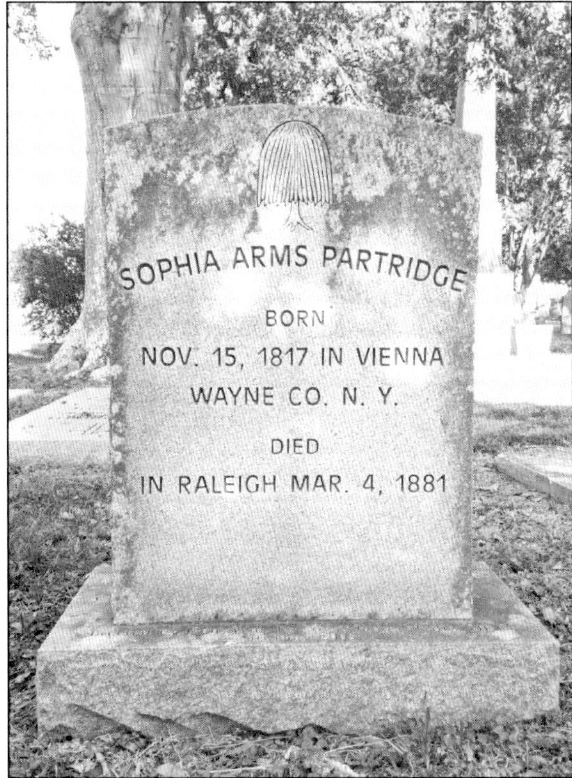

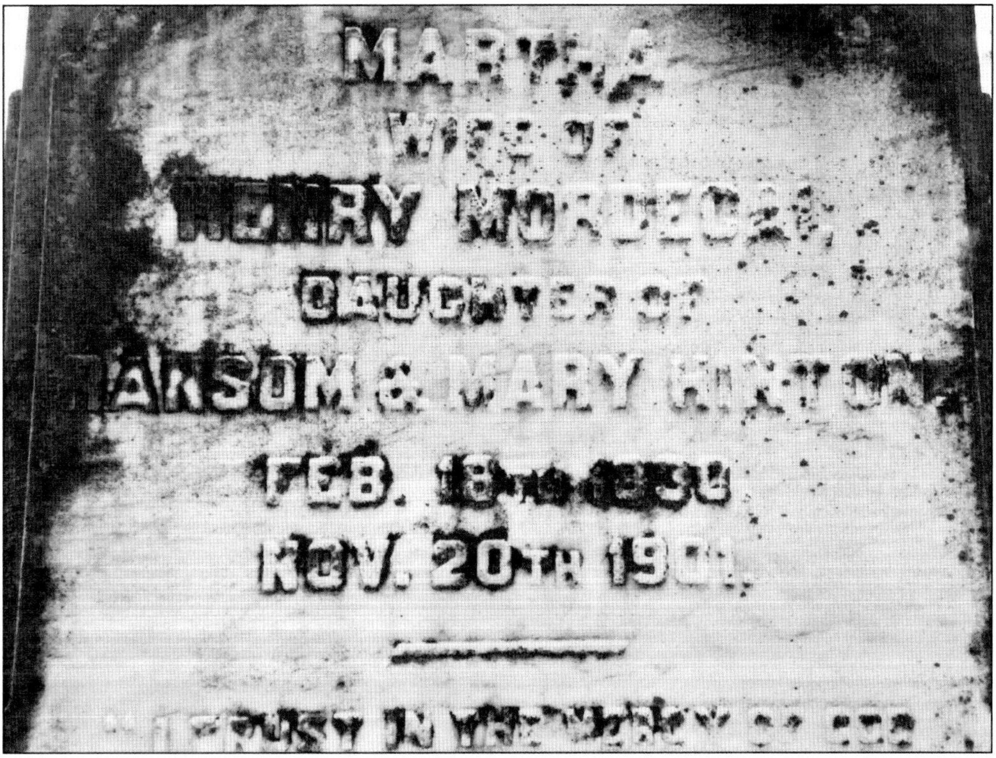

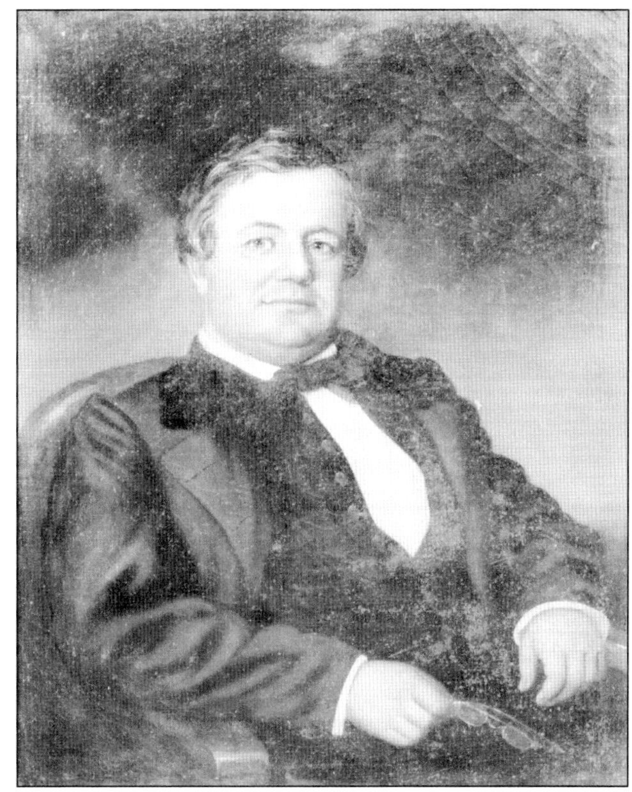

Martha Hinton (1830–1901), Mrs. Henry Mordecai, was a particularly valuable member of the Ladies Memorial Association initiated by Sophia Partridge. Descended from one of oldest families in Wake County (Raleigh's county), Martha married the primary heir to the extensive Mordecai plantation at the northern edge of the capital. The LMA went to Henry Mordecai (1819–1875; pictured) in 1866 to ask for plantation acreage for the Confederate Cemetery, and he granted what they wished: nearly three acres, surely with Martha's encouragement. It is said that it was Henry who later suggested the name of the larger cemetery, Oakwood, Sleeping Place among the Oaks. (Above, Palko; right, SANC.)

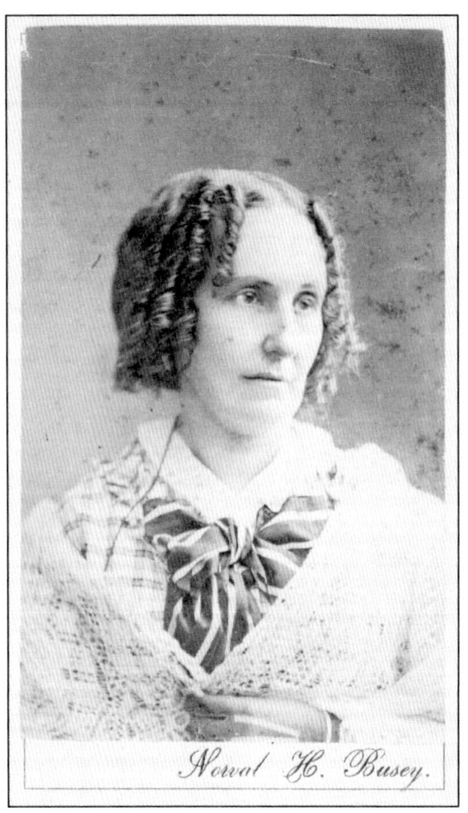

Margaret Lane Devereux (1824–1910) had several connections helpful to the Ladies Memorial Association in its campaign for a Confederate Cemetery. She was the half sister of Henry Mordecai, heir to the family plantation, and the wife of Maj. John Devereux Jr. (1819–1893), himself a wealthy antebellum landowner and the much-respected chief quartermaster of the state during the Civil War, successfully providing Tar Heel soldiers with the necessary clothing and equipment. The Devereuxes lived on a beautiful estate, Will's Forest, just north of downtown, a home that Margaret was forced to sell after John's death to settle debts brought on by the Civil War. (Left, SANC; below, Palko.)

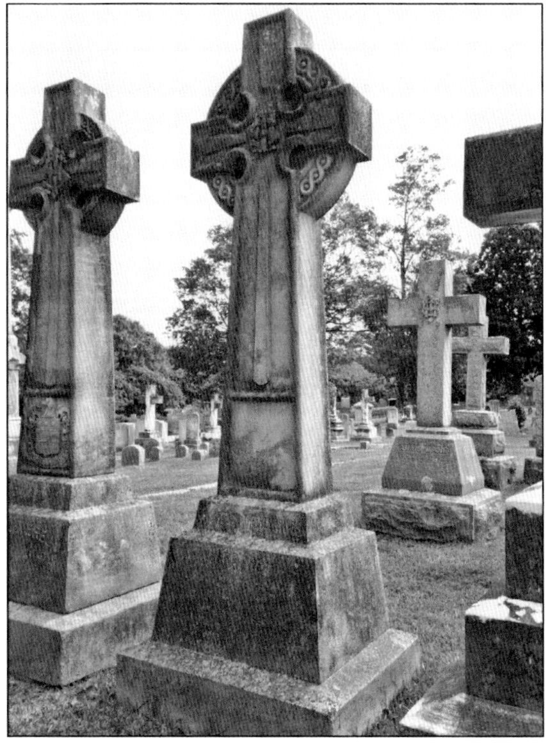

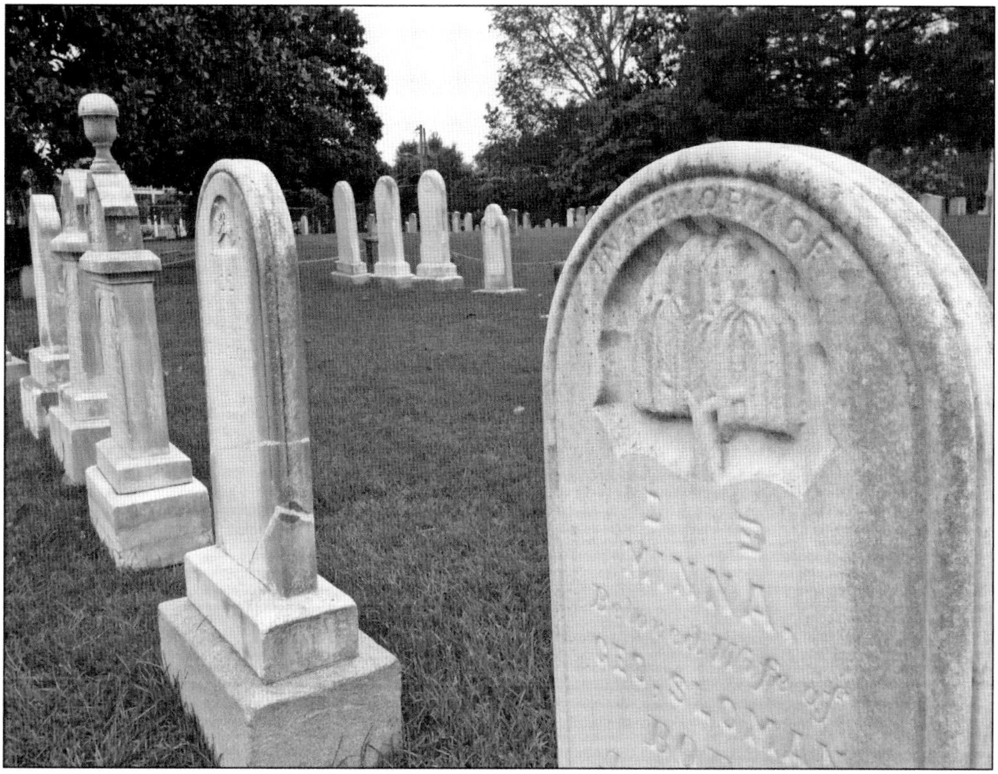

Although much "Christianized" over the years, the Mordecai (pronounced MOR-de-kee) family, in donating plantation land for the cemetery, ensured there would be a section for Raleigh's Jews, their family heritage. Thus the small Raleigh Hebrew Cemetery abuts the Confederate Cemetery to the east. In time, local Jewish families required more burial space and established the independent Raleigh Hebrew Cemetery in 1912 along the eastern edge of the larger Oakwood Cemetery. (Palko.)

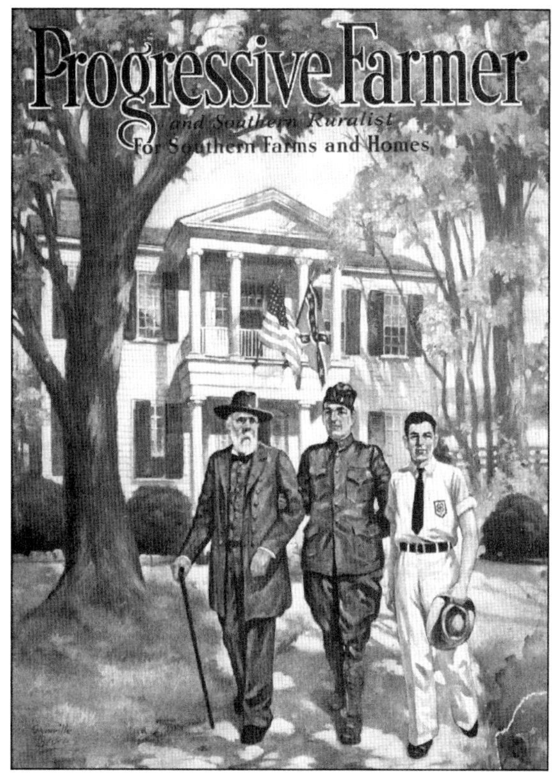

Shown here on a magazine cover (see Leonidas Polk, page 70), the Mordecai House (extant), several blocks west of the cemetery, was the hub of a huge antebellum plantation. The rear portion was built in the 1780s by then landowner Joel Lane for his son; the front portion, in 1826 by a widow of family patriarch Moses Mordecai (1785–1824). Moses and many of the Mordecai family are interred in Oakwood Cemetery. (SANC.)

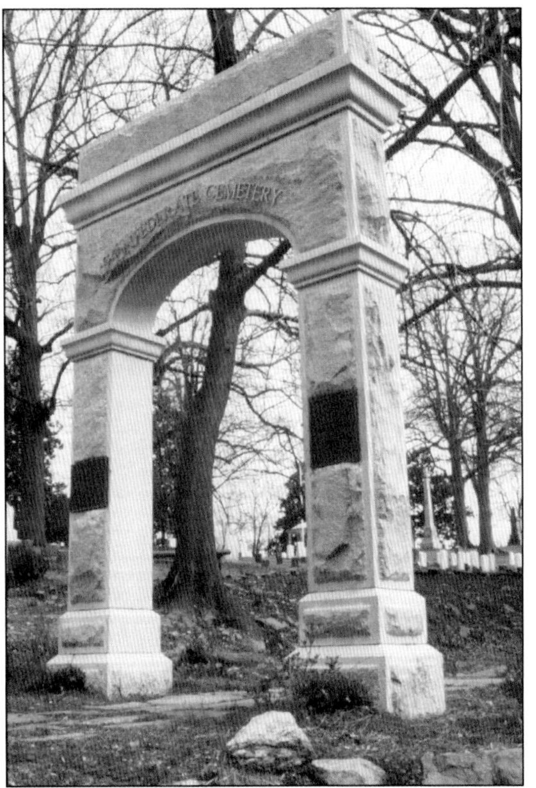

This arch, which now serves as the main entry to the Confederate Cemetery, was dedicated in 1910 by a local chapter of the United Daughters of the Confederacy, which earlier had absorbed the Ladies Memorial Association. It replaced the old gate that still stands at the south end of the Confederate Cemetery off Oakwood Avenue and is used today only for major ceremonies. (HOC.)

"Lieutenant Walsh," a Texas cavalryman, fired at General Sherman's Union cavalry as they entered Raleigh on April 13, 1865. The Federal horsemen chased him down and had Walsh hanged nearby. He has become a local symbol of the "Lost Cause," and for many years on April 13 this marker has been draped and decorated. There is no known photograph of Walsh; even his first name and birth date are uncertain. (SANC.)

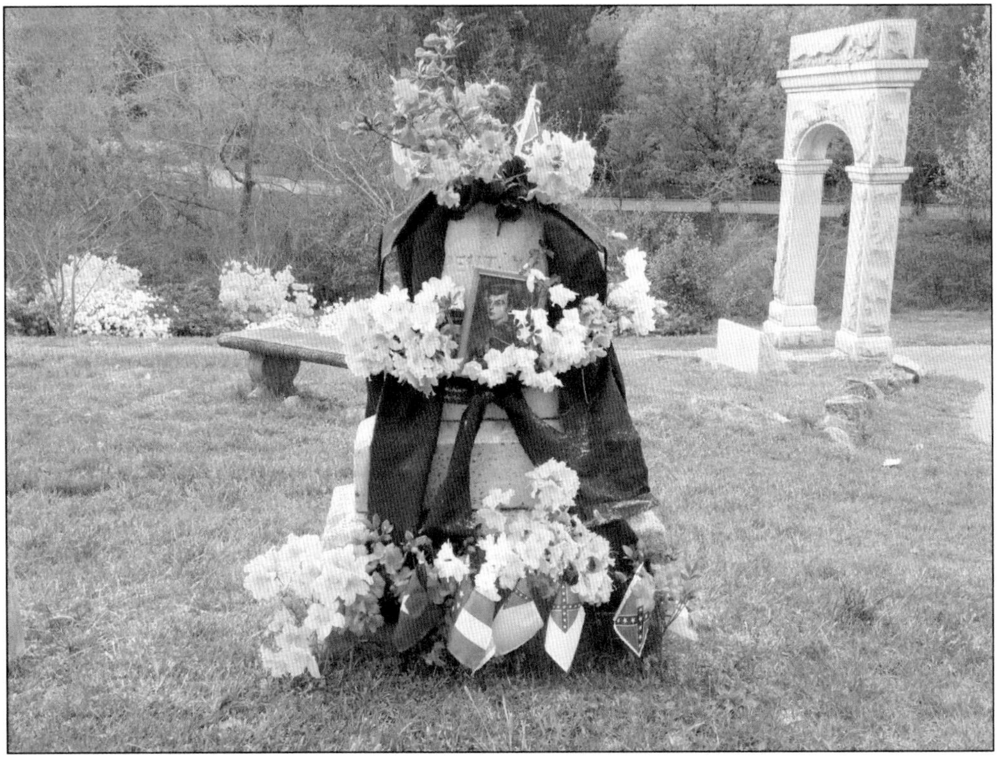

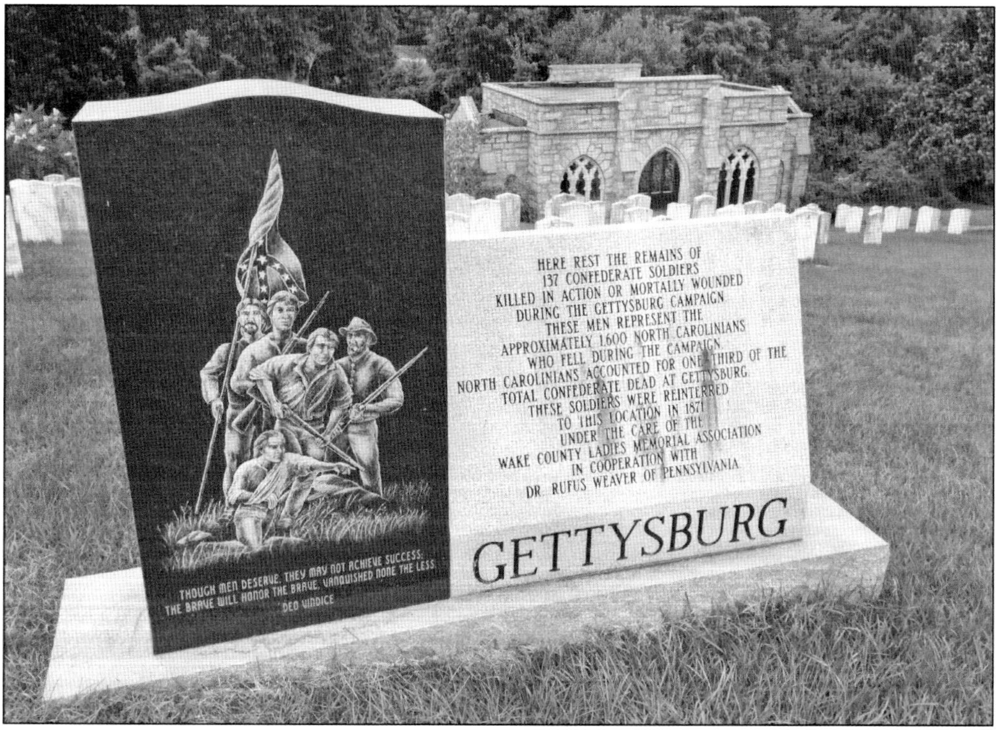

Over the years, the cemetery received the remains of Confederate soldiers not welcome in national cemeteries. In 1871, the Ladies Memorial Association made arrangements with Dr. Rufus Weaver of Pennsylvania to transfer some 137 Confederate remains from Gettysburg to Raleigh (other southern cities received remains also); most lie in individual, marked graves, with 14 in a mass grave. In 1883, some 107 remains in four caskets were transferred with great ceremony from an isolated corner of Arlington Cemetery to Oakwood; in 1993, the Sons of Confederate Veterans dedicated a bronze plaque including the name and unit of each known Arlington soldier, with tablet space for "unknowns." In all, some 10 percent of Confederate remains in Oakwood are "unknown," but research continues. (Both, Palko.)

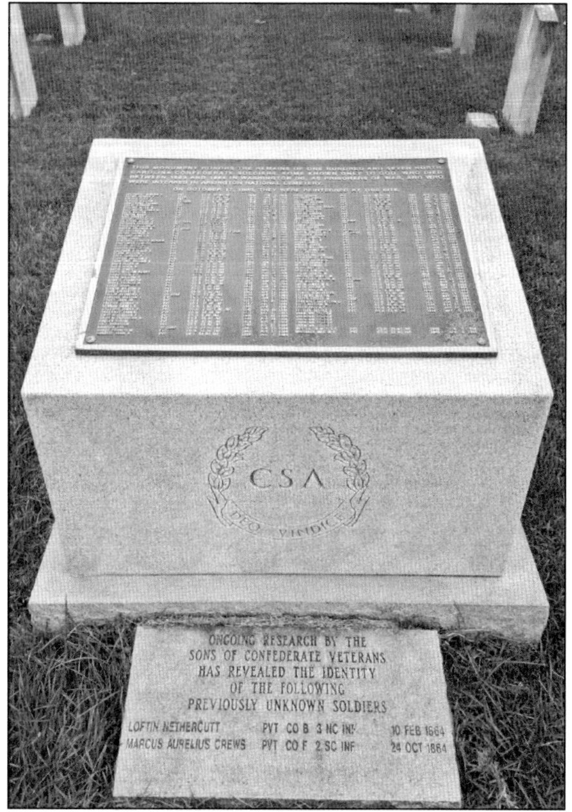

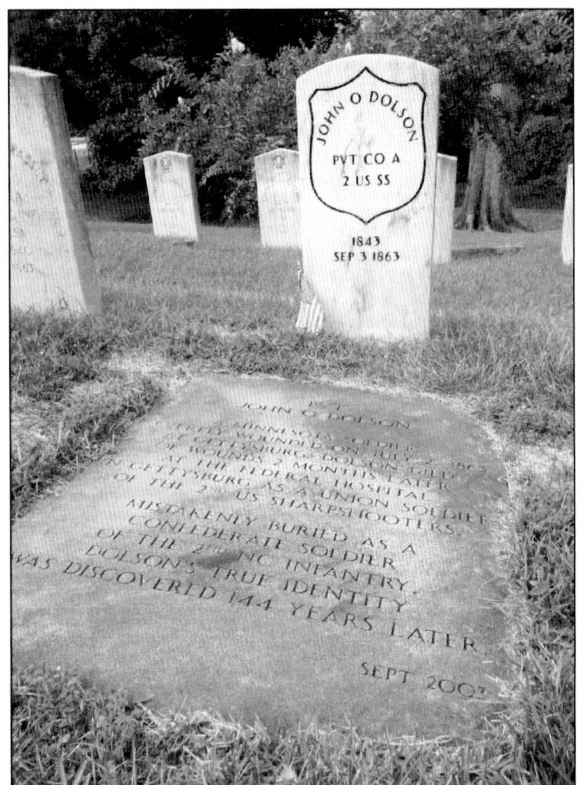

In the 1871 transfer of remains from Gettysburg, mistakes were made. Originally identified as a nonexistent Tar Heel soldier named Dobson, John O. Dolson was correctly identified in 2007 as a Union sharpshooter. A rounded US soldier's stone replaced the incorrect, pointed Confederate marker, now on display in Dolson's hometown of Richfield, Minnesota. In 2008, "George Piper" was properly identified as New Yorker Jacob Pfeiffer, US Army (one row behind Dolson). (Palko.)

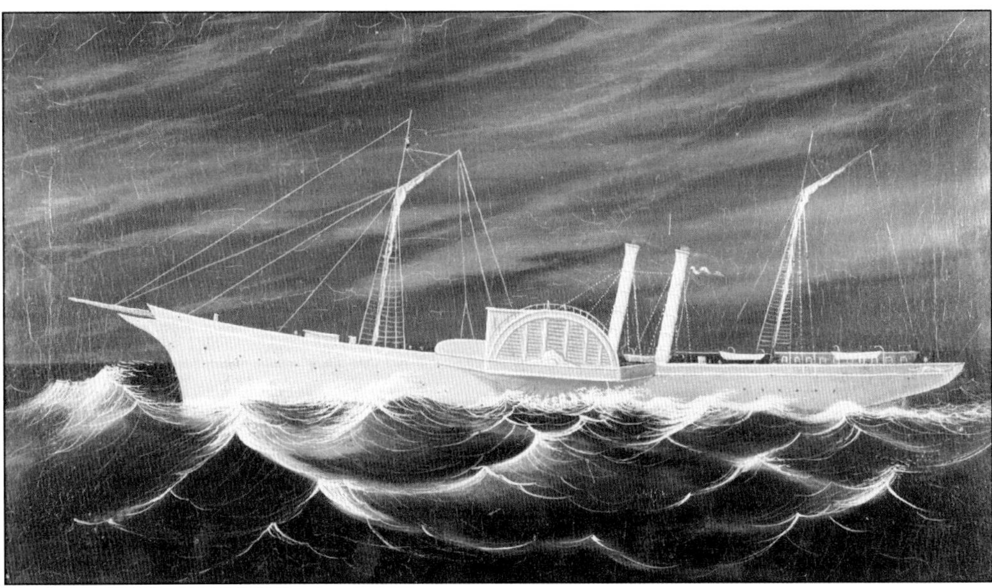

James Maglenn (1833–1914), interred at the edge of the Confederate Cemetery, was a locomotive engineer from Goldsboro who became the chief engineer on the blockade-runner *Advance*, bringing needed supplies through Wilmington to the Confederacy. A side-wheeler purchased in England and named for then governor Zebulon Vance, the *Advance* was captured in September 1864. Maglenn, himself Irish, claimed afterwards that, upon capture, the crew all feigned British accents to avoid arrest. (SANC.)

Henry "Harry" King Burgwyn (1841–1863), the "Boy Colonel," assumed command of the 26th North Carolina Infantry Regiment when then-commander Zebulon Vance assumed his duties as the state's governor. At Gettysburg, Burgwyn led the 26th in its successful assault of McPherson's Ridge against the Union's "Iron Brigade" on July 1, 1863, the first day of battle. The cost in casualties to the regiment was extraordinary, however, and included the young colonel, whose regimental colors were said to be in his hand when he was shot. At the news, Harry's Raleigh sweetheart, Annie Lane Devereux (1843–1912), wore black every day for the rest of her life; she rests in Oakwood's Mordecai Section, with a view of Harry's grave in the distance. (Right, SANC; below, Palko.)

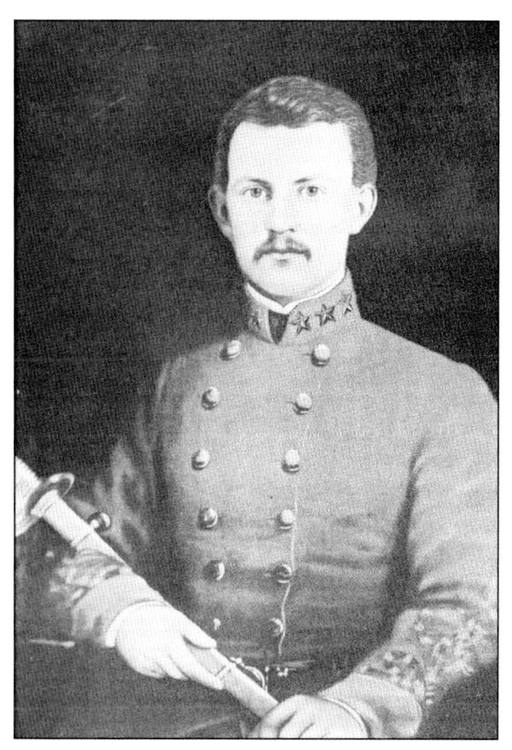

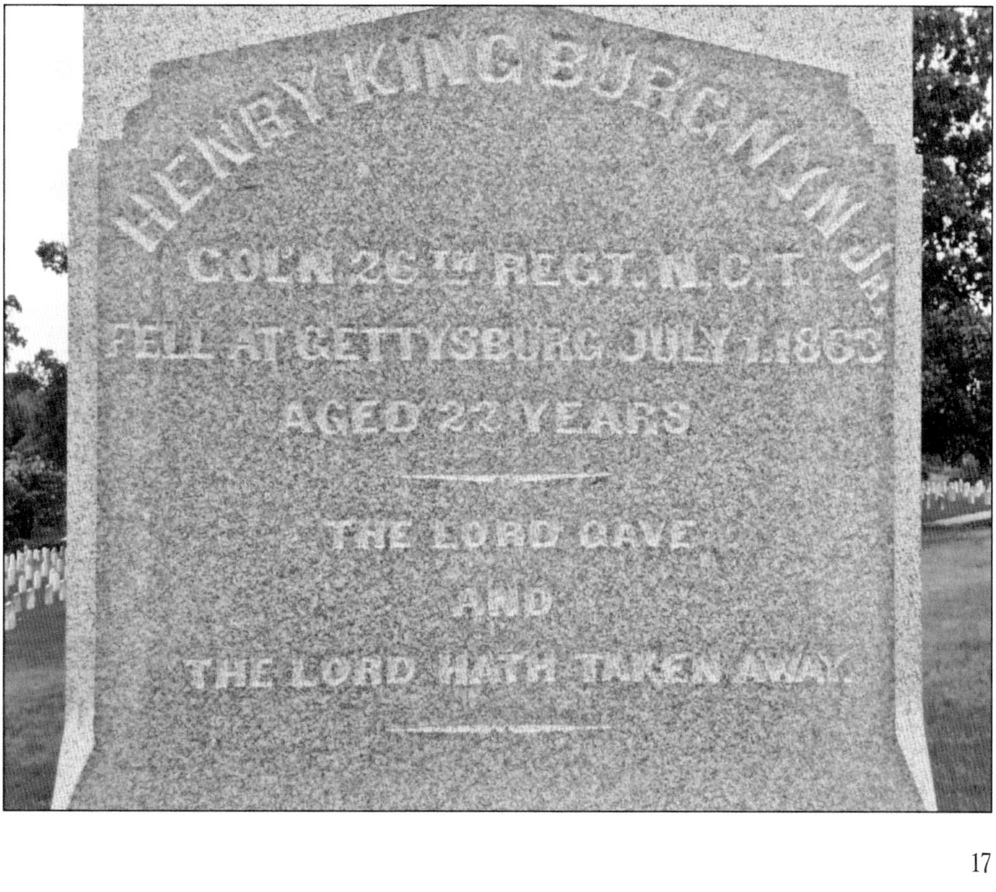

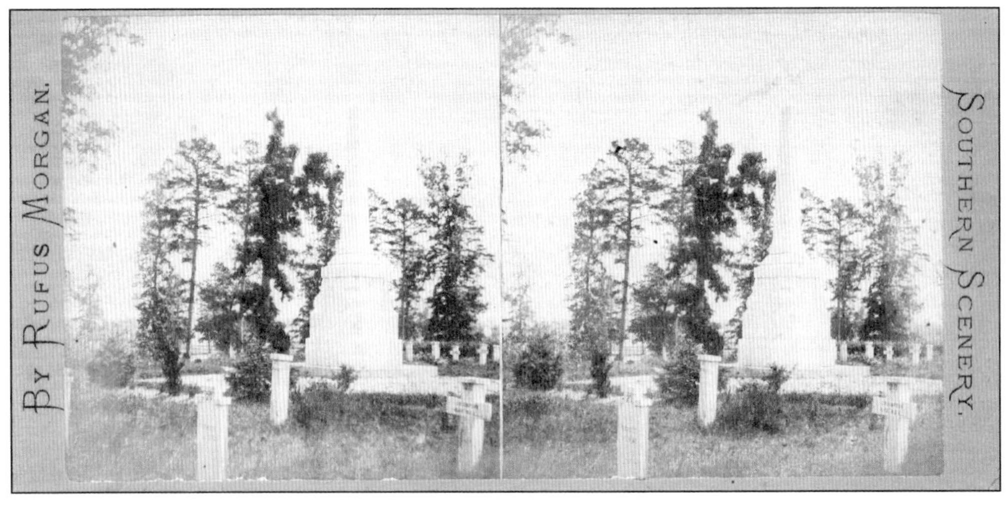

Around 1871, Raleigh citizens gave this tall Memorial to Confederate Dead; wooden markers surround it. The Ladies Memorial Association replaced the moldering "headboards" with numbered stone blocks, which were replaced in the 1990s with pointed markers for Confederate soldiers, acquired and set out by local Sons of Confederate Veterans. (Above, NCCUNCLCH; both below, HOC.)

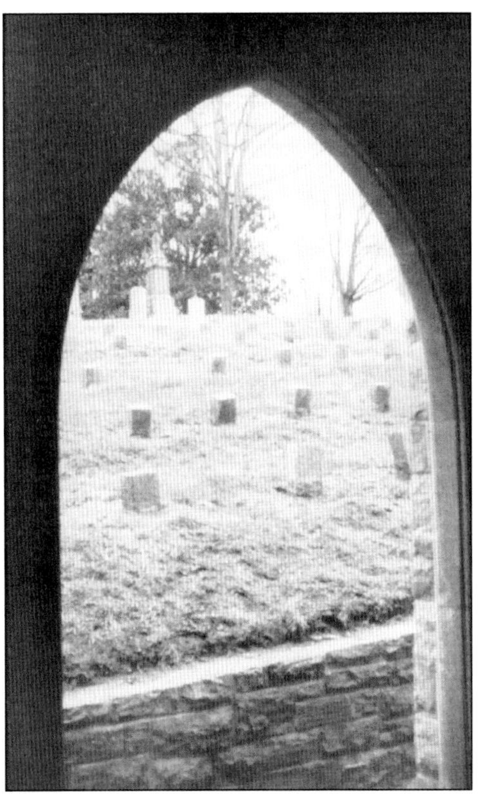

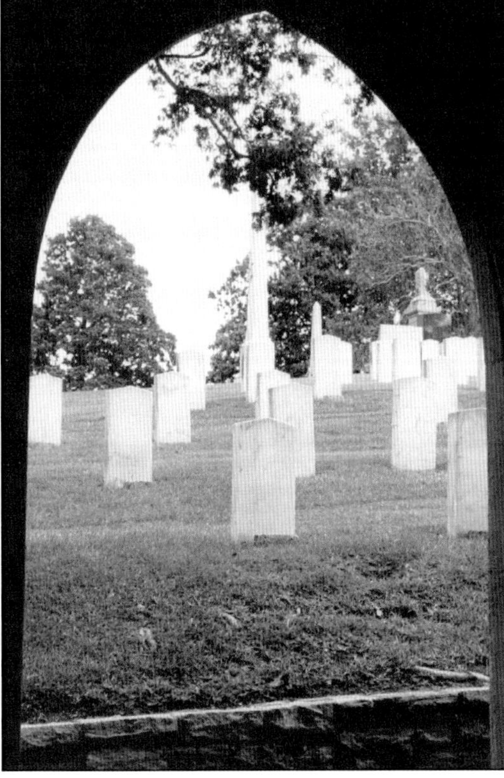

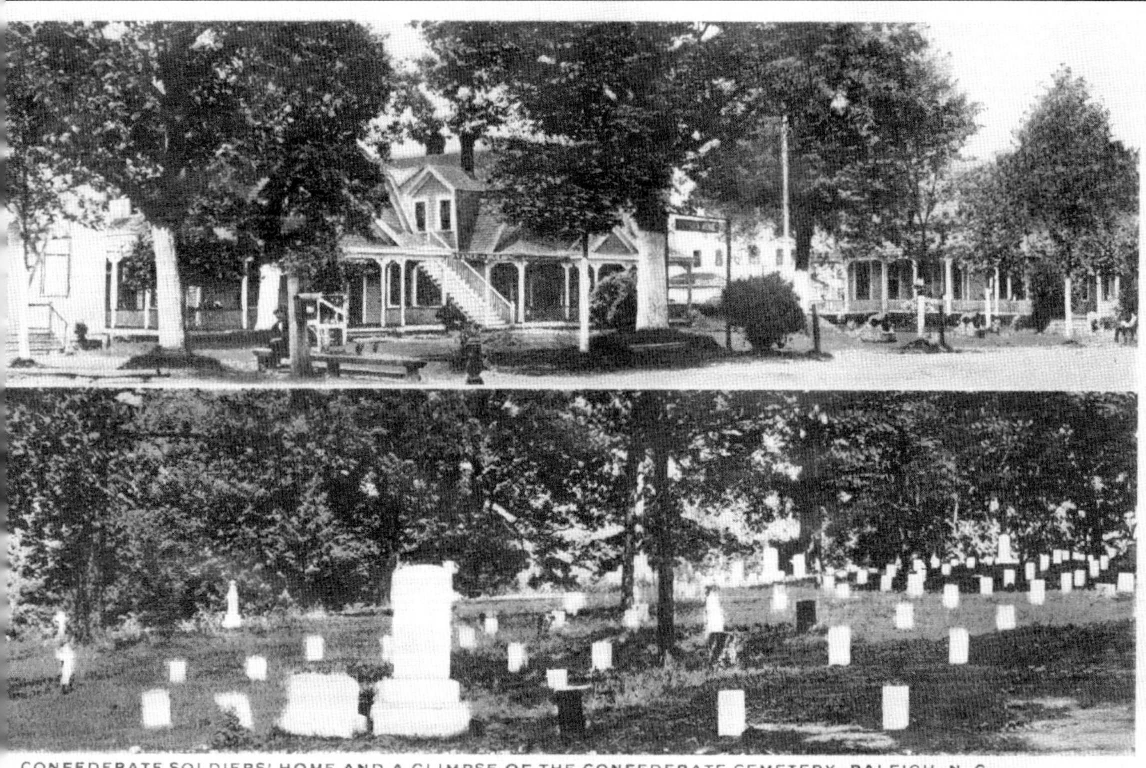

Many stones in the Confederate Cemetery mark the graves of veterans who spent their final years at the North Carolina Confederate Soldiers' Home, which stood east of town on New Bern Avenue, the site of the North Carolina Department of Motor Vehicles today but a hospital during the Civil War. This postcard depicts both the home and the cemetery. The final non-transfer veteran to be laid to rest here was Andrew J. Wise (1844–1938) from Buncombe County, Private, Company H, 29th North Carolina Regiment. Another veteran, George L. Cathey, a captain in a Georgia "legion," lived to be 100 years old (1822–1923) and died in the North Carolina Confederate Soldiers' Home hospital. He is one of the few male centenarians in Oakwood Cemetery. The North Carolina Confederate Soldiers' Home closed in 1938. (Olivia Raney Local History Library.)

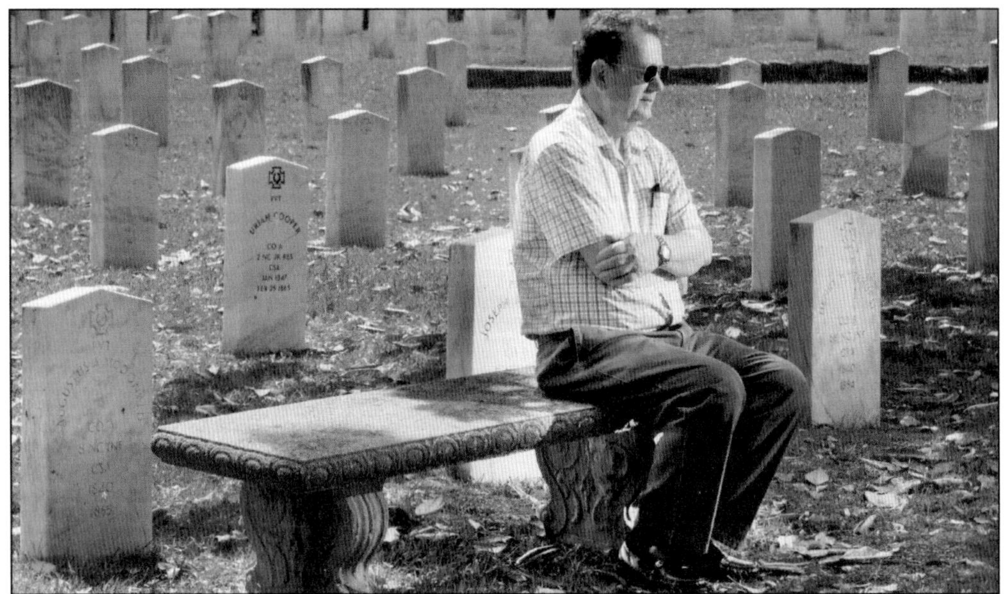

Much of the credit for the remarkable memorial that is Oakwood's Confederate Cemetery goes to Charles Everett Purser Jr. (1939–2013) of the Sons of Confederate Veterans (SCV), and to the women of Raleigh who, for a century and a half, have been members of local chapters of the Ladies Memorial Association (LMA) and the United Daughters of the Confederacy (UDC). Purser led research efforts and gravestone acquisition for many years and authored *A Story Behind Every Stone*, a guidebook. The LMA, SCV, and UDC have added to the infrastructure of the cemetery, including walkways, Summer House, and special markers. In the mid-1930s, the UDC built the House of Memory (pictured here), dedicated to all North Carolina men and women who have given their lives in America's wars. (Above, Robert Ringham; below, William Hutchins.)

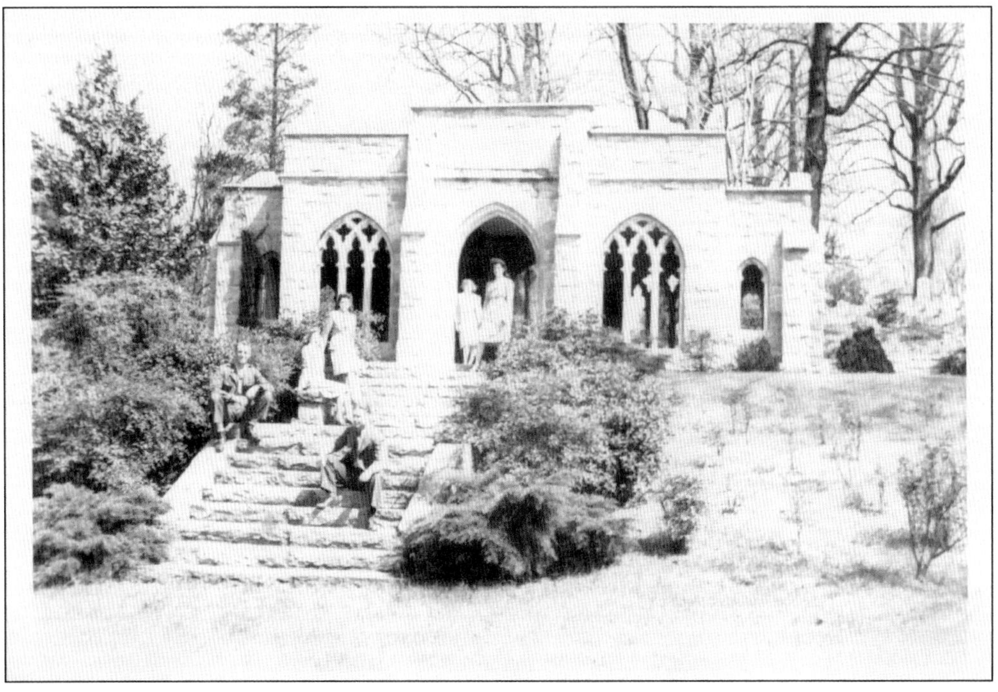

Two

Oakwood Cemetery, "Sleeping Place among the Oaks"

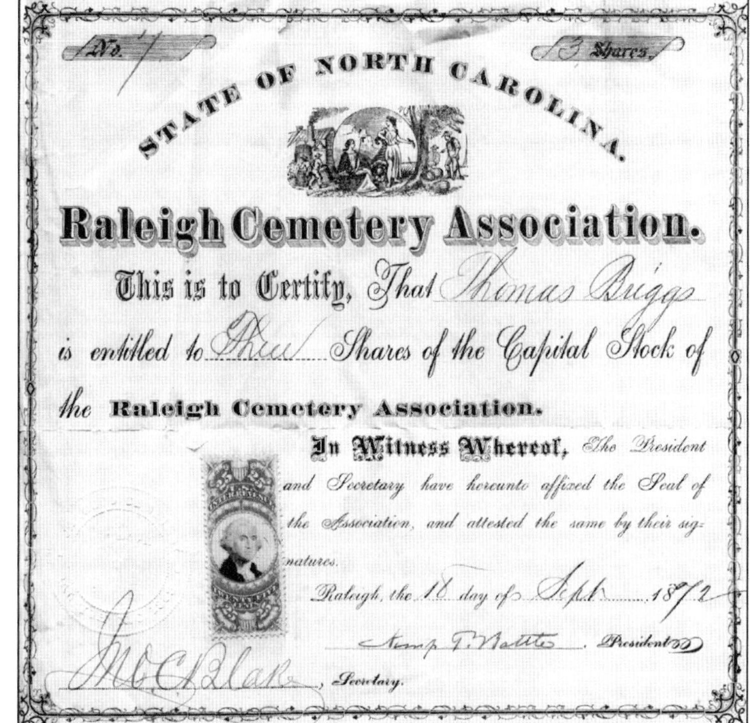
No. 1

3 Shares.

STATE OF NORTH CAROLINA.

Raleigh Cemetery Association.

This is to Certify, That Thomas Briggs is entitled to Three Shares of the Capital Stock of the Raleigh Cemetery Association.

In Witness Whereof, The President and Secretary have hereunto affixed the Seal of the Association, and attested the same by their signatures.

Raleigh, the 18 day of Sept 1872

President

Secretary.

The Raleigh Cemetery Association (RCA) received a charter from the State of North Carolina on February 26, 1869, marking the official beginning of Oakwood Cemetery, sited alongside the Confederate burial ground. Capitalized at $10,000 (about $180,000 in 2017), the new corporation sold $100 shares to many prominent Raleigh citizens who also bought some of the first burial plots, often marked by towering obelisks. (Evelyn Scruggs Murray.)

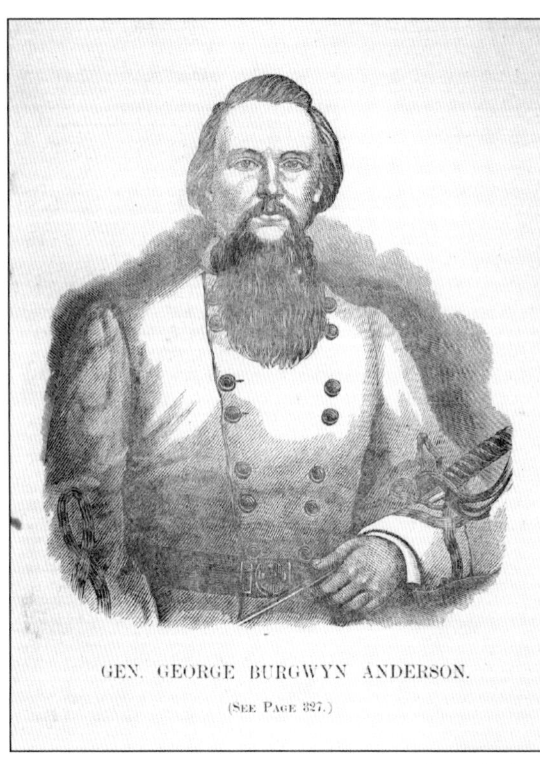

Confederate brigadier general George Burgwyn Anderson (1831–1862) was wounded at Sharpsburg/Antietam in September 1862 and came to Raleigh to recover. The wound eventually took his life, and his brother William Edward Anderson (1835–1890) moved George, after temporary interment elsewhere, to the edge of the then new Confederate Cemetery, erecting Oakwood's first obelisk monument to him. Accounts note that it was during this process that William, a banker and a vestryman at Christ Church on Capitol Square, envisioned a larger cemetery for military and nonmilitary interments—the future Oakwood. With City Cemetery filling up and little empty land downtown for church-side graveyards, Anderson's idea received enthusiastic support. (Left, SANC; below, Palko.)

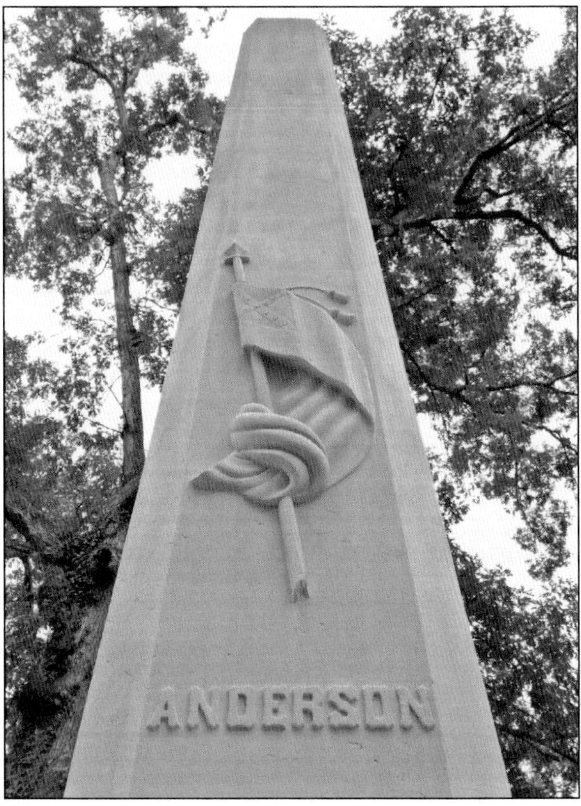

The early *Charter and By-laws of the Raleigh Cemetery Association* states that the purpose of the cemetery management is "to make [Oakwood] ideal." Among the original rules: "No refreshments, and no party carrying refreshments, will be permitted within the grounds; No horse is to be fastened except at the posts provided; Walking on the grass, fishing, firing guns or pistols, throwing stones, [and] interfering with birds or birds' nests . . . are absolutely prohibited." (HOC.)

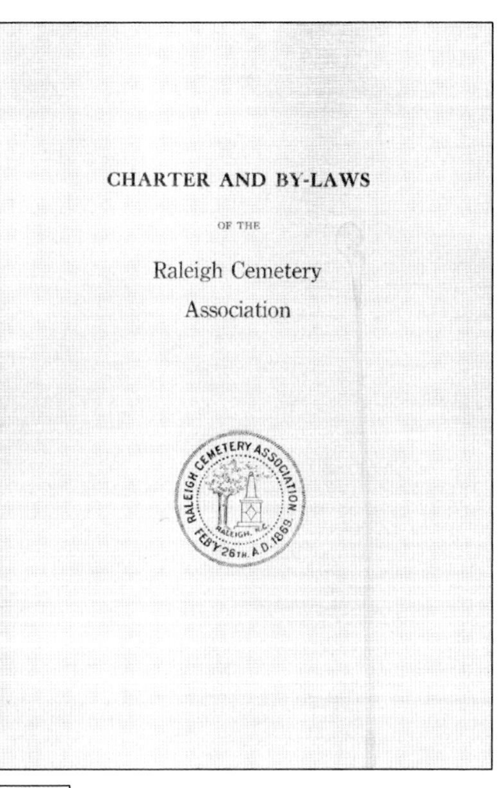

CHARTER AND BY-LAWS

OF THE

Raleigh Cemetery

Association

RALEIGH CEMETERY ASSOCIATION

RALEIGH, N.C.

FEB'Y 26TH. A.D. 1869

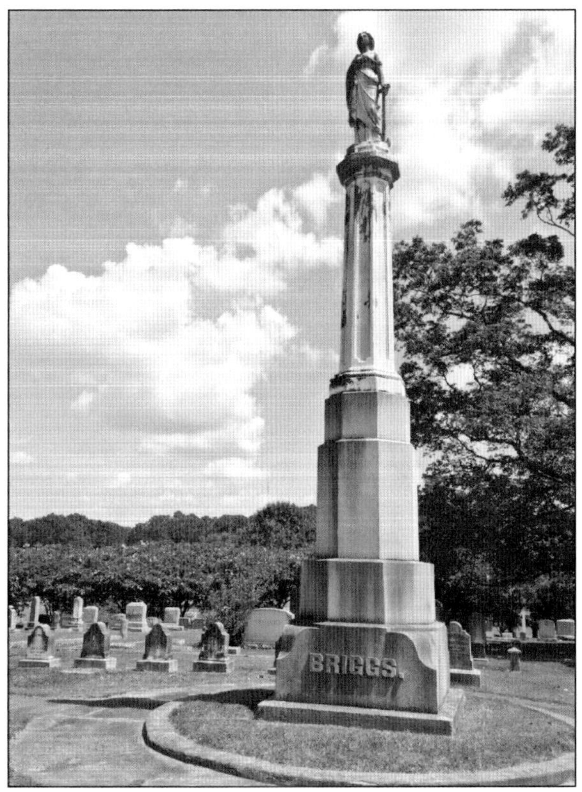

Thomas Henry Briggs (1821–1886) initially bought three cemetery shares (see page 21), two family plots, and over time would build the fine homes of many of the families interred here. However, today he is best remembered as a hardware merchant; the four-story Briggs Building (1874) that housed his store remains a downtown Raleigh landmark. A lofty monument topped by "Hope" towers over Oakwood's Briggs Section. (Palko.)

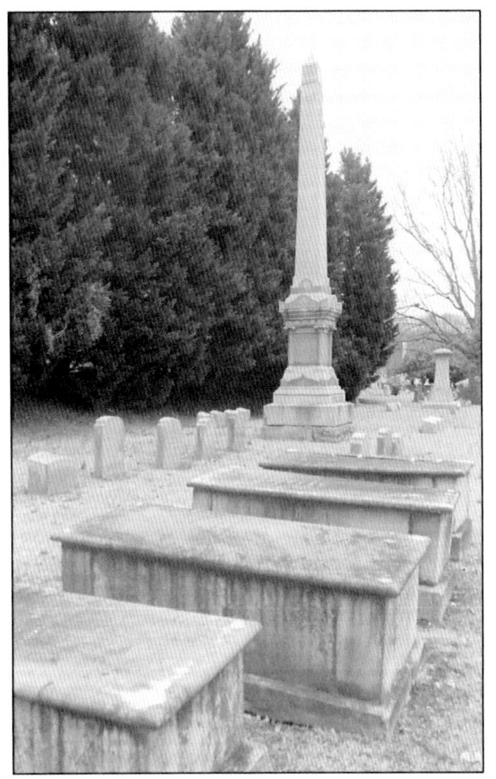

Richard Stanhope Pullen (1822–1895), a wealthy developer, bought five shares of the Raleigh Cemetery Association. A generous philanthropist, Pullen supported a number of other area institutions, providing the land for Raleigh's first public park and the North Carolina College of Agriculture and Mechanic Arts (today's North Carolina State University) and financing a struggling Peace Institute (now William Peace University). An early developer of the Oakwood residential district, Pullen and his servant Washington Ligon planted hundreds of trees throughout the city. Pullen, a modest bachelor, had no children and never allowed a portrait or photograph of him to be made. His large family plot, said to be the first such in Oakwood, is just inside the cemetery's main gate. (Left, Bruce Miller; below, HOC.)

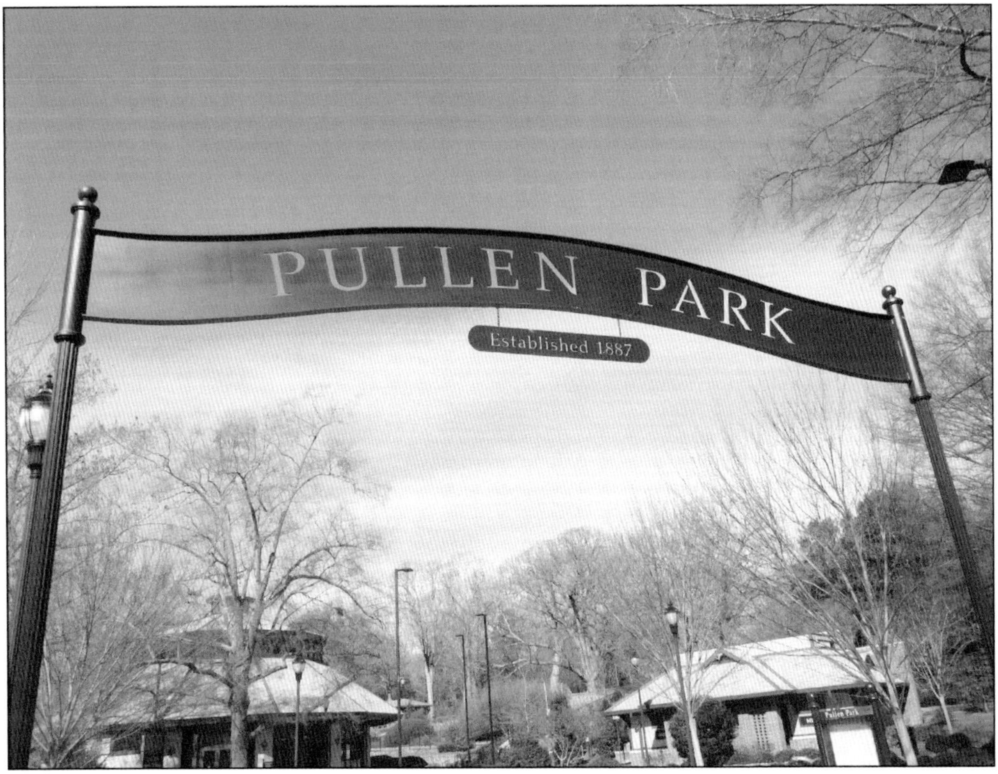

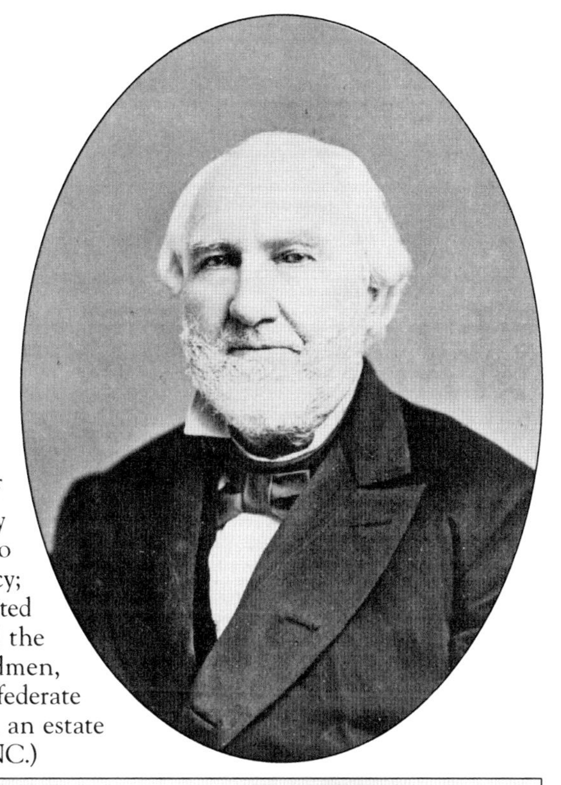

Bartholomew Figures Moore (1801–1878), born in Halifax County, has been called the "Father of the North Carolina Bar." An original Raleigh Cemetery Association shareholder, Moore served four terms as a legislator, became North Carolina attorney general (1848–1851), and led a revision of North Carolina's law code. Moore was strongly opposed to secession "madness," refusing to take an oath of allegiance to the Confederacy; however, he also resisted a Washington-dictated Reconstruction, during which he drafted the Black Codes for North Carolina's freedmen, considered liberal among the former Confederate states. Moore married two sisters and had an estate just east of downtown Raleigh. (Both, SANC.)

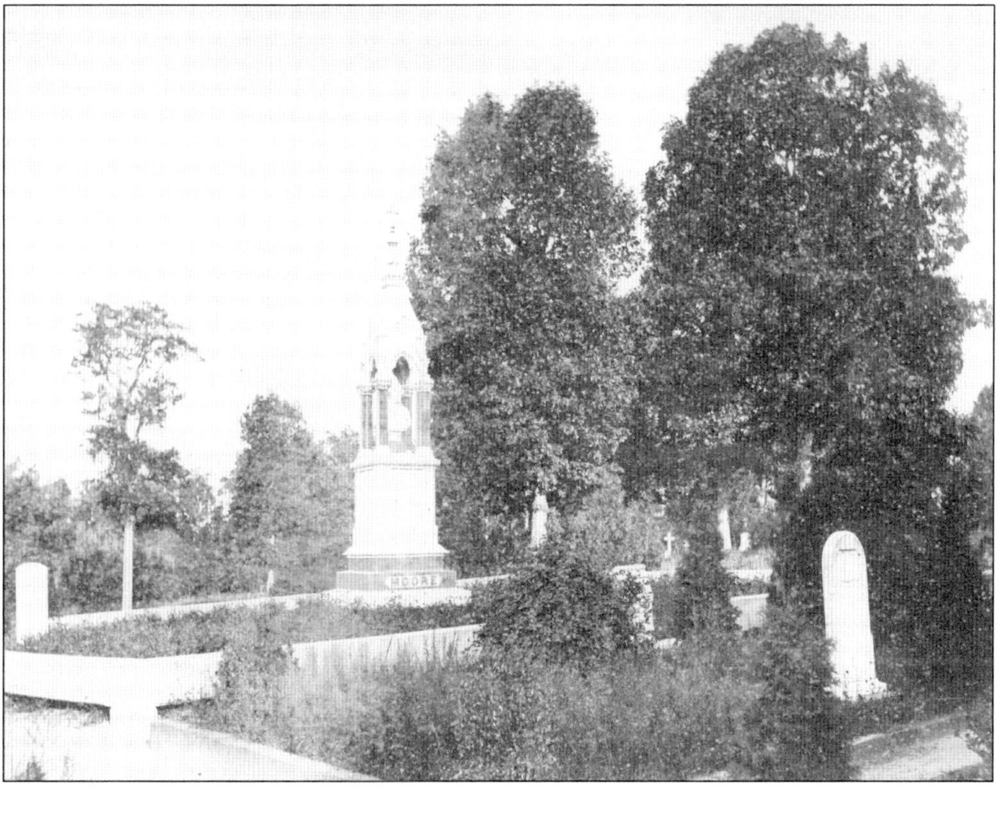

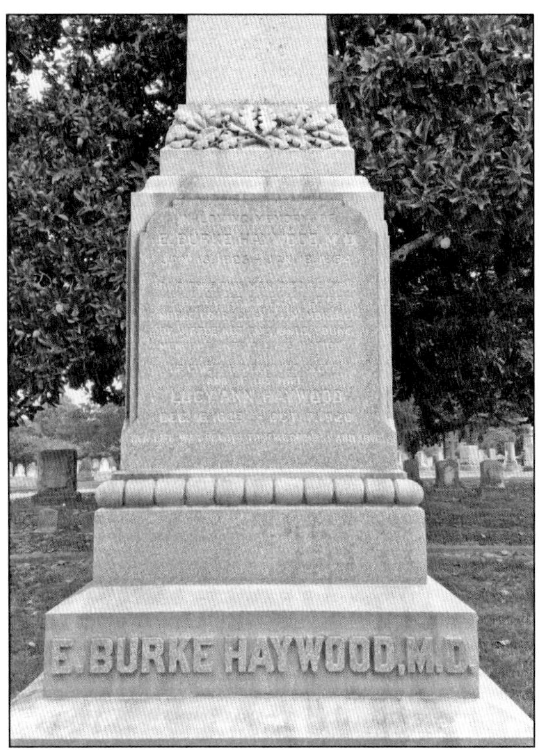

Edmund Burke Haywood (1825–1894) bought only one share of the cemetery association but made his contribution to his city in another way. A son of John Haywood, the city's first mayor, "E. Burke" went to undergraduate school at the University of North Carolina and medical school at the University of Pennsylvania, becoming a compassionate, innovative physician. He worked tirelessly in military hospitals during the Civil War (he supervised the three in Raleigh), and the diligence with which he served all—Union and Confederate, black and white—may have caused the pleurisy that eventually took his life. He grew up in one of Raleigh's most historic homes, Haywood Hall (extant), built around 1800 for his father, who, along with many of his family, rests in E. Burke's large Oakwood plot. (Left, Palko; below, SANC.)

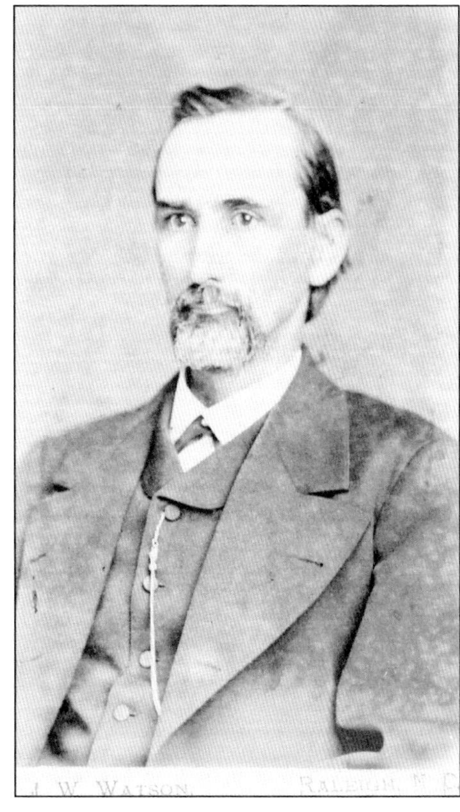

George Washington Mordecai (1801–1871) was a respected Raleigh lawyer, banker, and businessman. He was an early and enthusiastic supporter of railroads, including Raleigh's Experimental Railroad (1830s), powered by draft animals as it moved stone to the new capitol then under construction. A half brother of family head Moses Mordecai and guardian of Henry Mordecai, who had given the land for the Confederate Cemetery, George spent his final years as the first Raleigh Cemetery Association president. He married Margaret Cameron (1811–1886), a member of the landowning family for whom Raleigh's Cameron Village shopping area is named, and lived with her in a mansion (not extant) then across Hillsborough Street from St. Mary's School. (Right, SANC; below, Palko.)

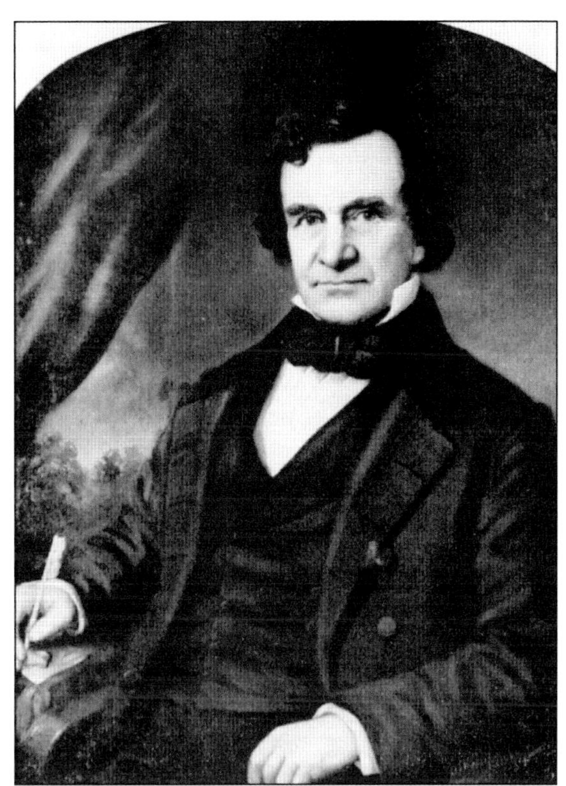

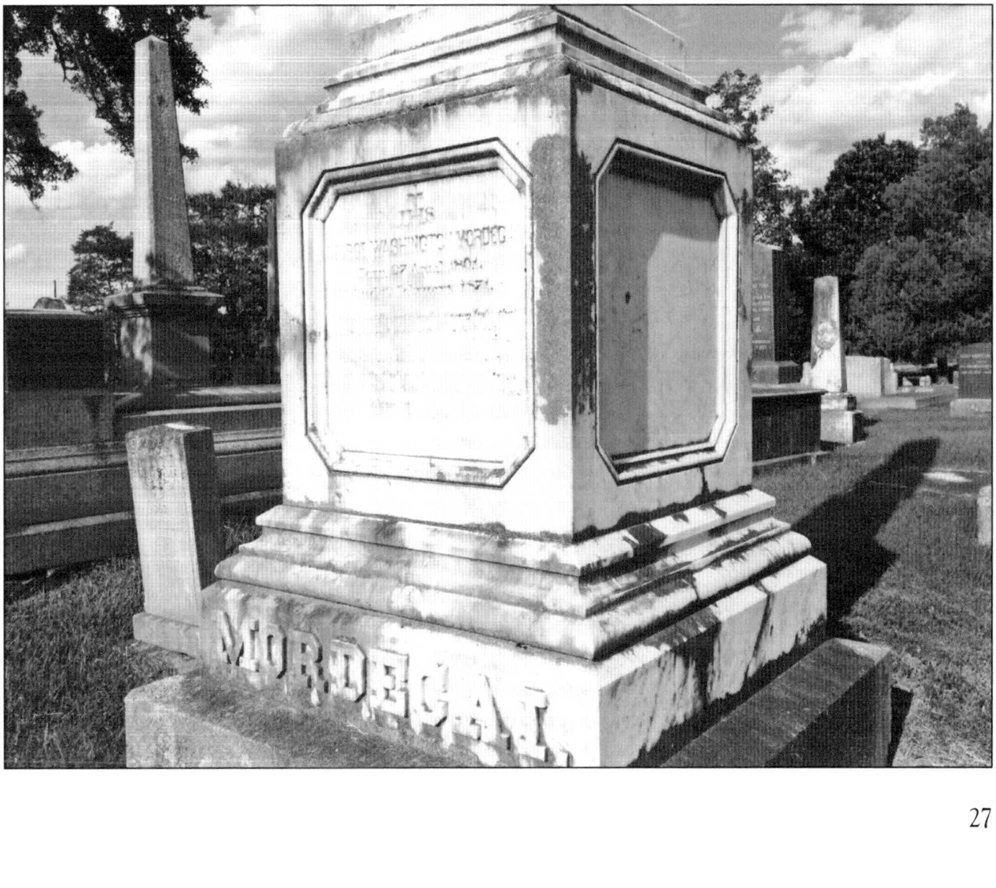

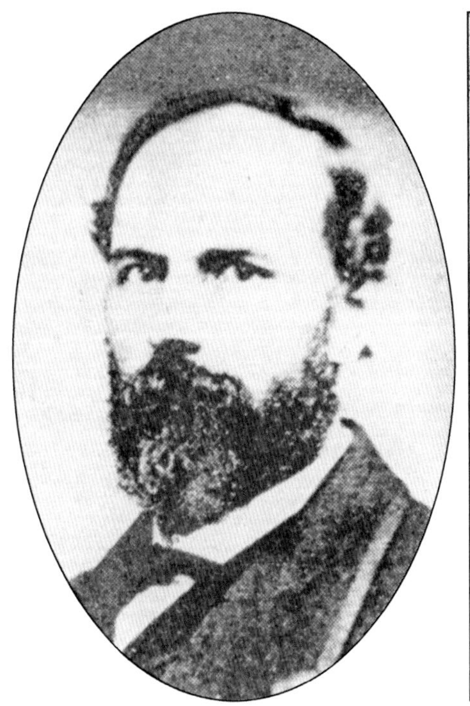

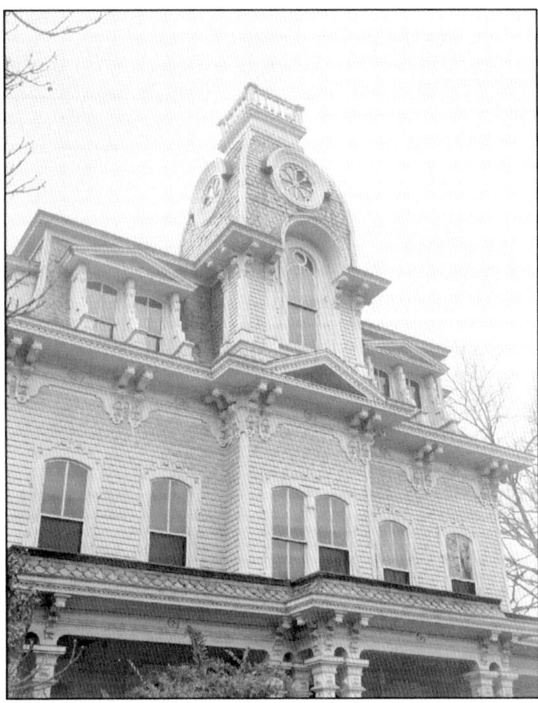

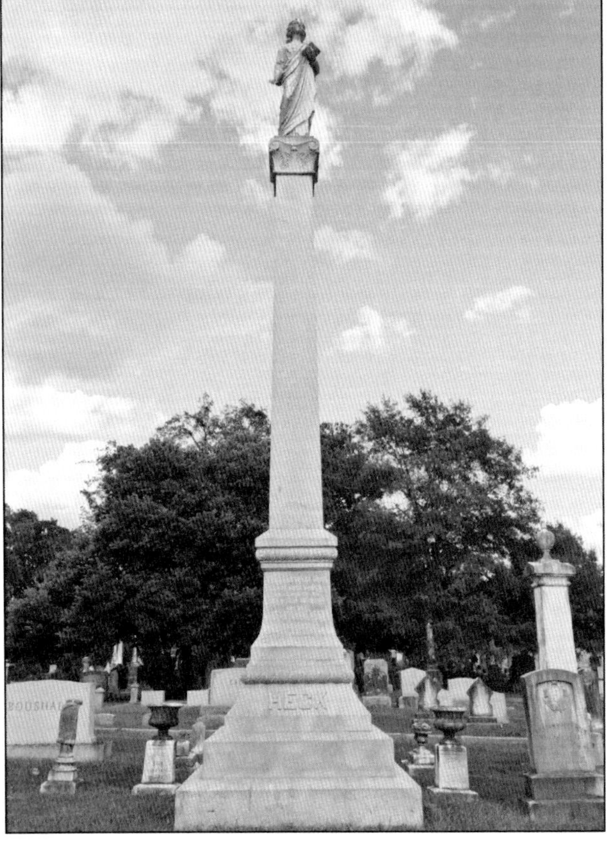

Col. Jonathan McGee Heck (1831–1894), a Confederate officer from (West) Virginia, became an industrialist and developer after the war, a cemetery association shareholder, and grand marshal in the city's 1892 centennial celebration. Heck's grand family home (built in 1870 and extant) and soaring cemetery obelisk speak of a resurgent postwar Tar Heel State. (Above, both, SANC; left, Palko.)

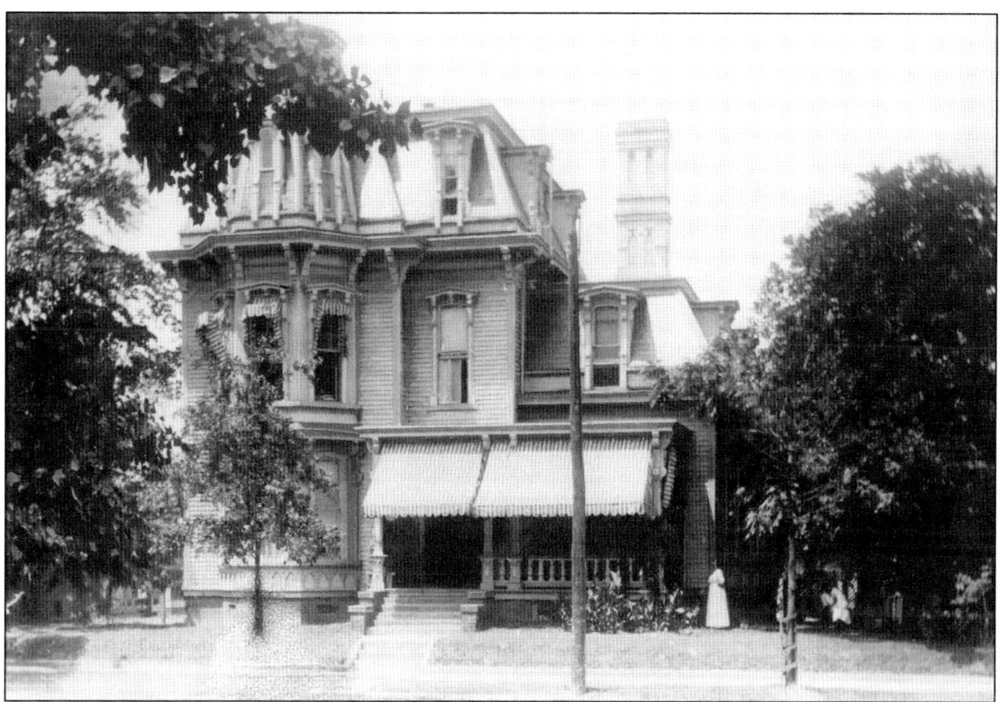

William Worrell Vass (1821–1896), a cemetery shareholder and plot owner, was treasurer of the Raleigh & Gaston Railroad for 48 years. That is said to be him standing on the locomotive. The Vass home, a Second Empire beauty built in the early 1880s at 3 East Edenton Street on Capitol Square, reflected both the family's wealth and the owner's occupation. The railroad yards in the early city were just a few blocks west. The Vass house, razed in 1971 to make room for the North Carolina Museum of History, was the last private mansion on Capitol Square. It is said Vass's daughter died at 96 on the day the state began demolition of the house. (Above, Karl Larson; below, SANC.)

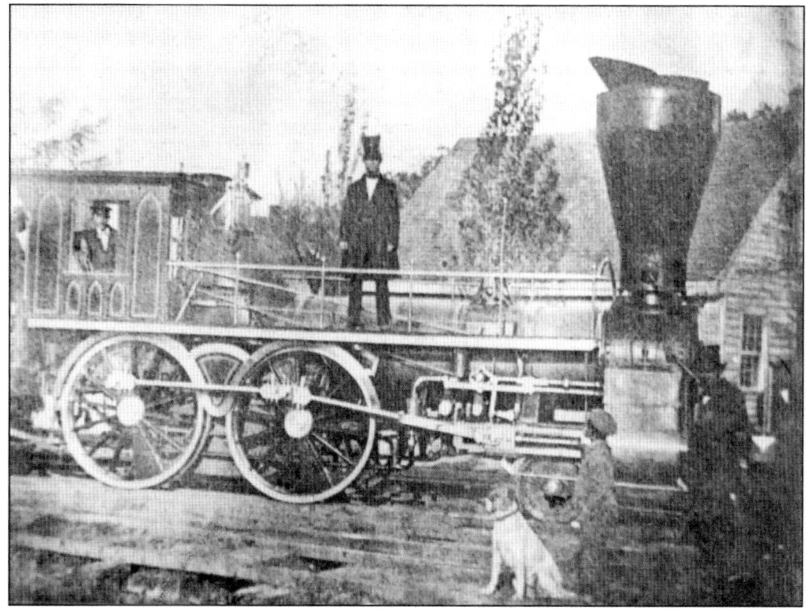

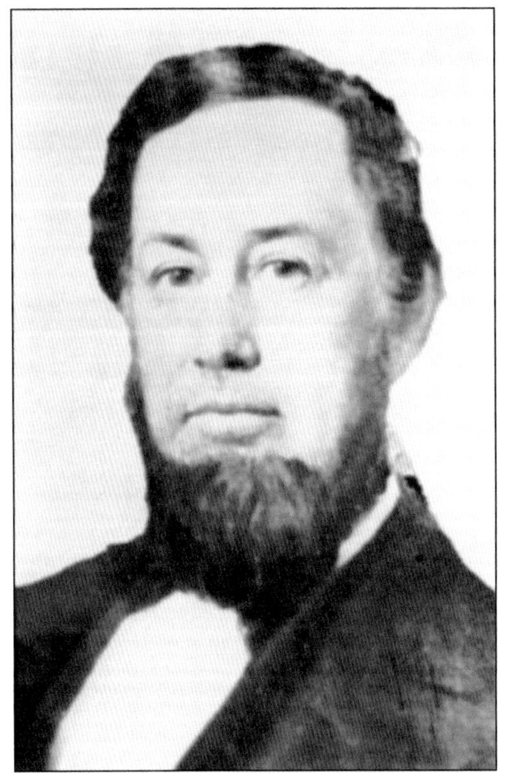

George William Swepson (1819–1883), a banker and Alamance County textile mill owner (Swepsonville, on the Haw River, is named for him), is remembered today chiefly as a Reconstruction-era rascal who, with a carpetbagger partner from New York named Milton Littlefield, defrauded the state of millions of dollars in tainted railroad bond and stock issues. Their "influence peddling" included bribes of food, drink, "loans," and other favors to members of the state legislature and other officials. Littlefield eventually fled the state, while Swepson, with substantial funds in his wife's name and with well-placed friends in government, escaped conviction; however, his single share of stock in the Raleigh Cemetery Association was rescinded and "reassigned." Swepson's home stood on Capitol Square next to First Baptist Church. (Left, SANC; below, Palko.)

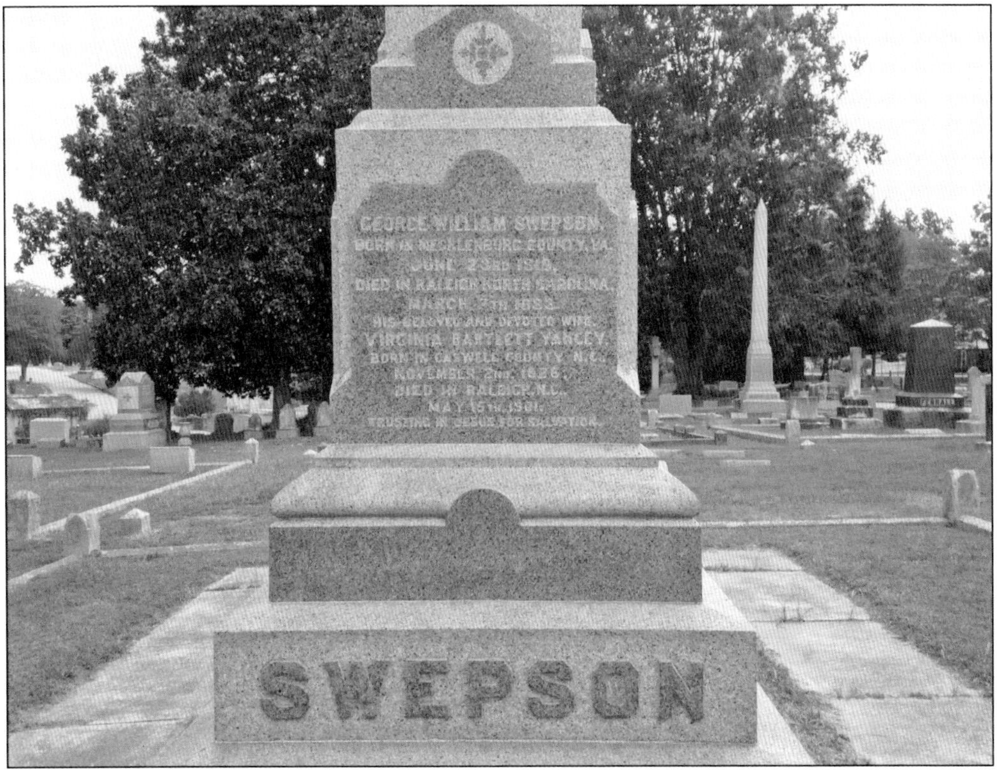

Asa B. Forrest (1846–1920) was a Pennsylvanian and a former Union soldier. As such, his appointment as the cemetery's second superintendent in 1874 was not without controversy. Forrest's background as a nurseryman made him an excellent choice, however, and he served Oakwood for nearly 50 years. For a short while, Forrest lived in a "sexton's [keeper's] house," once near today's main gate but long gone; he later lived on Polk Street within sight of the cemetery. He is credited with the early beautification of the place, notably with many trees, especially magnolias, which he also planted throughout the city. In Forrest's day, Oakwood had a lake, since filled in. A section of the cemetery is named in his honor. (Right, Johanna Grimes; below, SANC.)

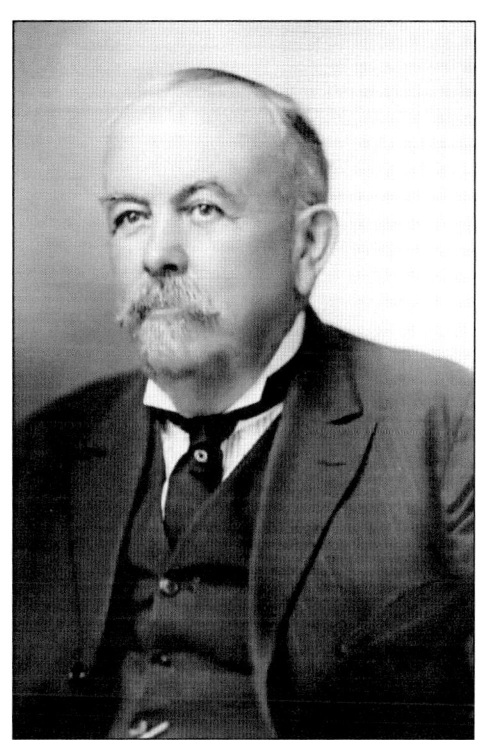

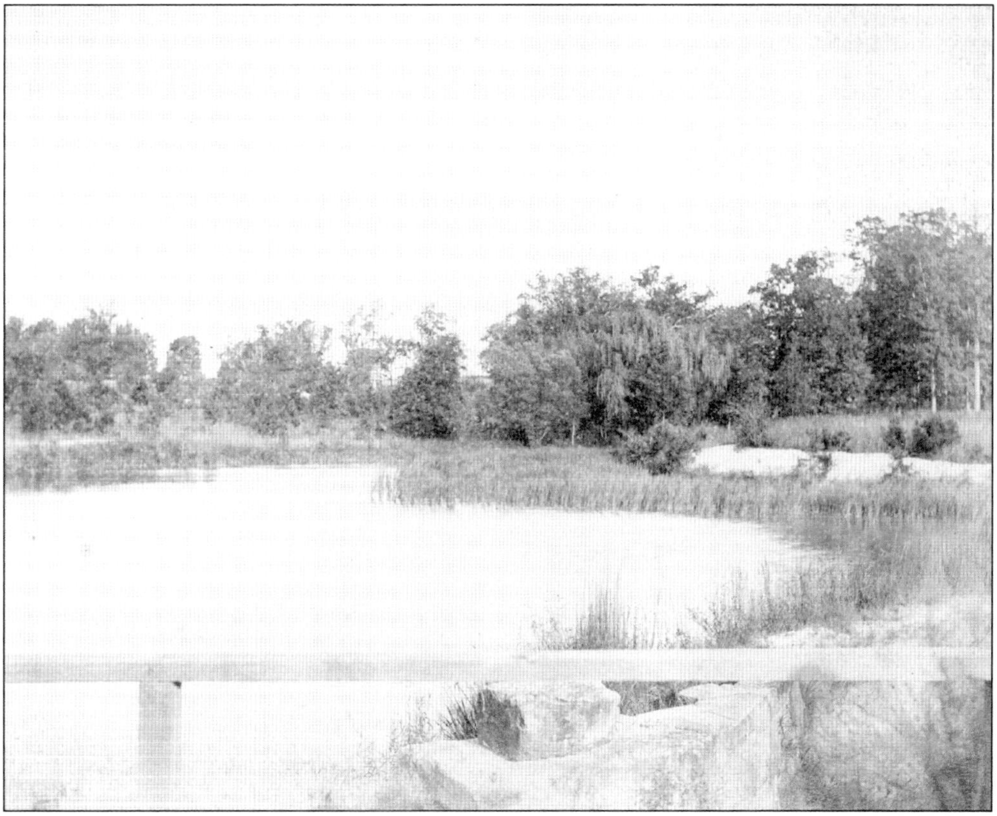

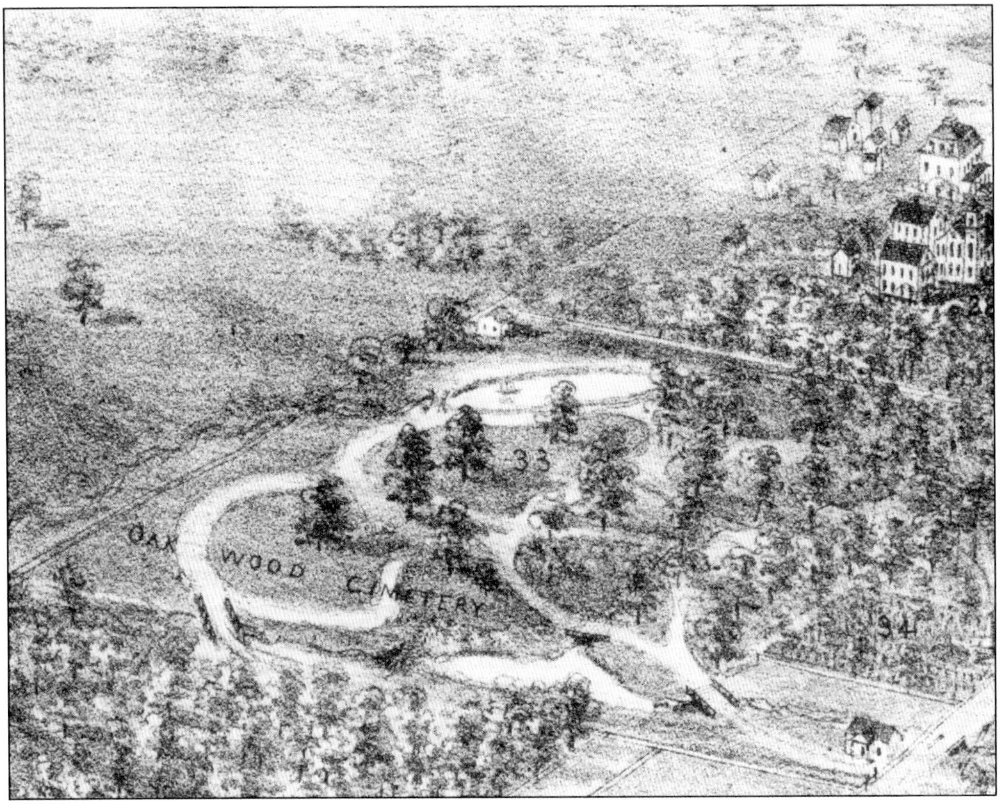

Oakwood Cemetery shows beyond "downtown" in this detail from the 1872 bird's-eye view of the city by famed mapmaker Camille Drie. The sinuous roads that wind through the historic section of the cemetery are clearly visible, as are the lake (with boat!) and the empty fields beyond into which Oakwood would expand in later years (to just over 100 acres, with nearly half yet to be utilized). Early photographs suggest that, in its early years, Oakwood had a more natural, less manicured look than it does today. (Above, HOC; below, NCCUNCLCH.)

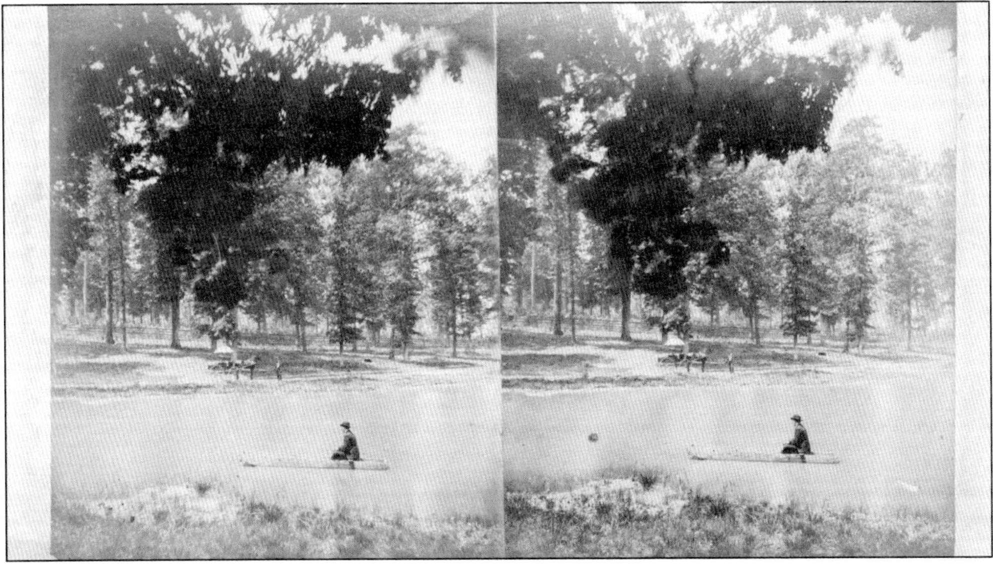

Three

Men and Women at Arms

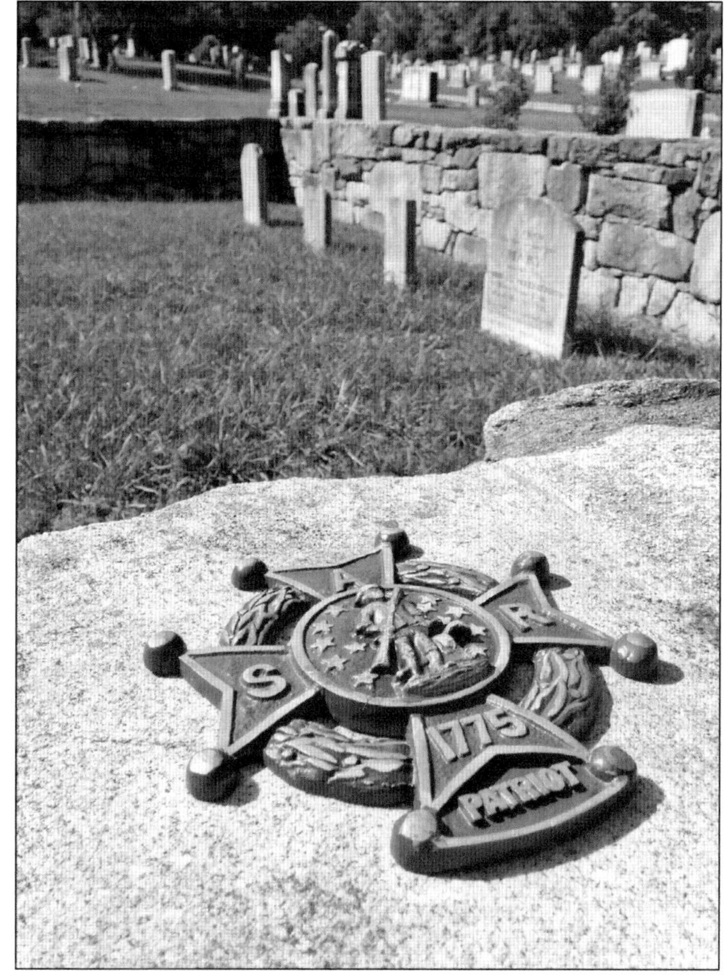

Interments in the larger cemetery include participants in most of America's major conflicts. The only known Revolutionary War veteran is Maj. John Hinton III (1748–1818), who fought with the local militia and later served as a legislator, judge, and sheriff. In 2007, the entire Hinton family cemetery—including its stone wall—was moved from the family's plantation to Oakwood; the dedication included a color guard of the Sons of the American Revolution. (Palko.)

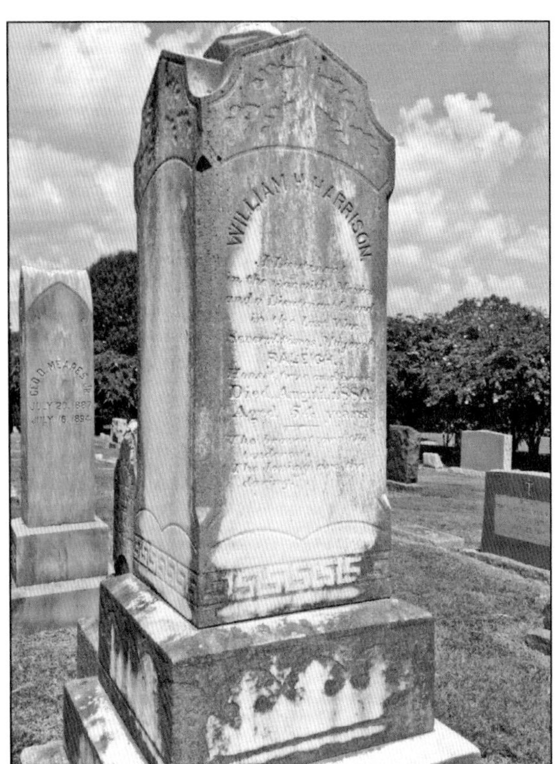

William Henry Harrison (c. 1826–1880), a US Army lieutenant in the Mexican War (1846–1848), served several terms as Raleigh's mayor (he may have been the first to be called that) during the period 1858 to 1872, broken by his service as a lieutenant colonel in the Confederate army. Harrison headed the small group of city leaders who surrendered Raleigh to General Sherman's Federals on April 13, 1865. (Palko.)

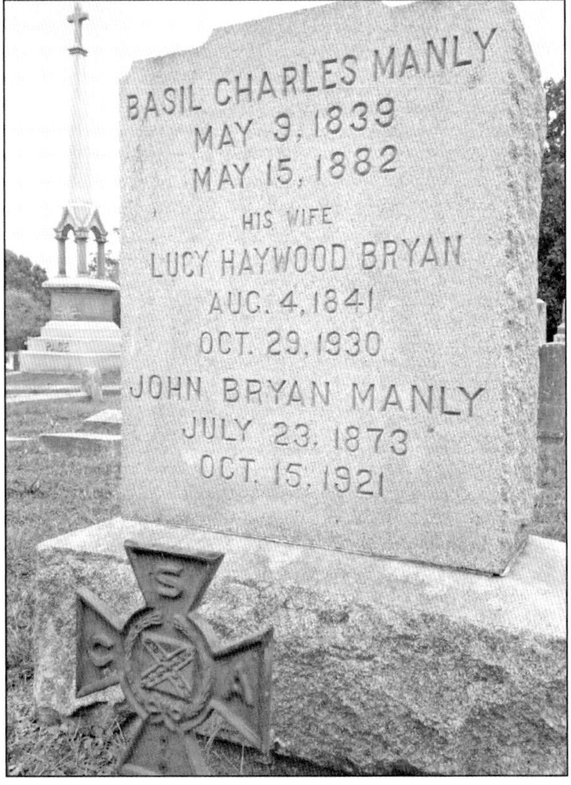

Maj. Basil Charles Manly (1839–1882), the son of a governor, was another veteran who served as mayor. "Manly's Battery" fought with Lee's Army of Northern Virginia and is said to have fired over 1,000 rounds at Gettysburg. After the war, this dashing Confederate artilleryman was elected to seven 1-year terms as Raleigh's mayor while managing the family estate, Ingleside, where Wake Medical Center is today. (Palko.)

Randolph Abbott Shotwell (1844–1884), a Virginian, left college in Pennsylvania to join Robert E. Lee's Army of Northern Virginia. His unit, the 8th Virginia Regiment, fought in 17 Civil War battles, and Shotwell led the sharpshooters of his regiment during Pickett's Charge at Gettysburg. He later spent time as a prisoner of war at Point Lookout and Fort Delaware. After the war, he became an "unreconstructed" newspaperman whose extreme views supporting the "Lost Cause" landed him in prison in 1871. Pres. Ulysses S. Grant granted Shotwell an unconditional pardon in 1872, after which he continued a newspaper career in Raleigh. (Both, SANC.)

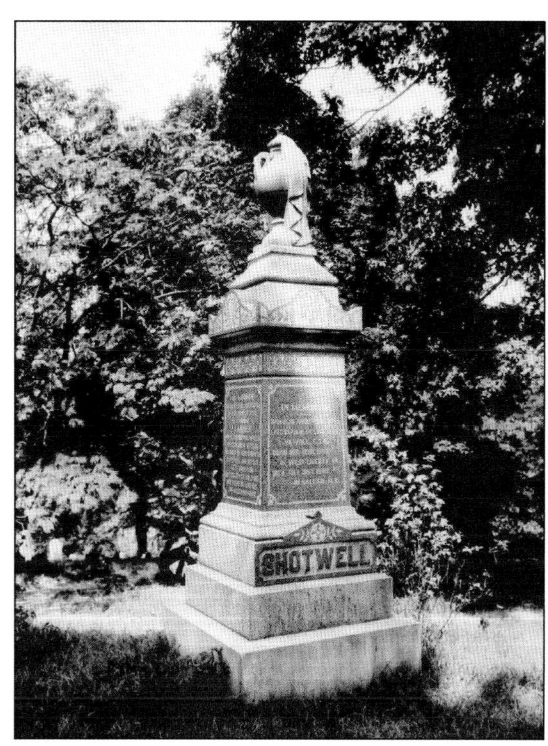

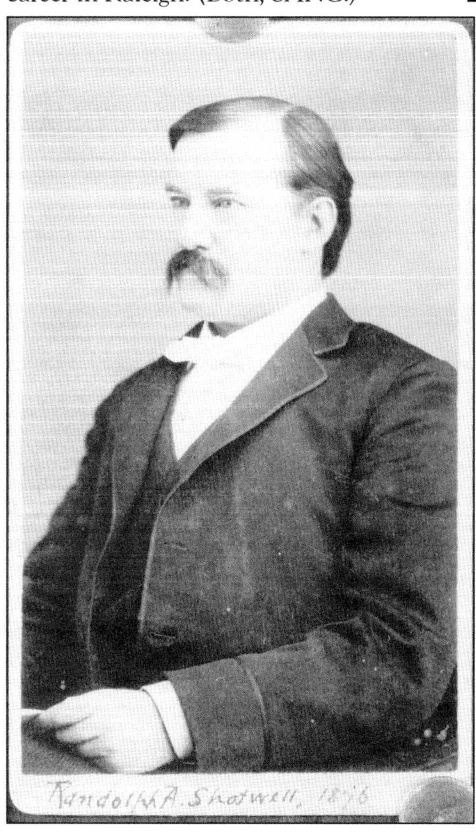

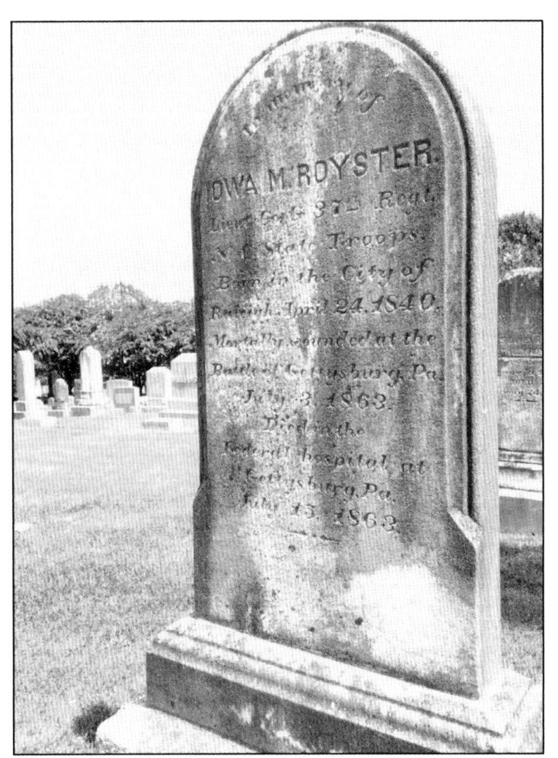

Iowa Michigan Royster (1840–1863), a member of a well-known Raleigh family with children named for states (such as Wisconsin Illinois, Virginia Carolina, and so forth), enlisted in the Confederate army soon after graduation from the University of North Carolina. He was mortally wounded at Gettysburg, probably during Pickett's Charge on July 3, and died in a field hospital 12 days later. Dr. Rufus Weaver, who sent the remains of thousands of Southern soldiers home from Gettysburg (including 137 to Oakwood, and others to Charleston, Savannah, and Richmond), kept Iowa's recovered remains in his Pennsylvania home until he could ship them, in 1871, to the young lieutenant's Raleigh brother, Arkansas Delaware Royster (1842–1884), later interred next to Iowa. (Left, SANC; below, Palko.)

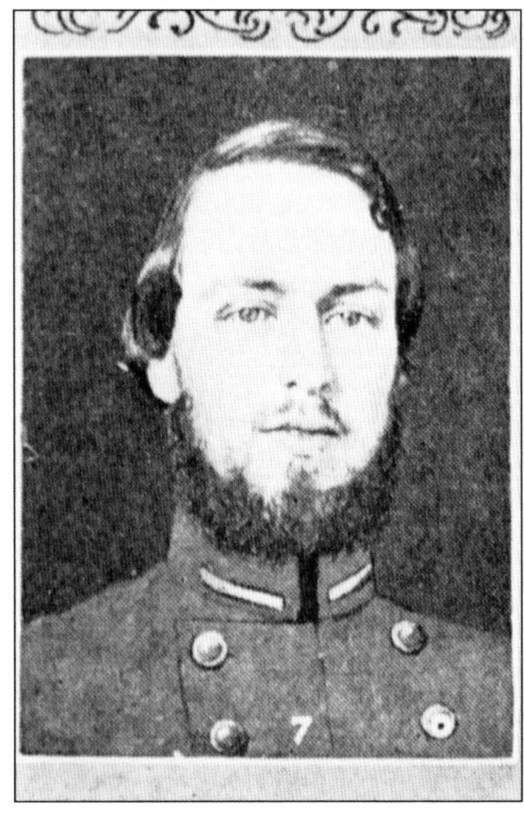

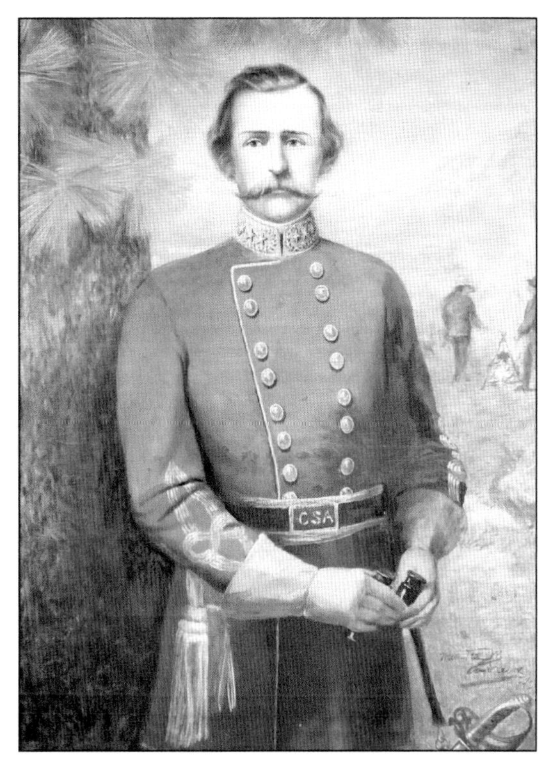

William Ruffin Cox (1832–1919) distinguished himself during the Civil War, rising to the rank of brigadier general (one of four Confederate generals in Oakwood, with none in the Confederate Cemetery). He was wounded in battle 11 times, and his giant obelisk memorial names the battles. It was his brigade that is said to have fired the last shots of Lee's army before surrender at Appomattox on April 9, 1865. After the war, Cox was active in politics and other civic affairs, serving three terms as a US congressman (1881–1887) and secretary of the US Senate (1893–1900). His home was in Raleigh off Hillsborough Street. (Right, SANC; below, Palko.)

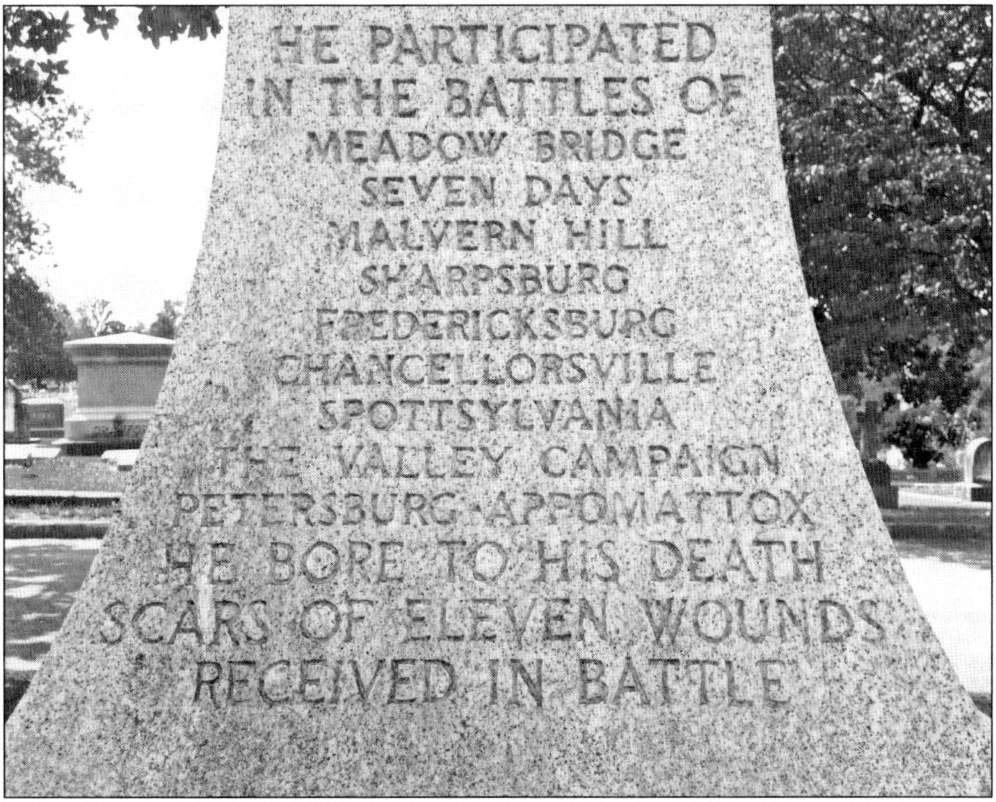

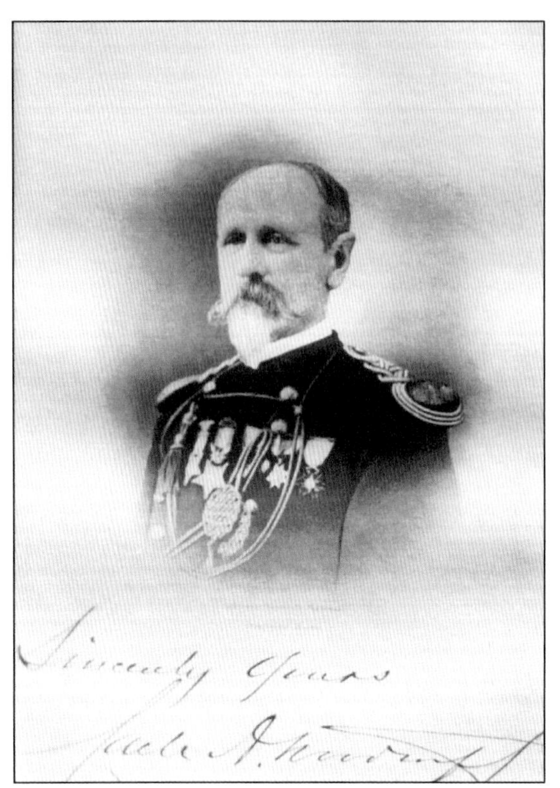

Carle Augustus Woodruff (1841–1913) won the Medal of Honor, America's highest military recognition, as an artillery officer with the Union army. In July 1863, while serving under Gen. George Armstrong Custer, he refused to abandon his guns in the heat of battle at Newby's Crossroads, Virginia, and saved the battery. A New Yorker by birth, Woodruff made the US Army a career, retiring as a brigadier general. He married a Raleigh girl, Euphemia Haywood, settled here, and made many friends among former Confederates, some of whom served as his pallbearers when he was buried as one of six known Union soldiers in Oakwood. A brother-in-law, US Army colonel Charles Winder Mason (1854–1913), died getting his wife, Marion Haywood Mason, to Woodruff's funeral and is buried behind him. (Left, SANC; below, Palko.)

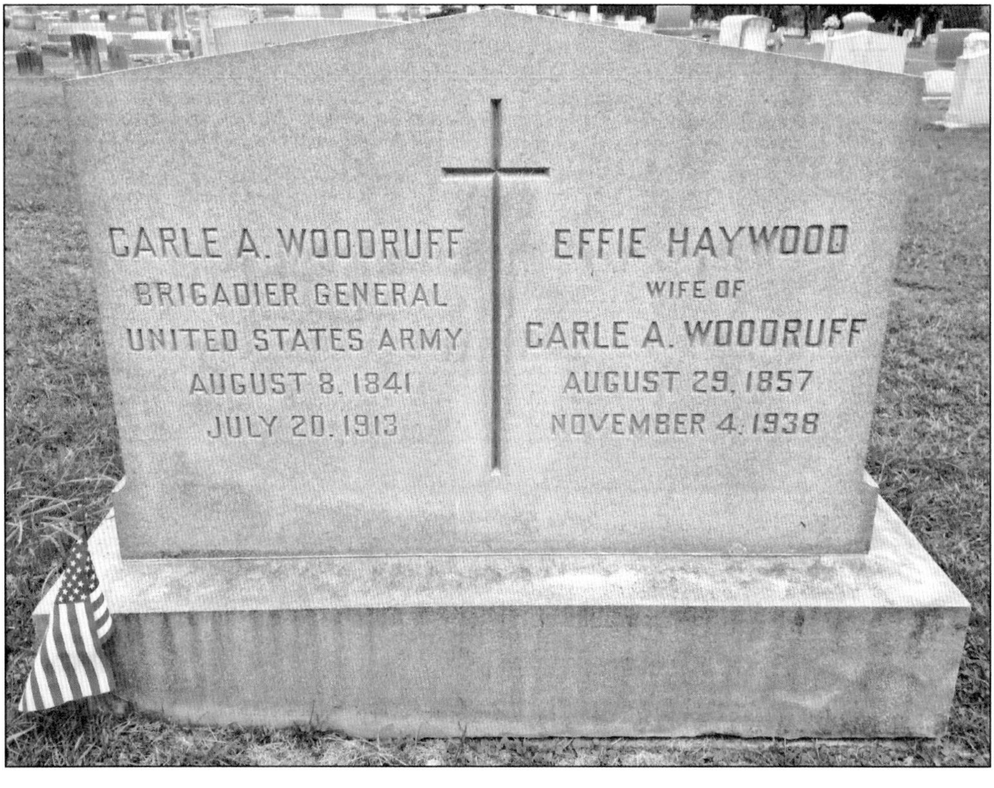

Ensign Worth Bagley (1874–1898) was the only US Navy officer to die in combat in the Spanish-American War, the result of "a terrible storm of fire and death" directed at his torpedo boat, USS *Winslow*, from Spanish guns at Cardenas, Cuba. A football star at Annapolis and brother-in-law of *News & Observer* owner Josephus Daniels, this Raleigh boy became a national hero; he lay in state at the North Carolina capitol, and some 15,000 mourners are said to have come to his funeral. In 1907, a statue of Bagley was placed on Capitol Square; next to it is a Spanish deck gun captured by the cruiser USS *Raleigh* at the Battle of Manila Bay (1898). Several US naval ships have been named in Bagley's honor over the years. (Both, SANC.)

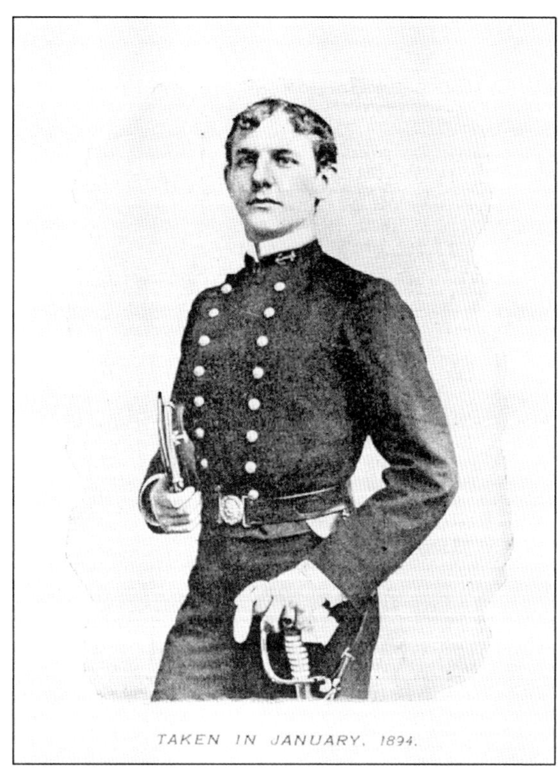

TAKEN IN JANUARY, 1894.

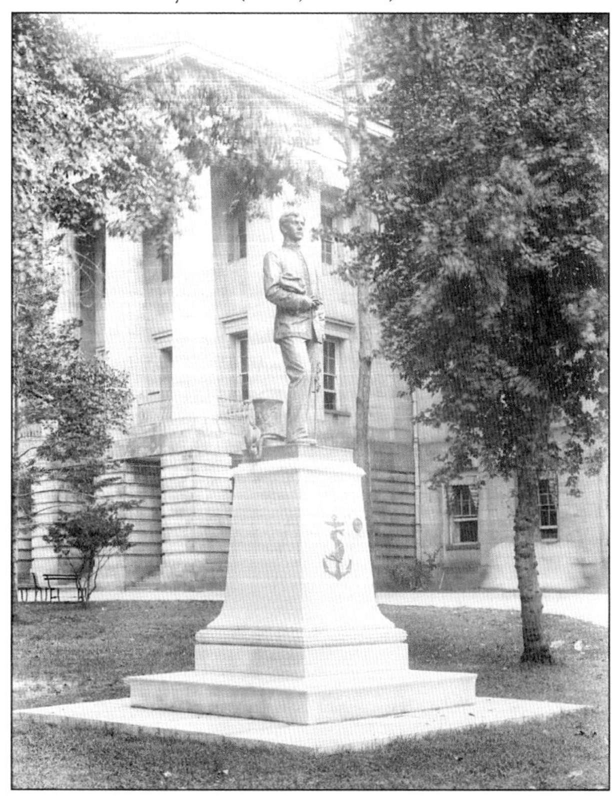

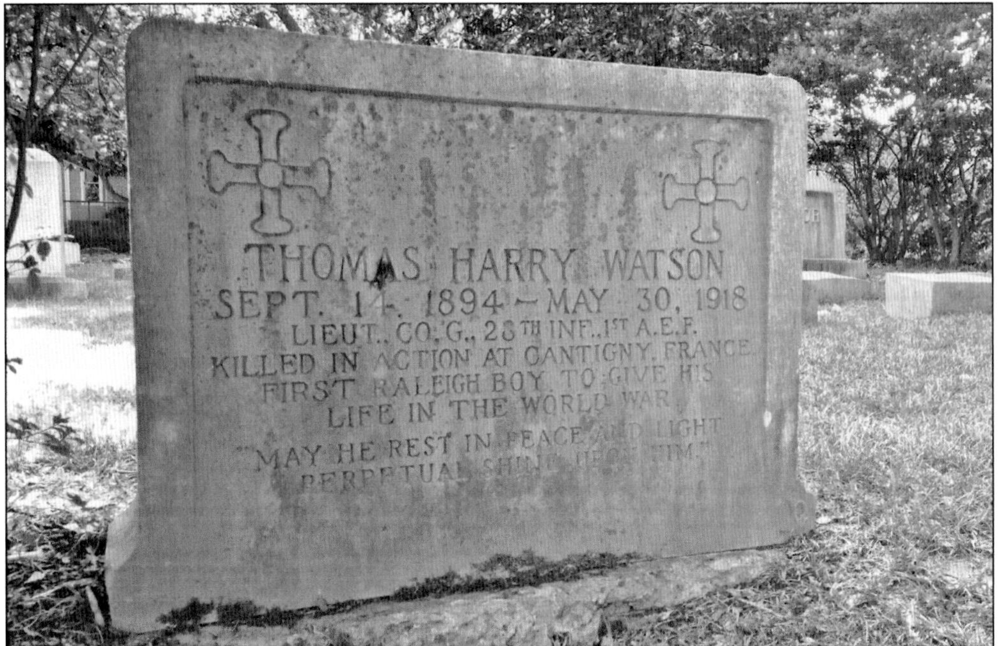

Thomas Harry Watson (1894–1918), a casualty of "the war to end wars," was the first World War I combat fatality from Raleigh. A lieutenant with the American Expeditionary Forces, he joined the assault on the French village of Cantigny in May 1918. Watson died, it is said, standing on a parapet, urging his troops: "Stick to it, boys. Give'em hell." (Palko.)

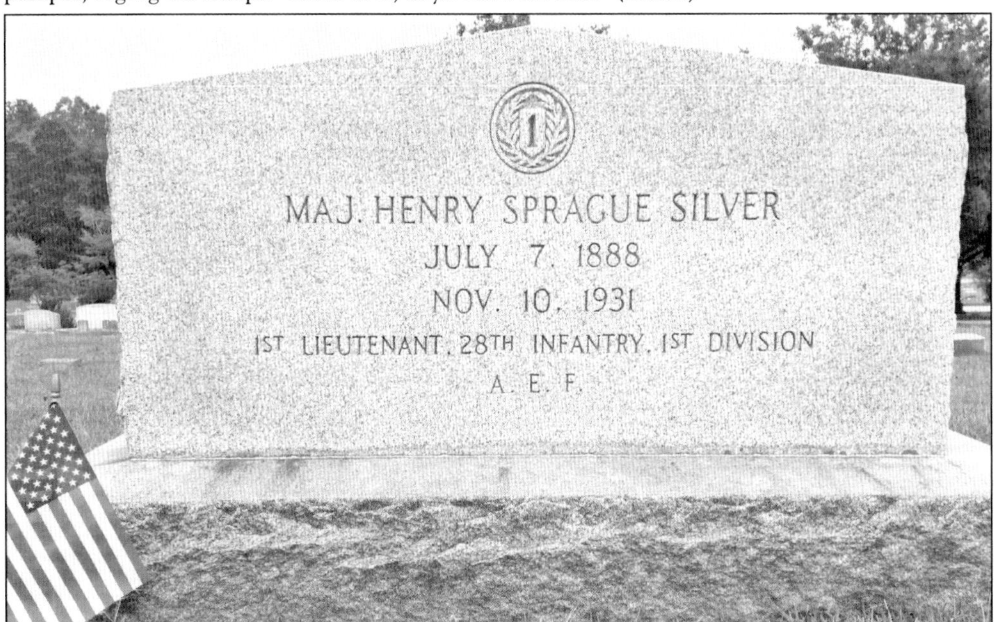

Henry Sprague Silver (1889–1931) enlisted in the US Army in 1917 and compiled a brilliant military record in France during World War I, earning the Distinguished Service Cross for heroism in action. After the war, he remained an officer with the National Guard; during a 1926 fire at the State Hospital for the Insane, Silver commanded a detachment of Guardsmen and ROTC students controlling hospital inmates. (Palko.)

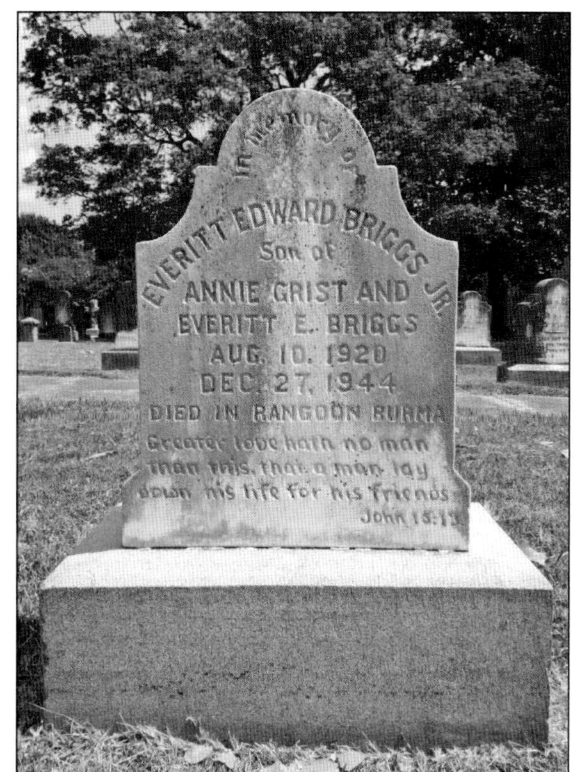

Everitt Edward Briggs Jr. (1920–1944), a Raleigh-born Army pilot in World War II, was shot down flying a P-51 fighter over Burma in 1943 and died in a prison camp in Rangoon (today's Yangon). After the war, the plane carrying home his remains and those of many others crashed after leaving Rangoon but (as of 2017) was never located. This remains a topic of controversy to this day. (Palko.)

Derward Blake Harper (1917–1944), from nearby Garner, North Carolina, was an Army Air Forces bomber pilot during World War II. During a mission on the China coast, his B-25 shot down an armed enemy seaplane in an unlikely dogfight, earning him a Silver Star. The award was posthumous as two days later bad weather caused his bomber to crash into a mountainside, killing Harper and his crew of five. (Palko.)

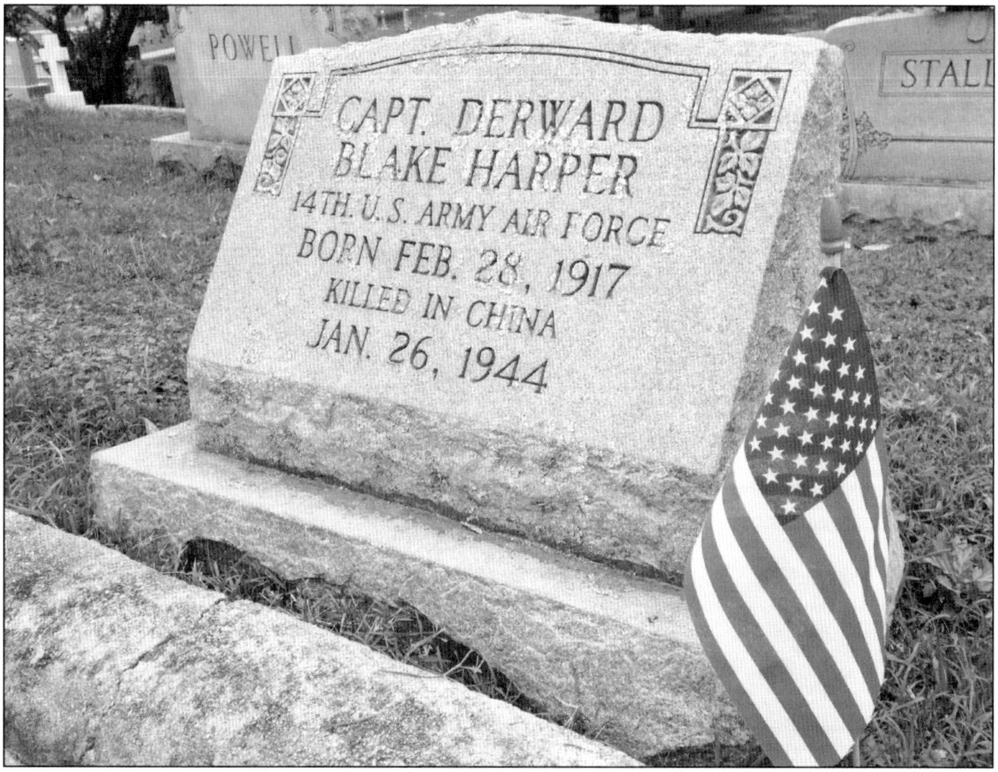

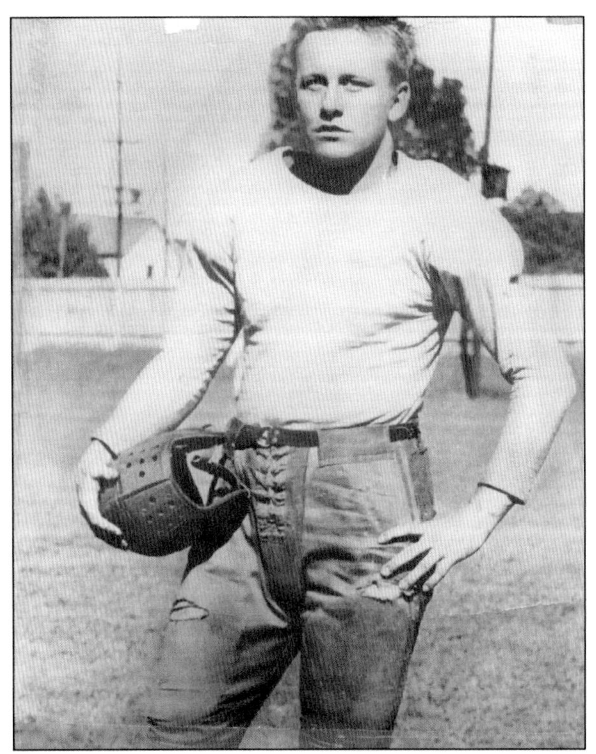

Robert Lafar Crocker Jr. (1925–1944) was a star football player with Raleigh High School when called to serve during World War II. He left Raleigh after the first half of his final football game, dedicated to him; those in the stands could watch as his train pulled away from the station near Devereux Meadow off Peace Street. As a marine, Crocker was sent to the Pacific and was wounded during the invasion of the Marshall Islands. Although the wound was mortal, Crocker sent a letter home the day before his death mentioning only a "minor mishap" so his parents would not worry. Initially buried on Eniwetok Atoll, his remains were later transferred to Oakwood Cemetery. (Both, Crocker family.)

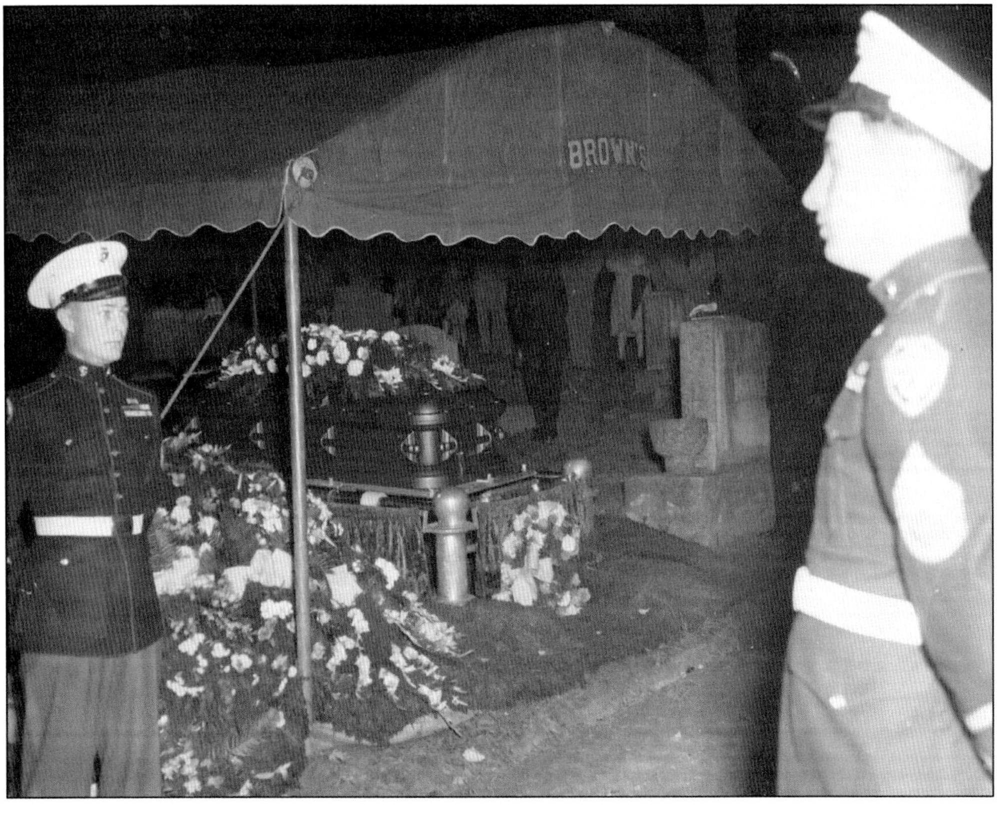

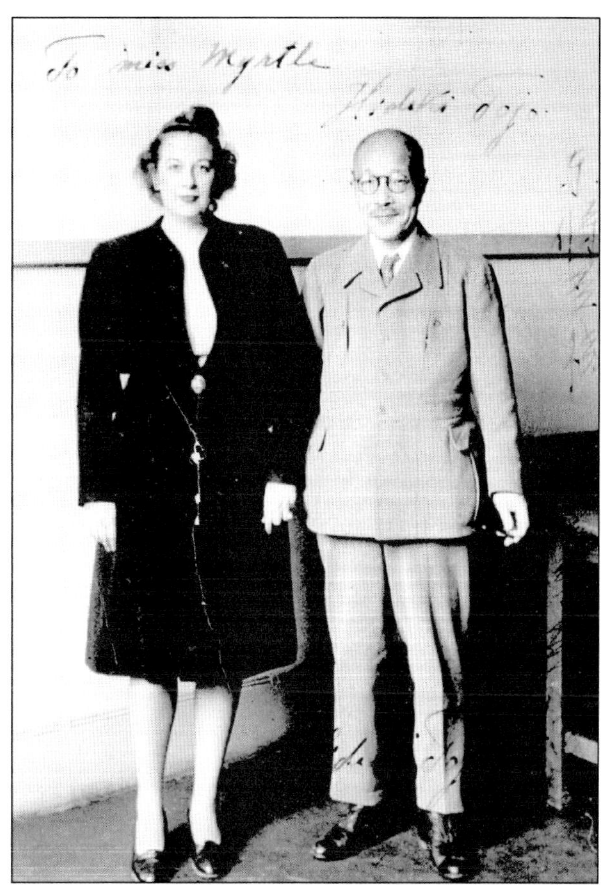

Myrtle Mills Hilton (1918–1988) was born into a prominent Raleigh family, attended Raleigh's Peace Institute, and worked for the Office of Strategic Services (OSS) as a court stenographer at the International Military Tribunal in Nuremburg, Germany (1945–1946). She later went to Tokyo in much the same capacity for the war crimes trial of Hideki Tojo, involved in planning the Pearl Harbor attack. She and the former Japanese premier developed a loose rapport, and she brought him chocolate bars from the Army PX. The photograph was taken as they said goodbye, she eventually returning to Raleigh as a legislative secretary. Tojo was hanged in December 1948. (Right, SANC; below, Palko.)

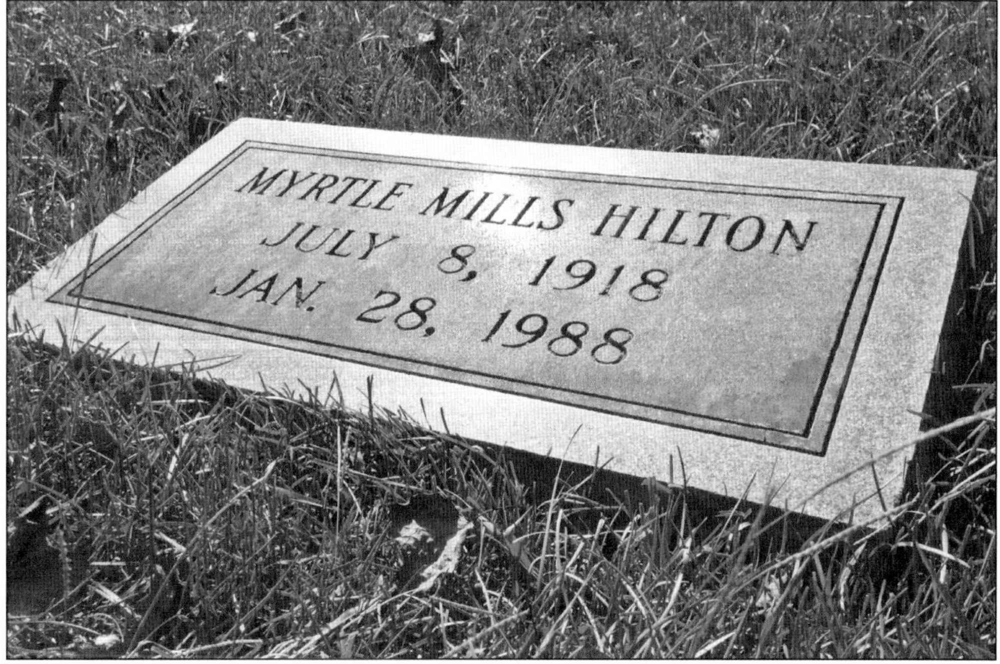

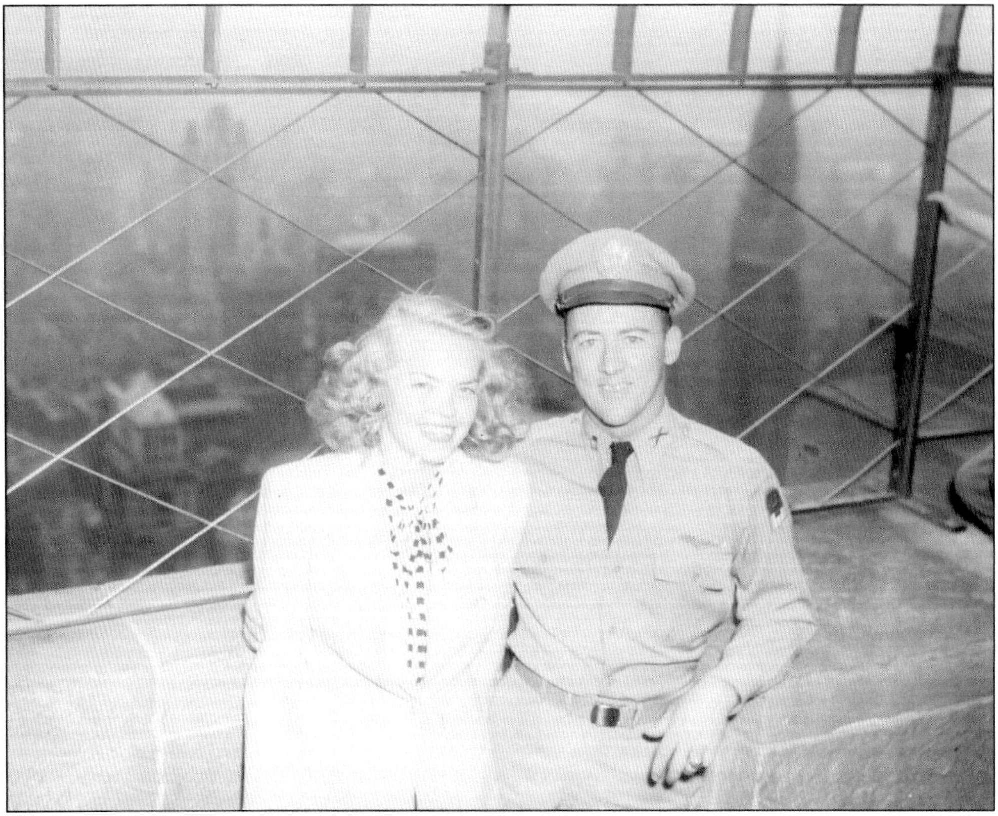

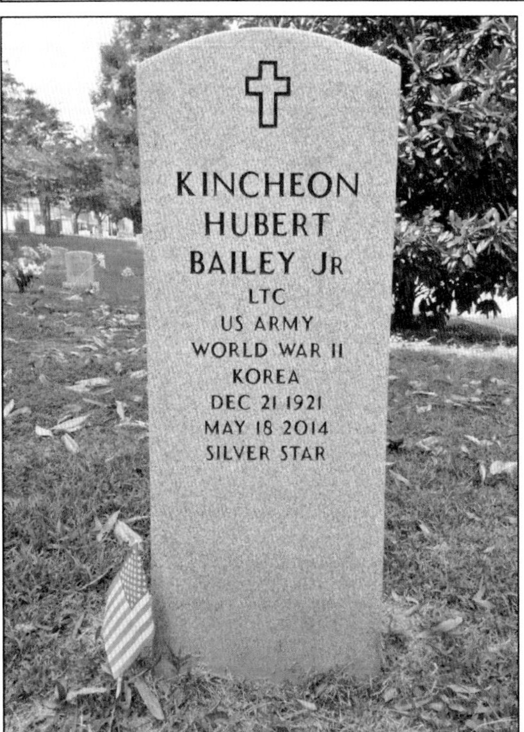

Kincheon Hubert "Bert" Bailey Jr. (1921–2014) received an appointment to West Point, class of 1945, and volunteered for service in Korea; there, he flew 614 combat hours, earning 10 Air Medals and the Silver Star. Later, he became a Green Beret with the 82nd Airborne, retiring from the military in 1966. He taught in a Raleigh community college for 25 years and ran marathons until age 74. Bert lies next to his beloved Tommye Lou ("T Lou," 1925–2009), his "Yellow Rose of Texas" and wife of 61 years, interred from a horse-drawn hearse. Their love story is on her stone and includes "KHB's" tour of duty in Korea, when he received from her "a box of cigars each month." (Above, Bailey family; left, Palko.)

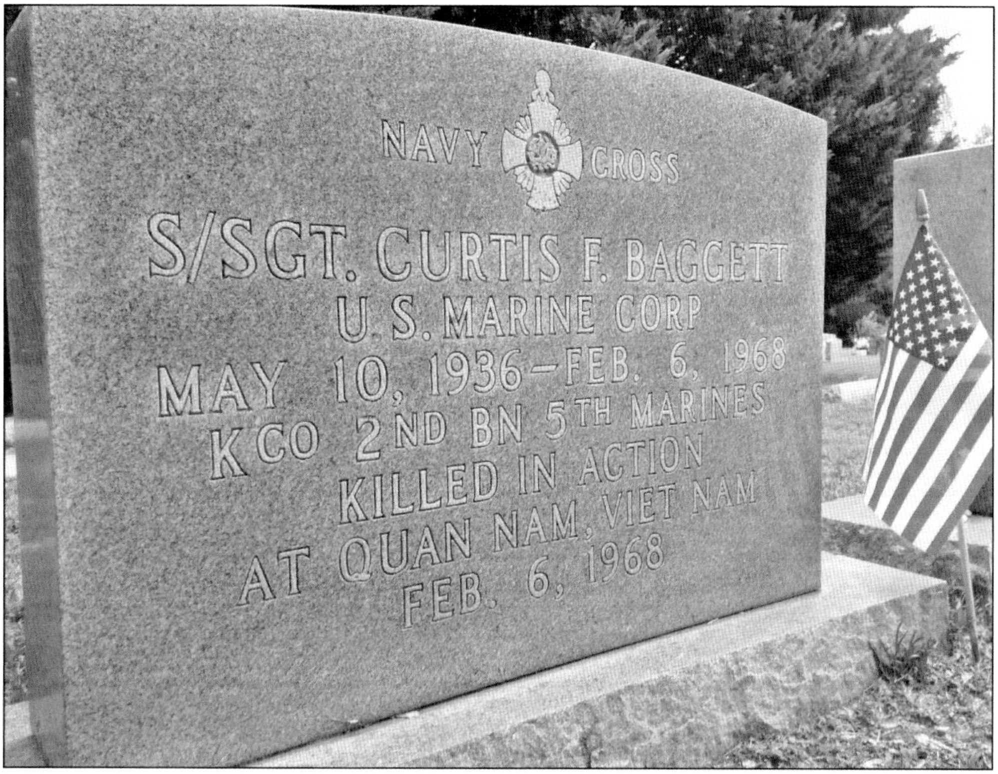

Curtis Franklin Baggett (1936–1968), Staff Sergeant, US Marine Corps, was posthumously awarded the Navy Cross (a recognition for valor second only to the Medal of Honor) for extraordinary heroism during an intense engagement between his platoon and a numerically superior North Vietnamese army force in Quang Nam Province, Republic of Vietnam. Baggett was killed in that firefight by an enemy rocket. (Palko.)

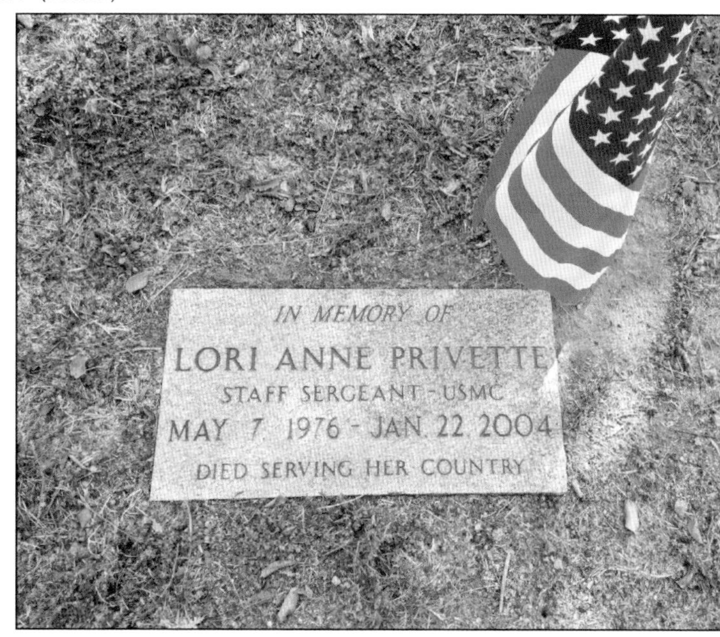

Marine staff sergeant Lori Anne Privette (1976–2004), a native of nearby Zebulon, North Carolina, was stationed at Camp Pendleton, California, as the corps' first female Huey helicopter crew chief when she and three fellow marines were killed in a helicopter crash during a routine training exercise. Sergeant Privette and a number of other military dead are honored with memorial tablets, called "battle blocks," in Oakwood's Field of Honor. (Palko.)

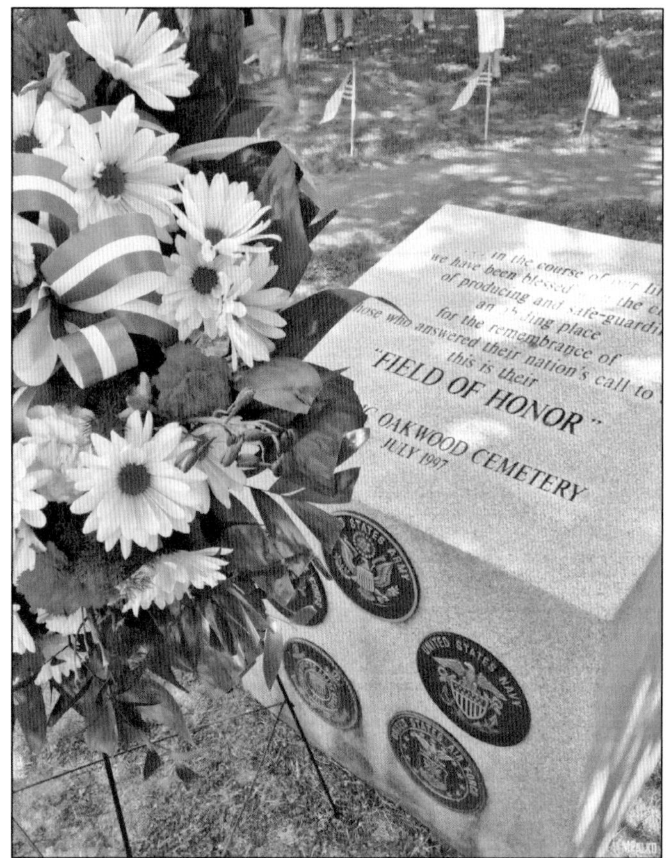

Oakwood Cemetery's Field of Honor was developed in the 1990s as a memorial to men and women who have served in America's military. Interred here are veterans from World War I to recent conflicts, many with family members beside them. Although relatively small, the facility in many ways resembles national cemeteries and follows similar protocols. Battle blocks occasionally memorialize service members not interred here but whose sacrifice inspired the donation. A columbarium holds cremated remains of service members and families (see page 122). (Both, Palko.)

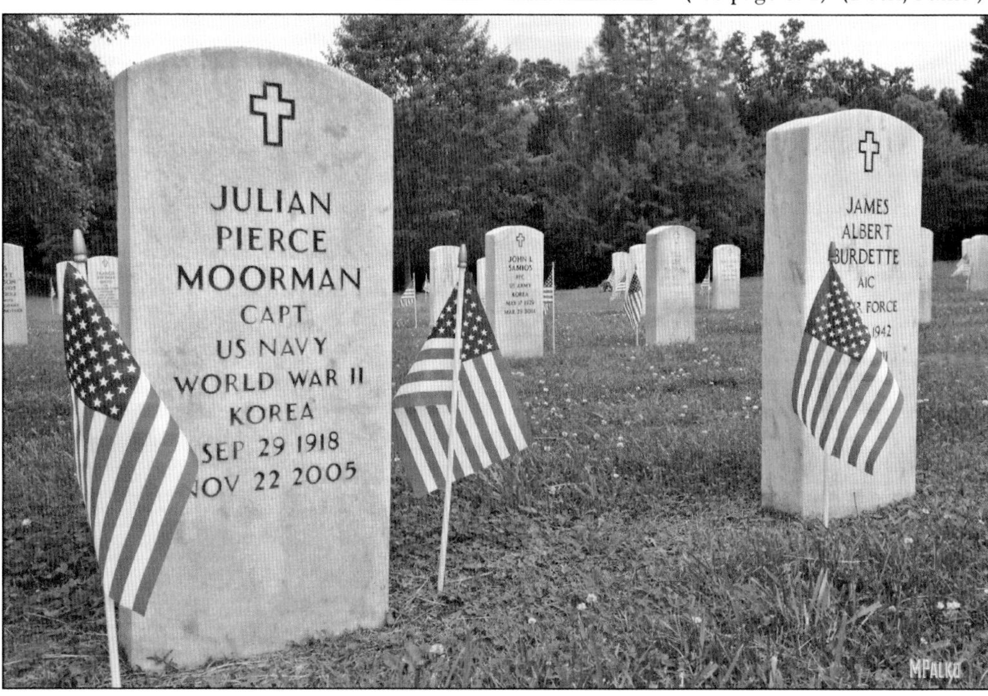

Four

Politicos

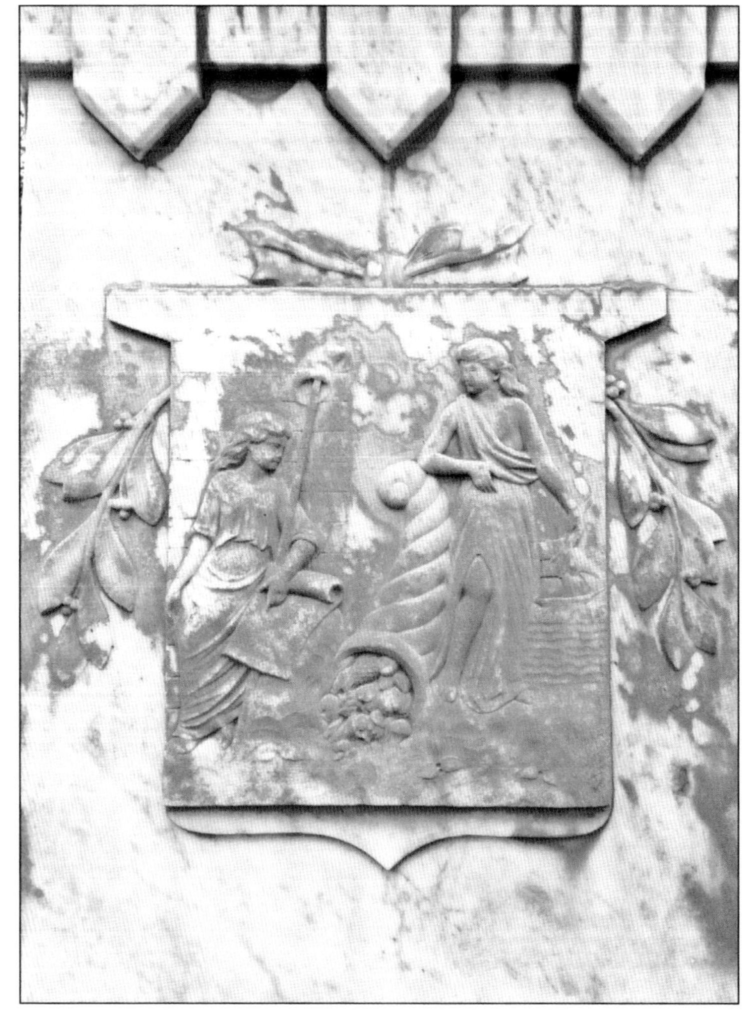

This carved seal of the state of North Carolina—from the grave marker of Jonathan Worth, governor from 1865 to 1868—reflects many in Oakwood Cemetery who determined the political history of the state. Seven Tar Heel governors rest here, as do a number of US senators and congressmen, state supreme court justices, legislators, and local officials. Several who are buried here served North Carolina under both the American and Confederate flags. (Palko.)

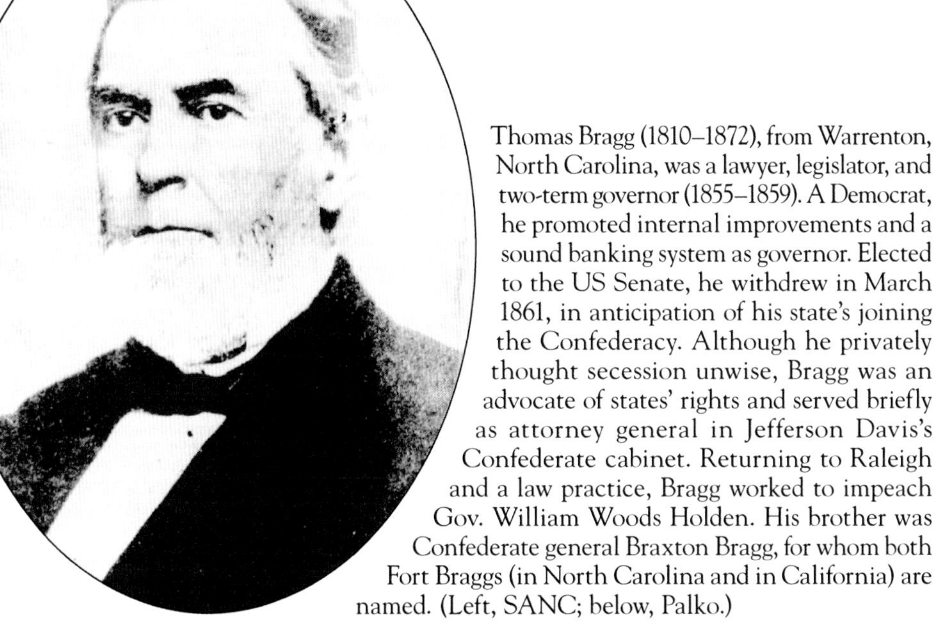

Thomas Bragg (1810–1872), from Warrenton, North Carolina, was a lawyer, legislator, and two-term governor (1855–1859). A Democrat, he promoted internal improvements and a sound banking system as governor. Elected to the US Senate, he withdrew in March 1861, in anticipation of his state's joining the Confederacy. Although he privately thought secession unwise, Bragg was an advocate of states' rights and served briefly as attorney general in Jefferson Davis's Confederate cabinet. Returning to Raleigh and a law practice, Bragg worked to impeach Gov. William Woods Holden. His brother was Confederate general Braxton Bragg, for whom both Fort Braggs (in North Carolina and in California) are named. (Left, SANC; below, Palko.)

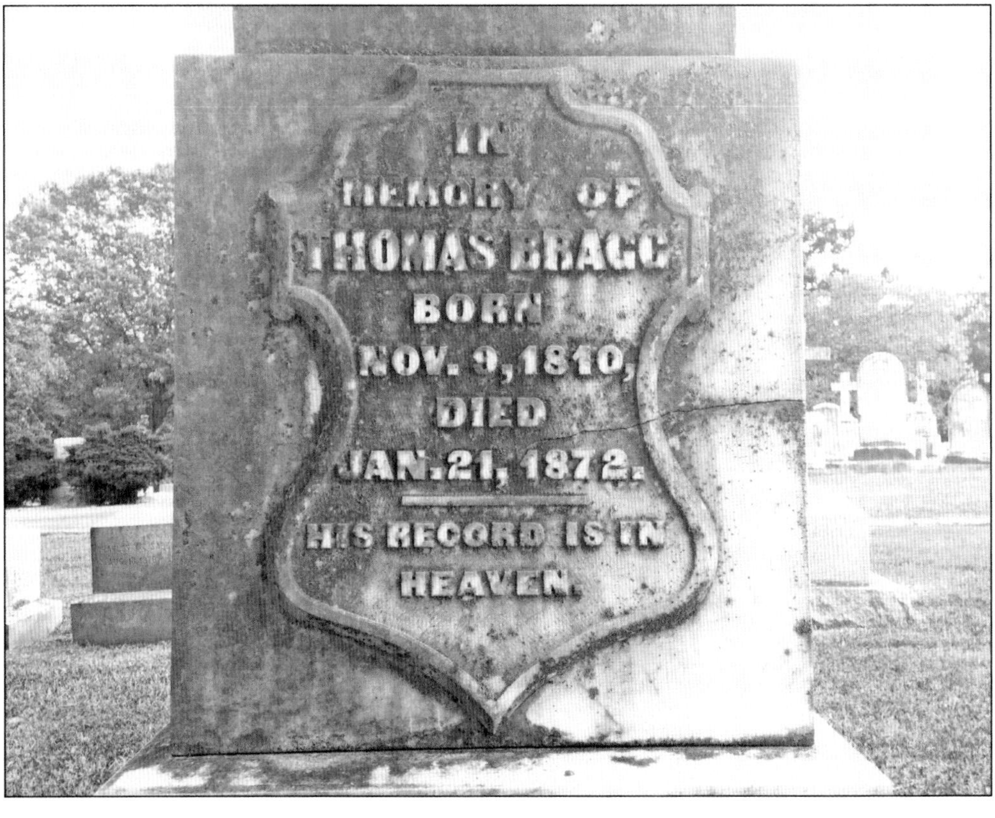

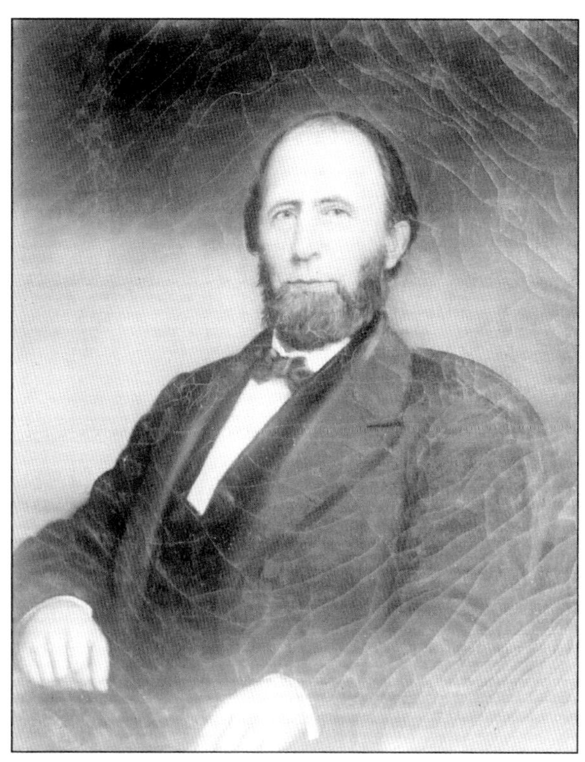

William Woods Holden (1818–1892), born near Hillsborough, became a newspaperman professionally and a "lightning rod" politically. Initially a Democrat and a secessionist (he was a signer of the state's Secession Ordinance), he later led the peace movement in the state during the Civil War and after Appomattox became the state's first Republican governor (1865; 1869–1871). As a Reconstruction-era opponent of the Ku Klux Klan, Holden ran afoul of conservative political forces, who had him removed. He was the first US governor to lose his office through impeachment. Holden ended his days living quietly at Nash Square in what was considered one of the finest homes in downtown Raleigh. (Right, SANC; below, Palko.)

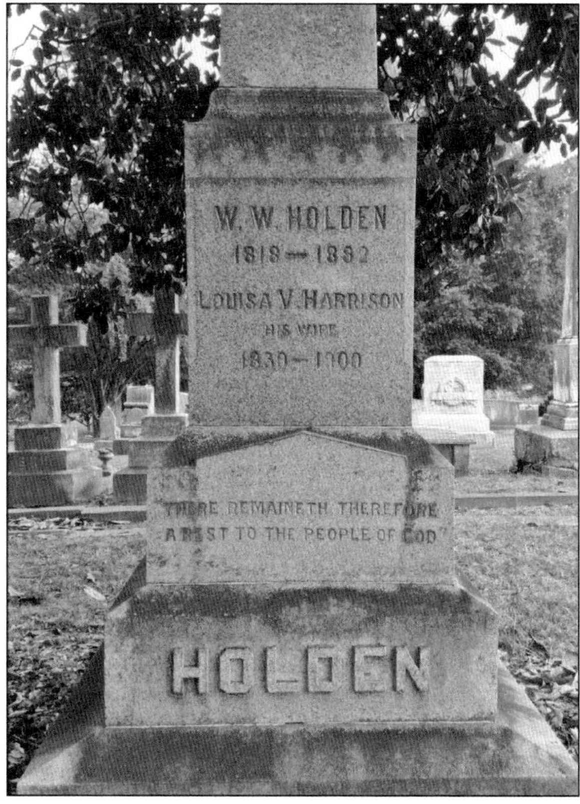

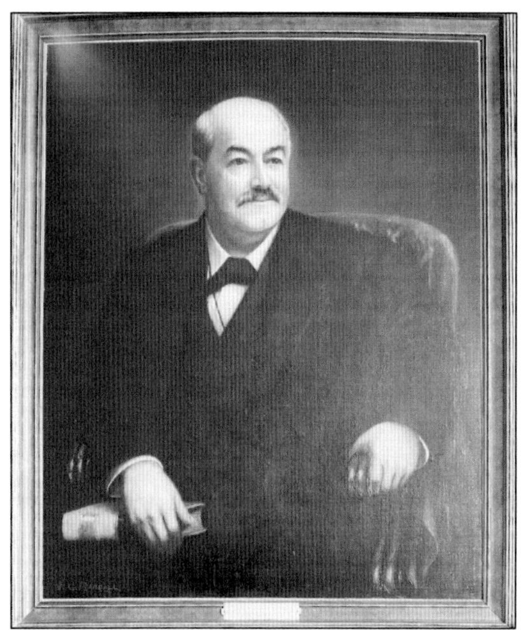

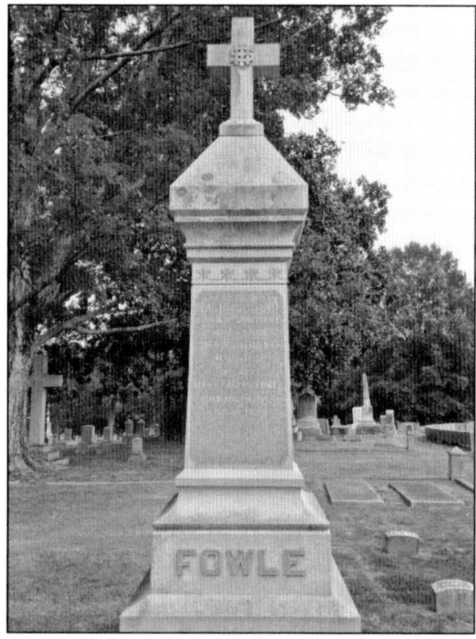

Daniel Gould Fowle (1831–1891), an attorney and a Democrat, was elected governor in 1888 and, as a widower with several children, was the first to live in the Governor's Mansion (1891). He also was the first to die in it, and subsequent residents believed his ghost haunted the place. (Above left, SANC; above right, Palko; below, SANC.)

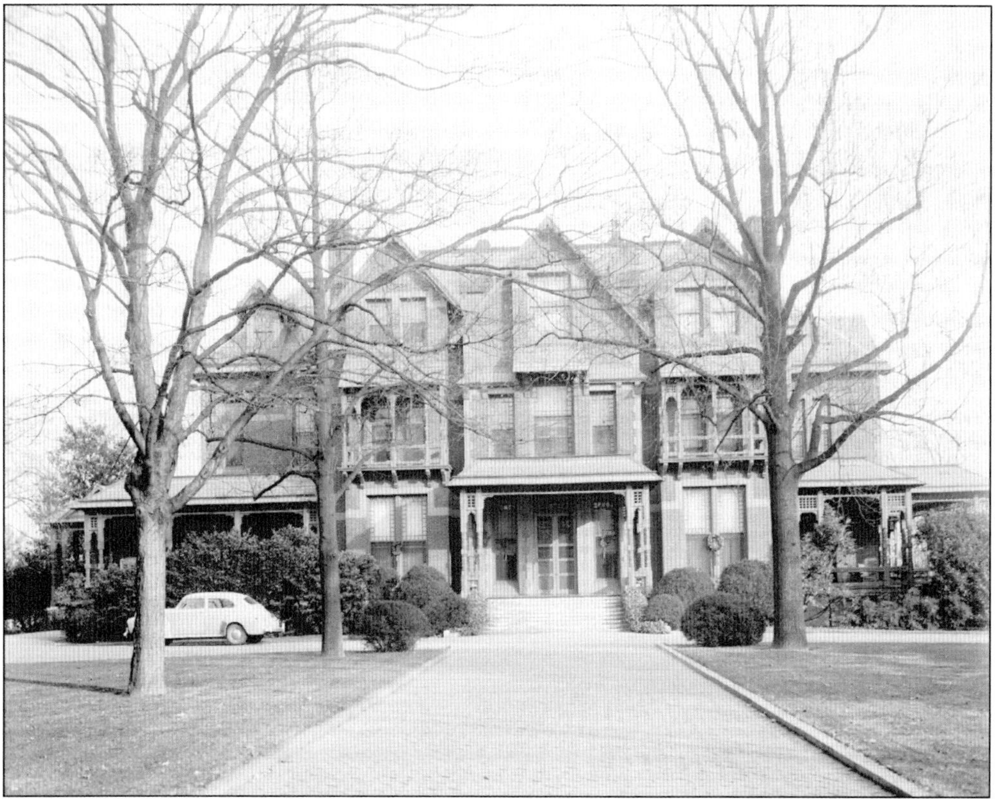

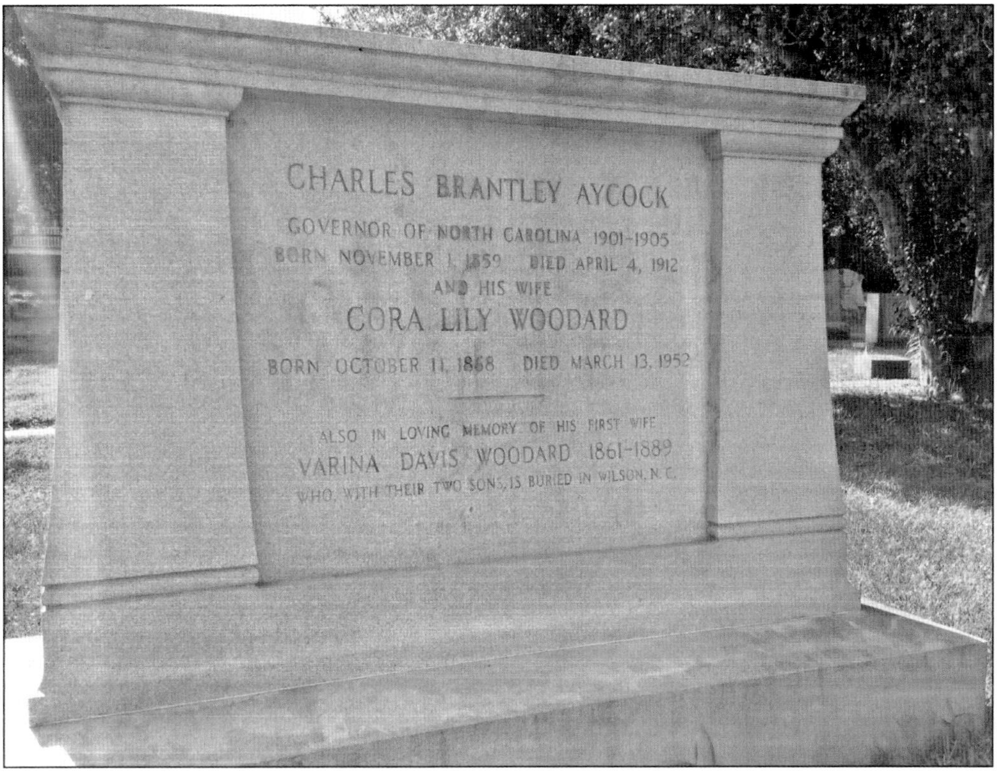

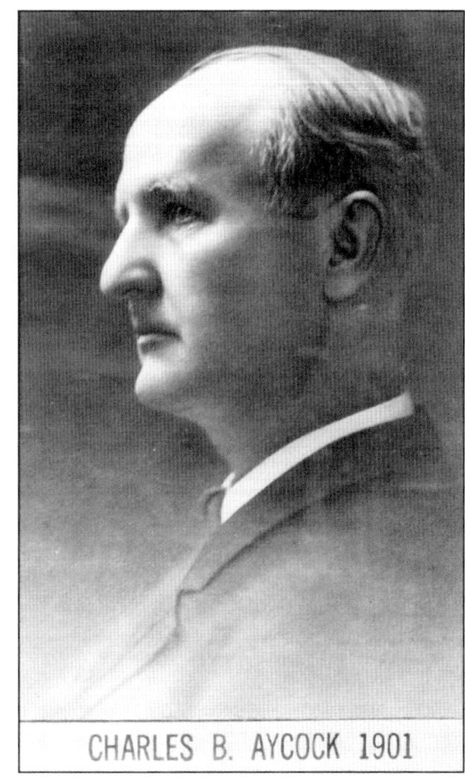

Charles Brantley Aycock (1859–1912), from Wayne County, North Carolina, taught school for a short time as a teenager but later practiced law. Active in politics and a friend of the influential Josephus Daniels of the *News & Observer*, Aycock was elected Democratic governor in the controversial campaign of 1900. As the state's chief executive, he spoke widely on the need for better schools, worked to improve them for whites and blacks, and became known as the state's "education governor." After he left the governorship, Aycock reestablished himself as a lawyer, purchasing a home in the Oakwood Historic District in 1910. His death came during a speech in Birmingham, Alabama, in which his final spoken word was "education." (Above, Palko; right, SANC.)

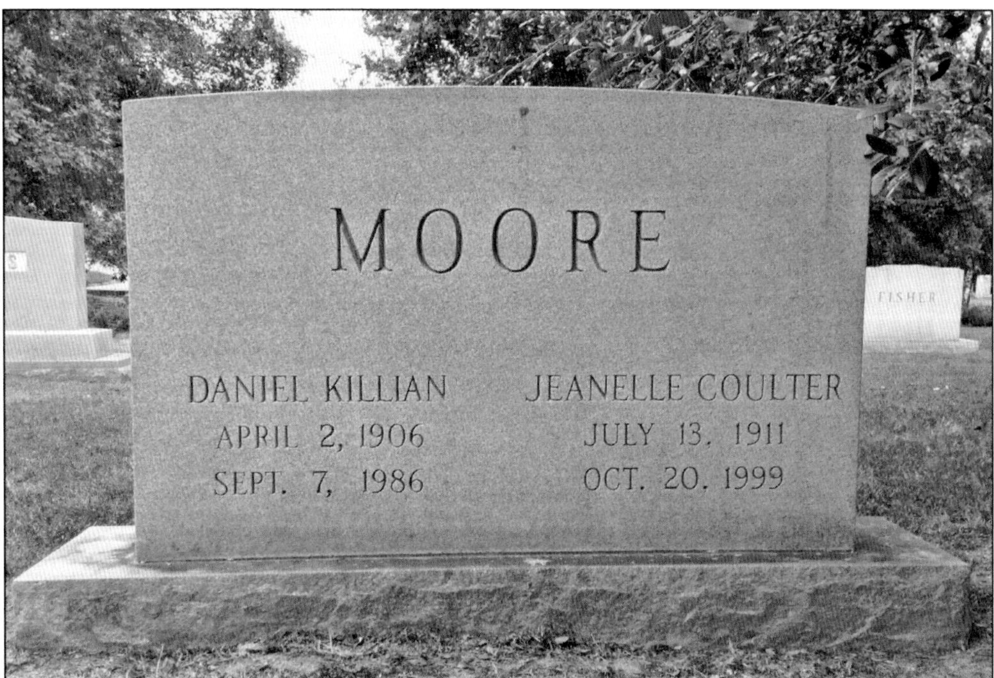

Daniel Killian Moore (1906–1986), an Asheville-born University of North Carolina graduate, US Army paratrooper during World War II, and superior court judge, was elected 66th governor of North Carolina in 1964. A Democrat, Moore was seen as a centrist during a term in office that saw a significant increase in teacher pay, the passage of a major road-improvement bond, and a moderate approach to emerging civil rights issues. After leaving the Governor's Mansion, Moore was appointed to the state supreme court. Jeanelle Coulter Moore (1911–1999), an active first lady, supported the arts, promoted the beautification of highways and of the Governor's Mansion, and authored a book, *The First Ladies of North Carolina*. (Above, Palko; below, SANC.)

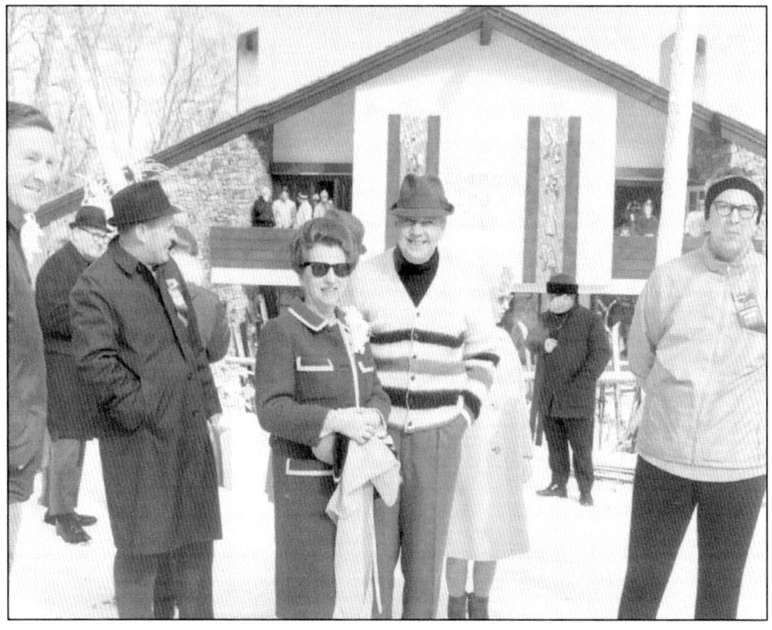

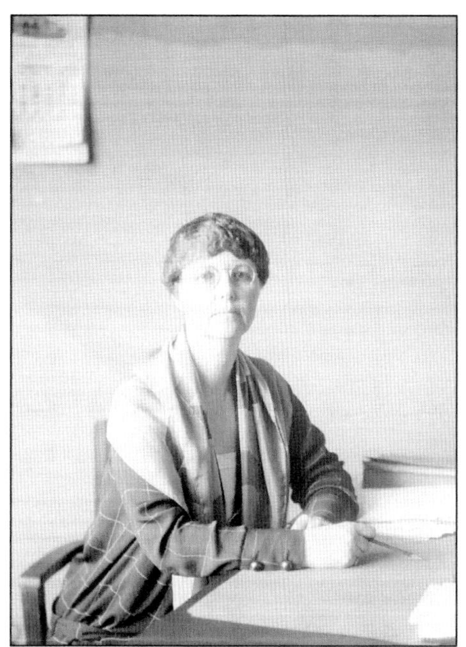

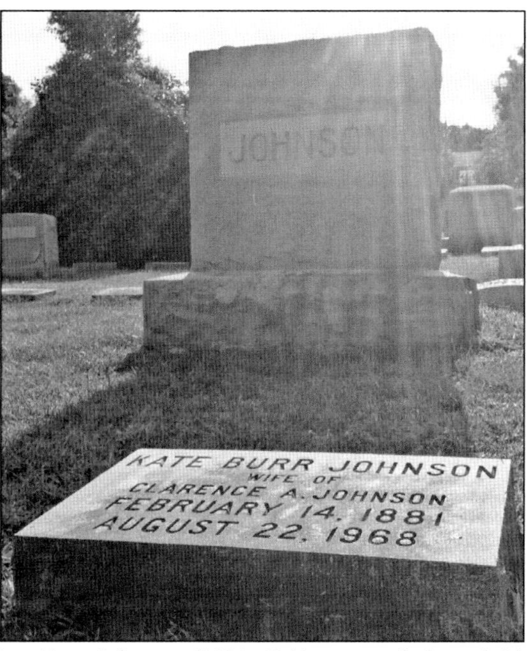

Carrie Lougee Broughton (1879–1957) and Kate Burr Johnson (1881–1968; pictured above left) were two of the first women to head major departments of state government—Broughton as head of the State Library of North Carolina (1918–1955) and Johnson of the Department of Public Welfare (1921–1930), now the Department of Health and Human Services. (Above left, SANC; above right and below, Palko.)

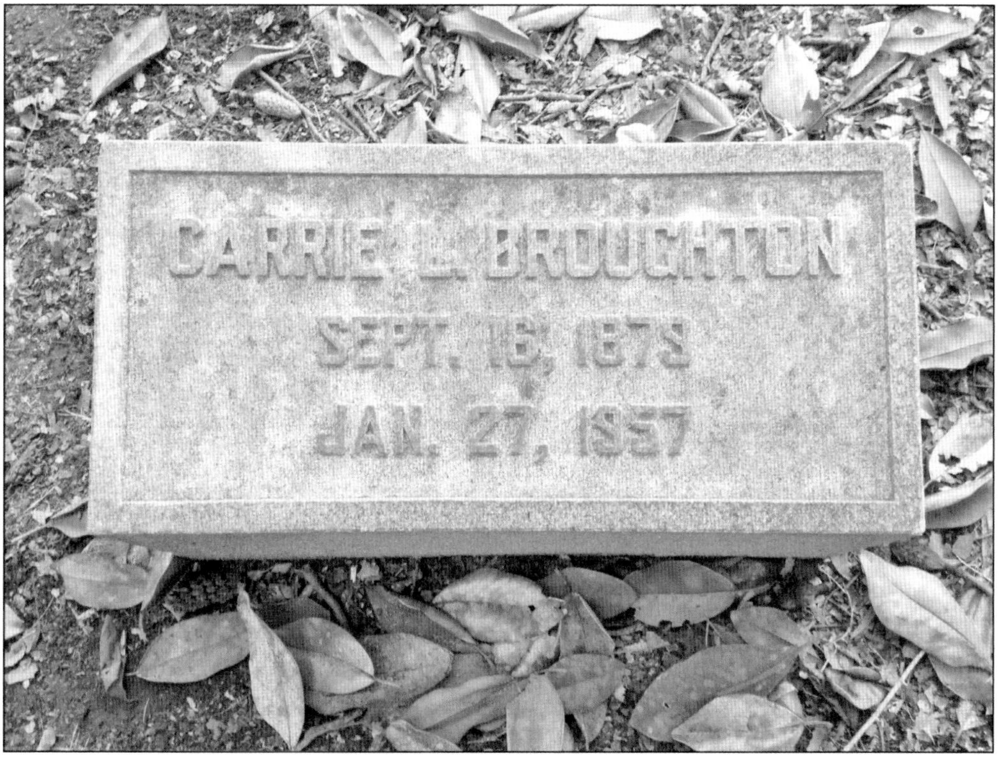

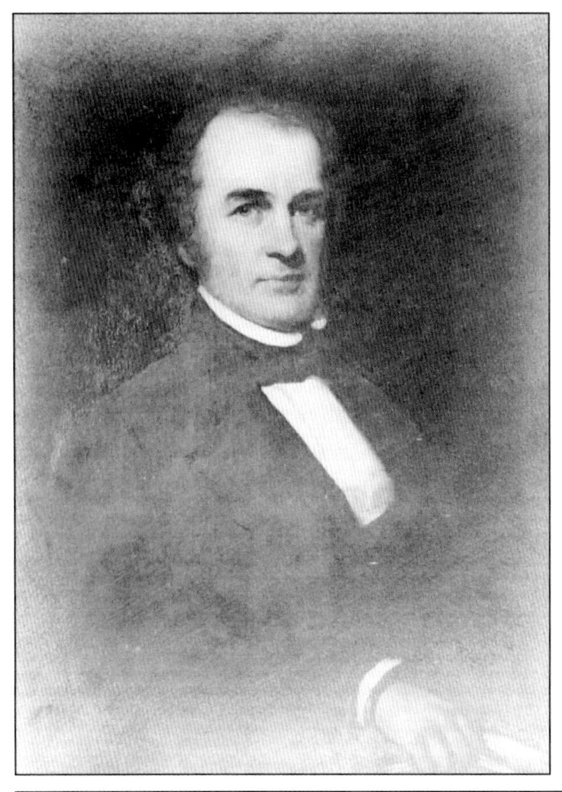

George Edmund Badger (1795–1866), a Yale student and a lawyer by training, served his state and nation in a variety of political roles: judge, legislator, and US senator (1846–1855). He briefly was secretary of the Navy (1841), recommending the establishment of a home squadron and technology upgrades for naval units. In 1853, Senate Democrats, distressed at his support for a national bank and lack of enthusiasm for slavery, blocked the nomination of this Whig to the US Supreme Court by one vote. As of 2017, Badger's small law office still stands on the grounds of Raleigh's Mordecai House; he married three times, and his wives were all from prominent families. (Left, SANC; below, Palko.)

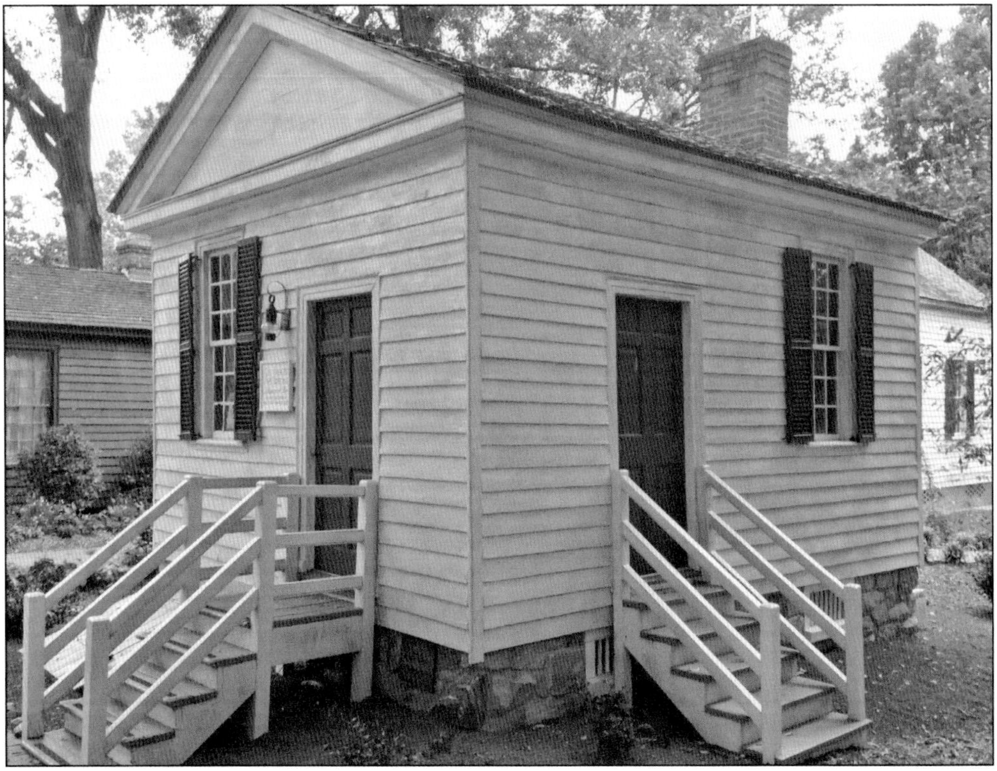

Josiah William Bailey (1873–1946) grew up in Raleigh and graduated from Wake Forest University. For many years, Bailey and his family were associated with the Baptist *Biblical Recorder* (Bailey was editor from 1895 to 1907), and he later joined the state bar and became active in politics. Elected US senator in 1930, Bailey is remembered as a "progressive" Democrat at home but a "conservative" Democrat in Washington, where he opposed much of Roosevelt's New Deal as creating too much federal power but supported preparedness for World War II. He and his wife, Edith Walker Pou Bailey (1890–1966), had five children. When he died in office, Bailey was replaced by William B. Umstead, who was later governor. (Right, SANC; below, Palko.)

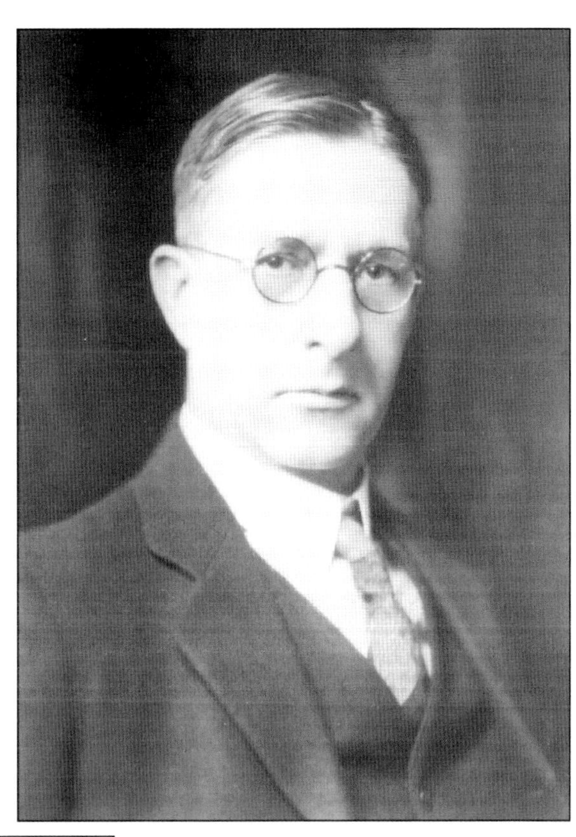

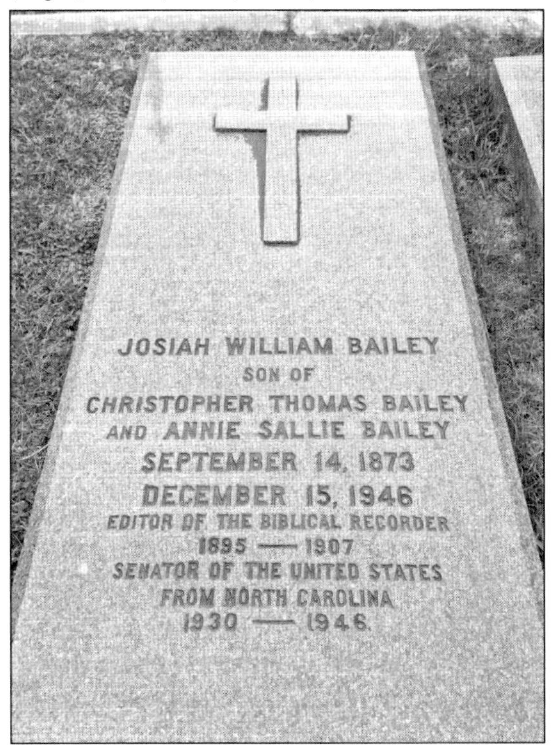

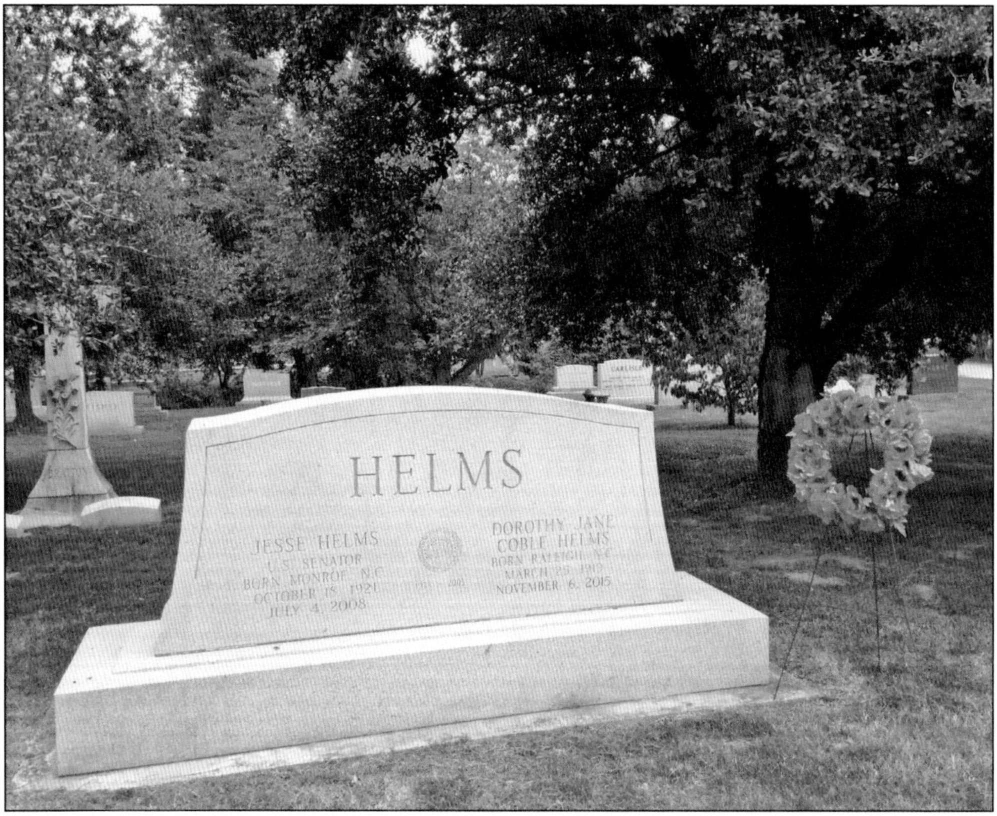

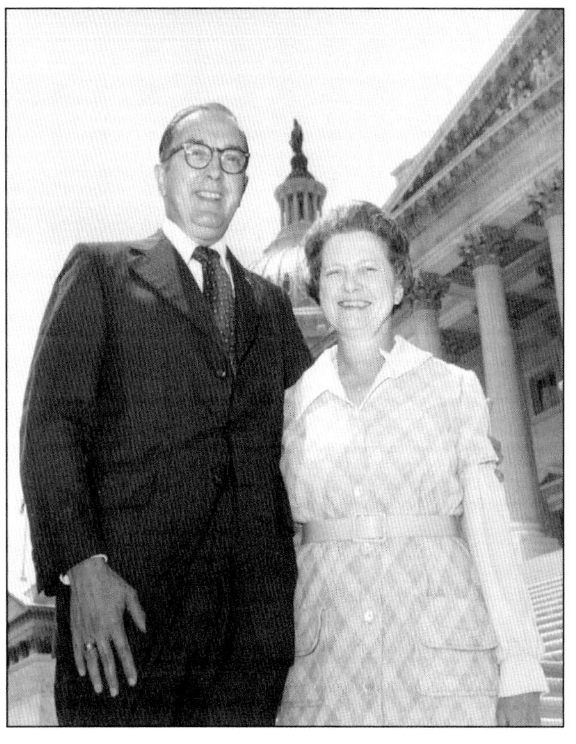

The son of a police chief, Jesse Alexander Helms Jr. (1921–2008) was born in Monroe, North Carolina. He began his career as a journalist with Raleigh newspapers; later, he worked with Democrat Willis Smith (1887–1953; interred in Oakwood), a US senator from 1950 to 1953, and other conservatives before entering politics himself as a city councilman. Helms's time as a commentator on a Raleigh television station launched him into his first Senate campaign (1972) as a Republican; his five terms in that office set a state record. Principled and uncompromising, Helms remains a controversial figure. His beloved wife, Dorothy Jane "Dot" Coble Helms (1919–2015), whom he met in his newspaper days, was a mother to two daughters and an adopted son. (Above, Palko; left, Helms family.)

John Louis Taylor (1769–1829), the first chief justice (1819–1829) of the state supreme court, was born in London, came to America as an orphan, attended William & Mary, and schooled himself in law. He built his Raleigh home, Elmwood (extant in 2017), around 1813 off Hillsboro Street, where a number of state leaders resided over the years. A simple "chest tomb" (see page 115) marks Taylor's grave. (SANC.)

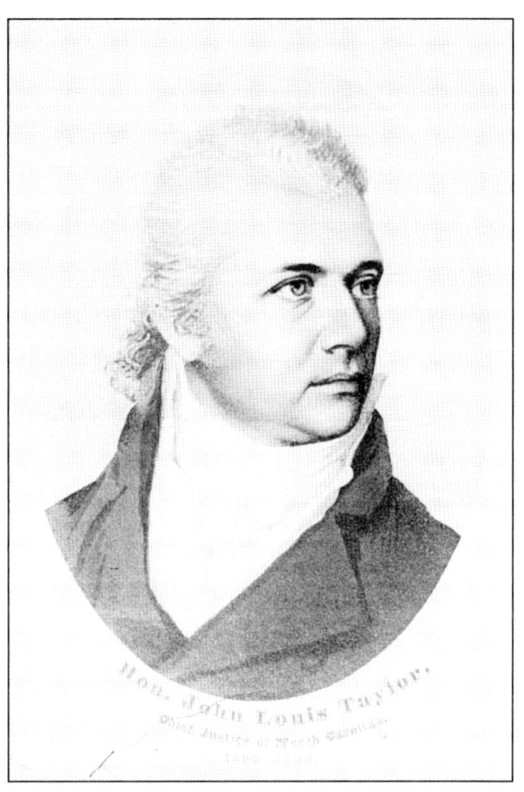

Walter McKenzie Clark (1846–1924) was a Confederate veteran, lawyer, and, for 35 years, supreme court justice (chief justice, 1903–1924). He championed "progressive" causes, helped persuade North Carolina to adopt *Esse quam videre* ("To be rather than to seem") as its motto, and authored the famed Clark's Regiments histories of the Civil War. (Palko.)

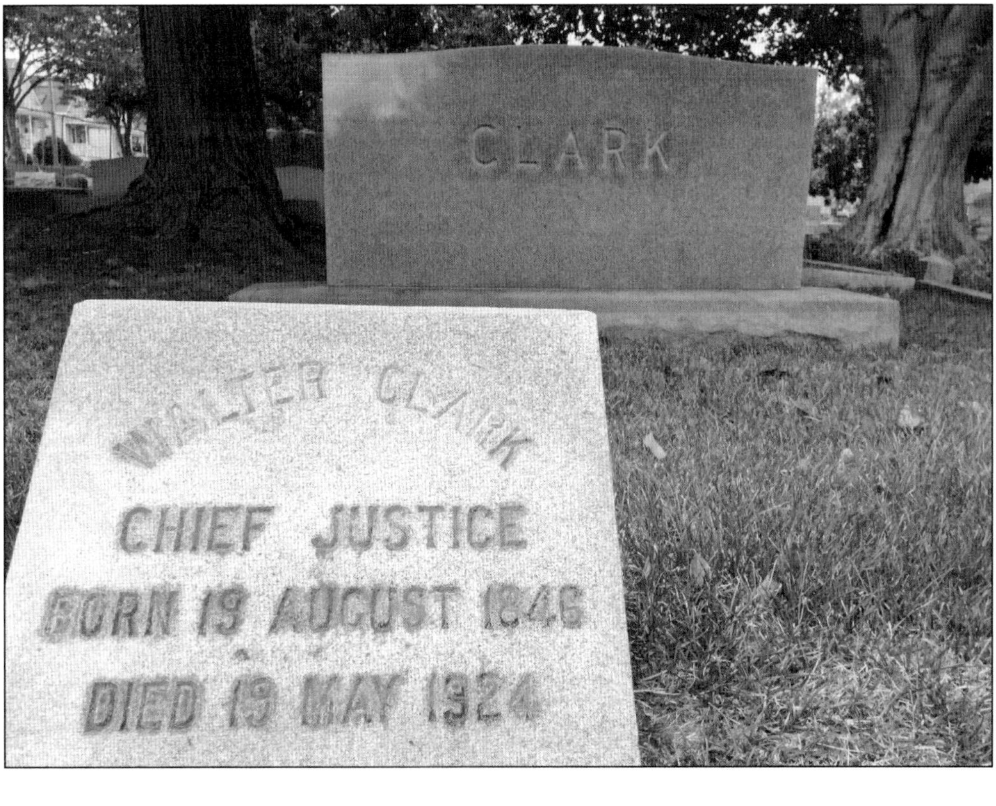

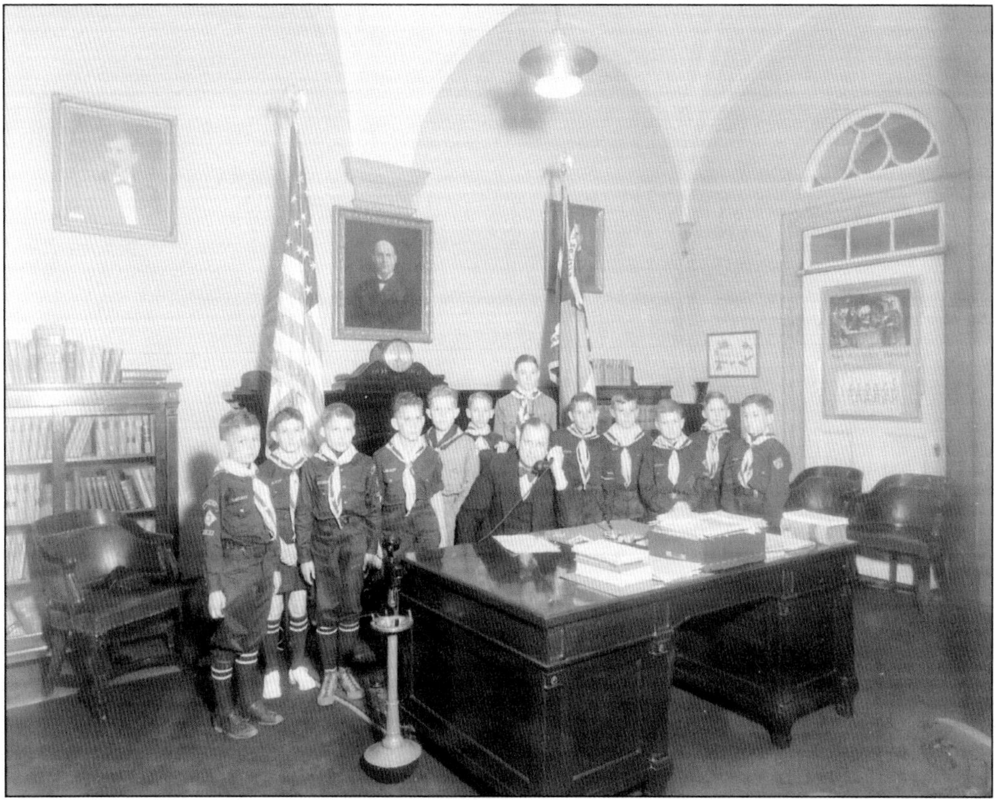

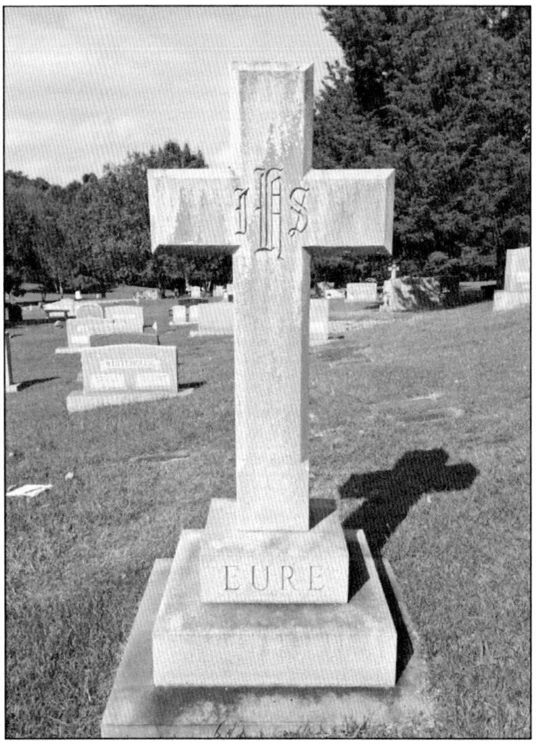

Thaddeus Armie Eure (1899–1993), from Gates County, North Carolina, is remembered fondly for his red bow tie and his longevity. Called "the oldest rat in the Democratic barn," he served as North Carolina secretary of state from 1936 to 1989, a record. Before "Thad" retired, Pres. Ronald Reagan recognized him as the then longest-serving public official in the nation. His son, also Thad (1932–1988), became a well-known area restaurateur as a founder of the Angus Barn. (Above, SANC; left, Palko.)

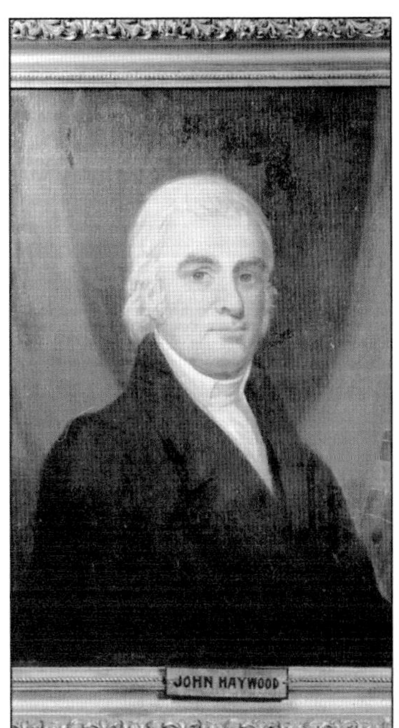

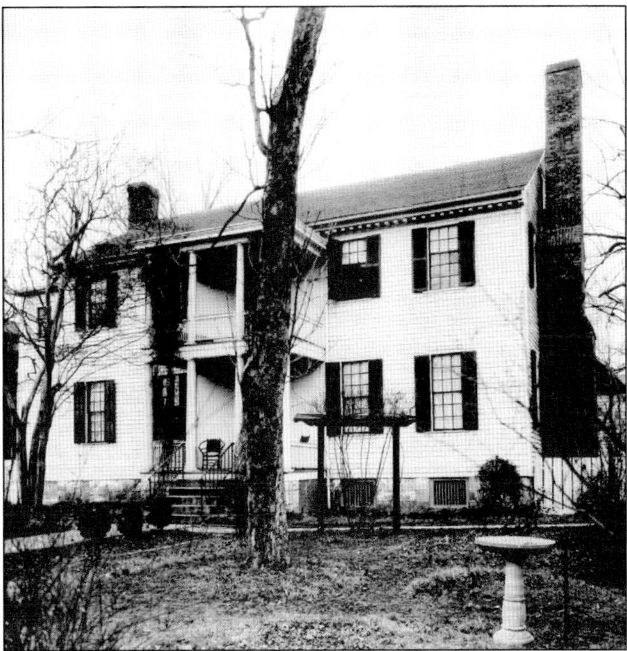

John Haywood (1755–1827), father of 14 children, served as Raleigh's first "intendant of police" (mayor) from 1795 to around 1802 and was state treasurer for 40 years (1786–1827). His house, Haywood Hall, was built around 1800 and is extant downtown. Haywood County, North Carolina, is named for him. (Above, both, SANC; below, Palko.)

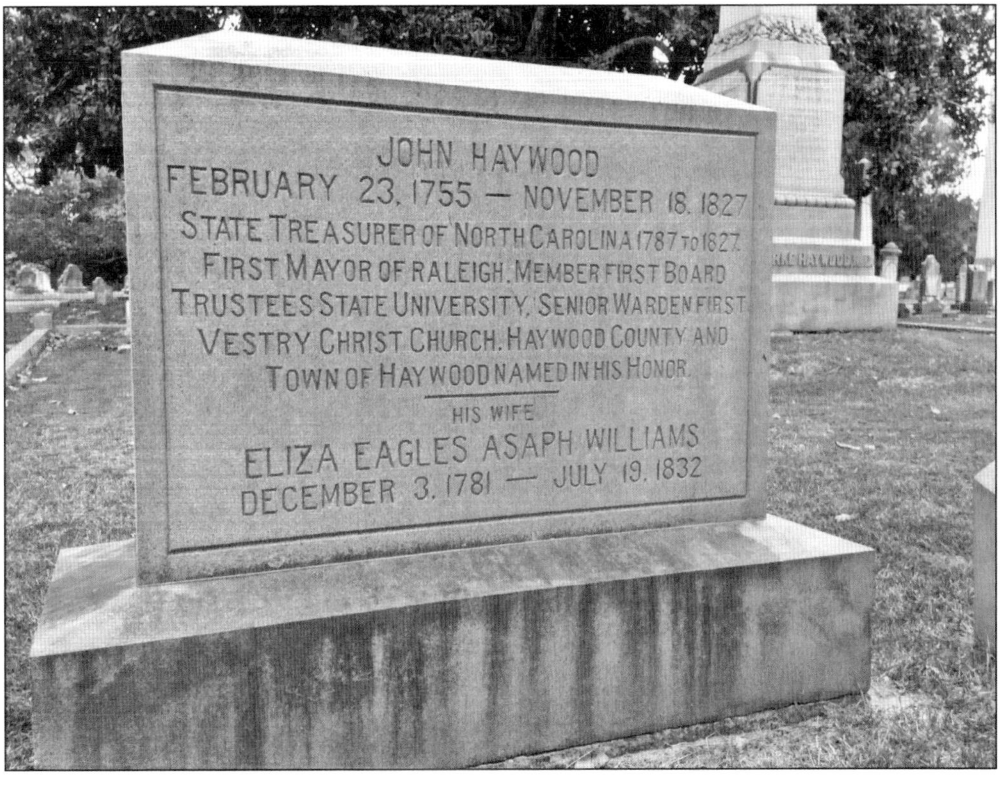

JOHN HAYWOOD
FEBRUARY 23, 1755 — NOVEMBER 18, 1827
STATE TREASURER OF NORTH CAROLINA 1787 TO 1827.
FIRST MAYOR OF RALEIGH. MEMBER FIRST BOARD
TRUSTEES STATE UNIVERSITY. SENIOR WARDEN FIRST
VESTRY CHRIST CHURCH. HAYWOOD COUNTY AND
TOWN OF HAYWOOD NAMED IN HIS HONOR.
HIS WIFE
ELIZA EAGLES ASAPH WILLIAMS
DECEMBER 3, 1781 — JULY 19, 1832

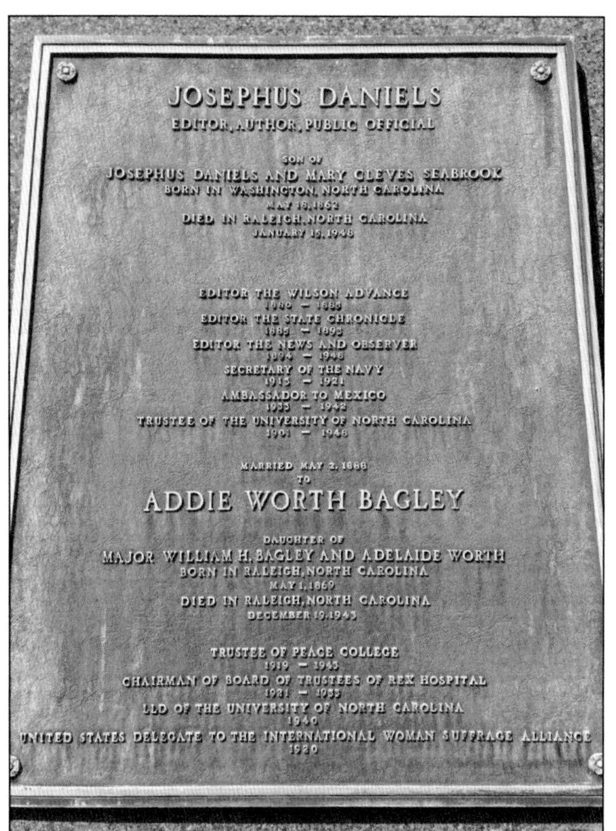

Josephus Daniels (1862–1948), although never holding an elected political office, was probably the most powerful political operative in the state in the first half of the 20th century. Born in Washington, North Carolina, he went into the newspaper business as a young man and gained control of Raleigh's *News & Observer* in 1895. A dedicated if controversial Democrat, Daniels built his newspaper into a political force in the state and nation. He also served as secretary of the Navy during World War I under Woodrow Wilson and as US ambassador to Mexico (1933–1941) under Franklin Roosevelt. Both presidents were friends of his. Daniels's statue stands in Nash Square in downtown Raleigh; his former home, officially declared a "naval base," still (in 2017) displays a giant deck gun in the front yard. (Left, Palko; below, Goodwin.)

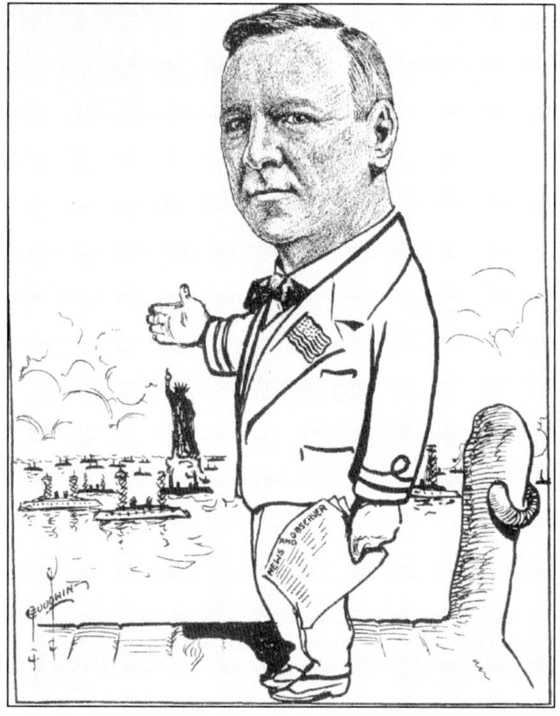

Five

Company Men and Women

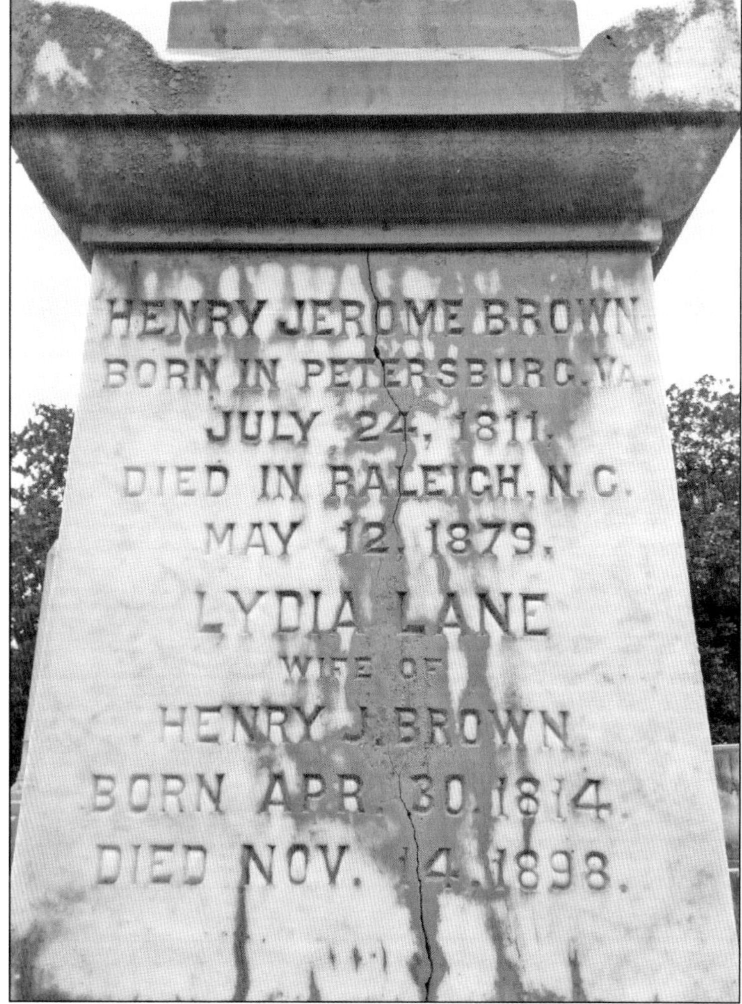

In the years after its founding, Raleigh's focus on government plus its relative isolation and lack of the transport and power provided by a river made it slow to attract business. Time and technology changed that. Henry Jerome Brown (1811–1879), cabinetmaker turned coffin maker (he helped reinter Confederate remains in 1867), reflects the growth of enterprise: In 1836, he established Raleigh's oldest surviving business, today a nationally affiliated funeral home. (Palko.)

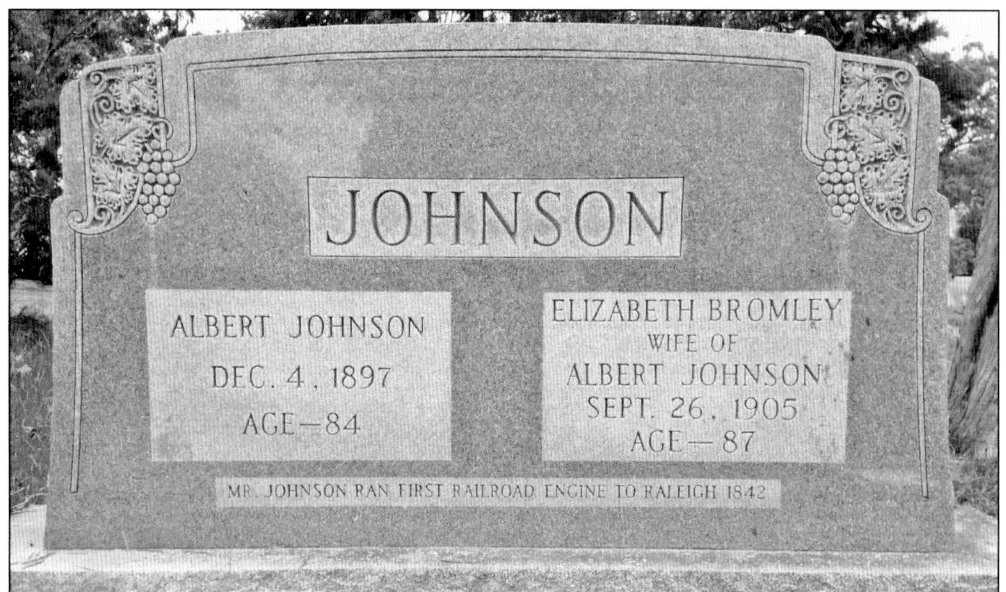

Railroading became big business after Albert Johnson (c. 1813–1897) drove the first locomotive, named *Tornado*, into Raleigh in 1840 (his headstone is incorrect) for the Raleigh & Gaston Railroad. Over time, the city—with lines running through it east-west and, especially, north-south—became a major hub for the Seaboard Air Line and a center for railroad personnel and activity (see Vass, page 29). (Palko.)

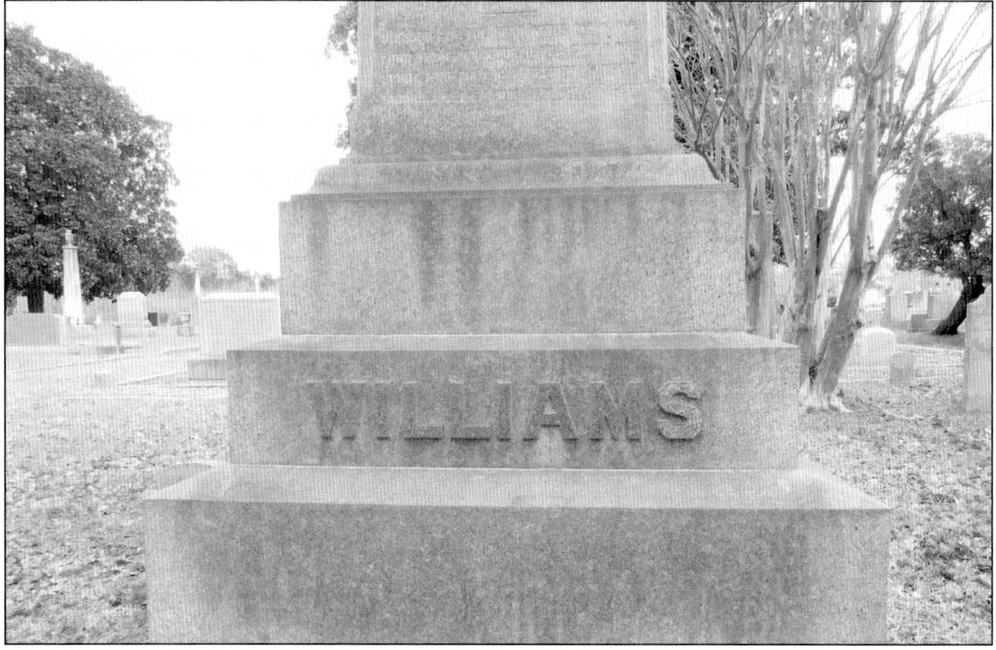

Miriam Carson White Williams (1831–1910), born in Wake County, became the nation's first female bank president (by four years) in 1879 upon the death of her husband, John Griffith Williams, the founder of Raleigh's State National Bank. Family relatives, however, betrayed her and robbed the bank in 1888, causing its collapse. Nevertheless, Miriam, also a real estate developer, was a local pioneer for women entering the world of business. (HOC.)

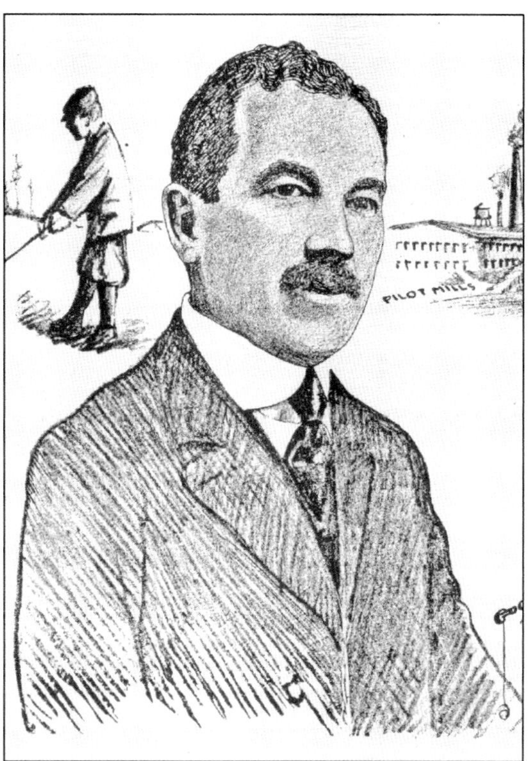

William Holt Williamson (1867–1926) made money from "King Cotton," as did many in Raleigh in the years between the Civil War and the 1920s. As if to underscore the industry's importance, a steam-driven cotton press was placed downtown where the legislature building is today. Related to the Holt family of Alamance County who produced world-famous Alamance Plaids, Williamson ran Pilot Mill (pictured), a textile factory just west of the cemetery. The looms and the mill village are gone, but the building has been a high school and office space in the past few decades (see page 111). (Right, Goodwin; below, SANC.)

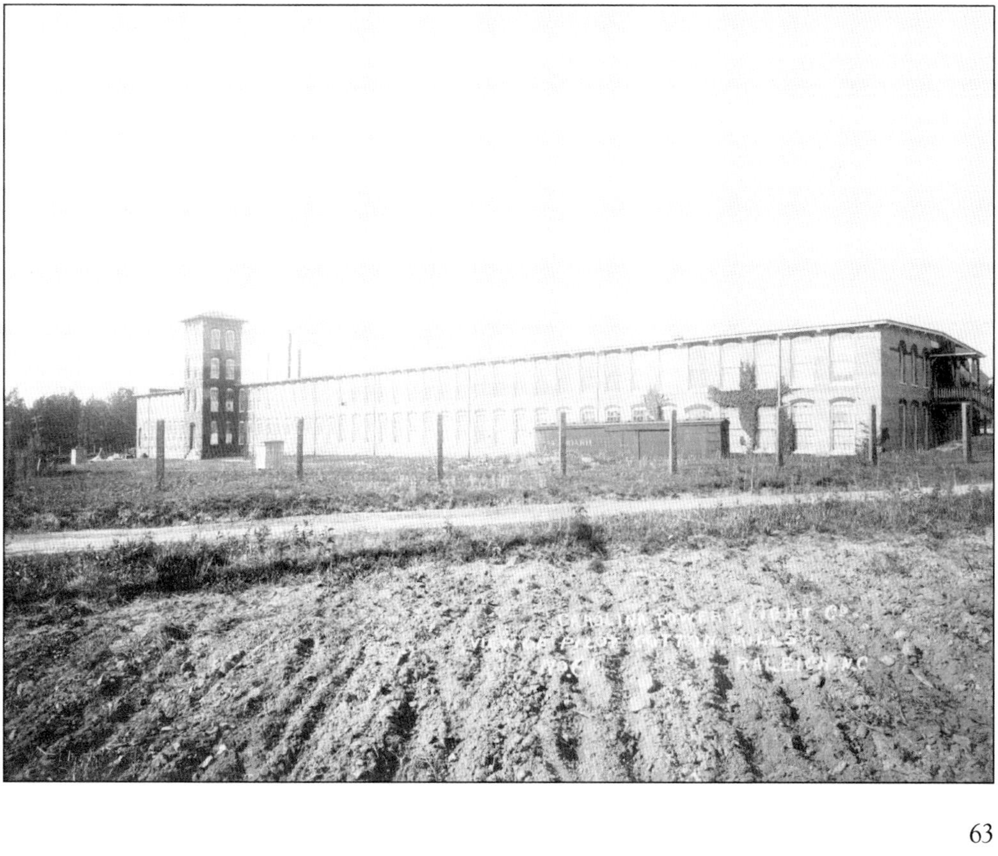

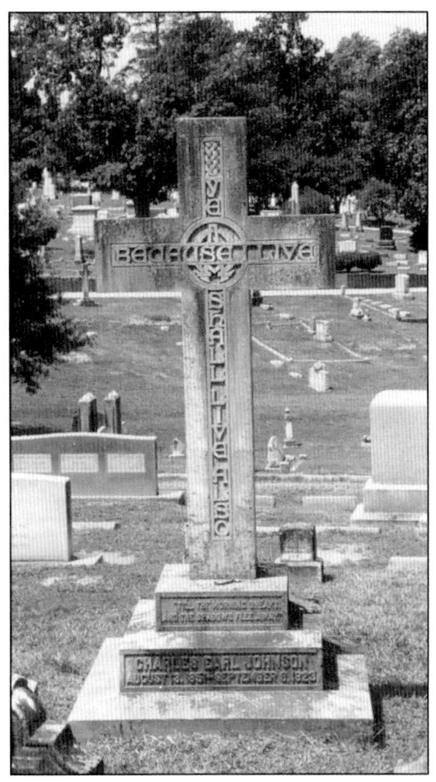

Charles Earl Johnson (1851–1923) and Robert Burton McGehee (1943–2007) made their marks in business with the same firm. Johnson, the son and namesake of a renowned Raleigh physician, was the first president of the newly formed (1908) Carolina Power & Light electric company (CP&L), which for years provided power and ran the city's streetcars. In 2004, with CP&L by then Progress Energy, Bob McGehee, a Mississippi native and nuclear submarine veteran, became CEO and chairman before dying unexpectedly of a stroke while in London. Both men were able leaders of what is now part of Duke Energy Progress, the nation's largest electric utility in 2017. (Both, Palko.)

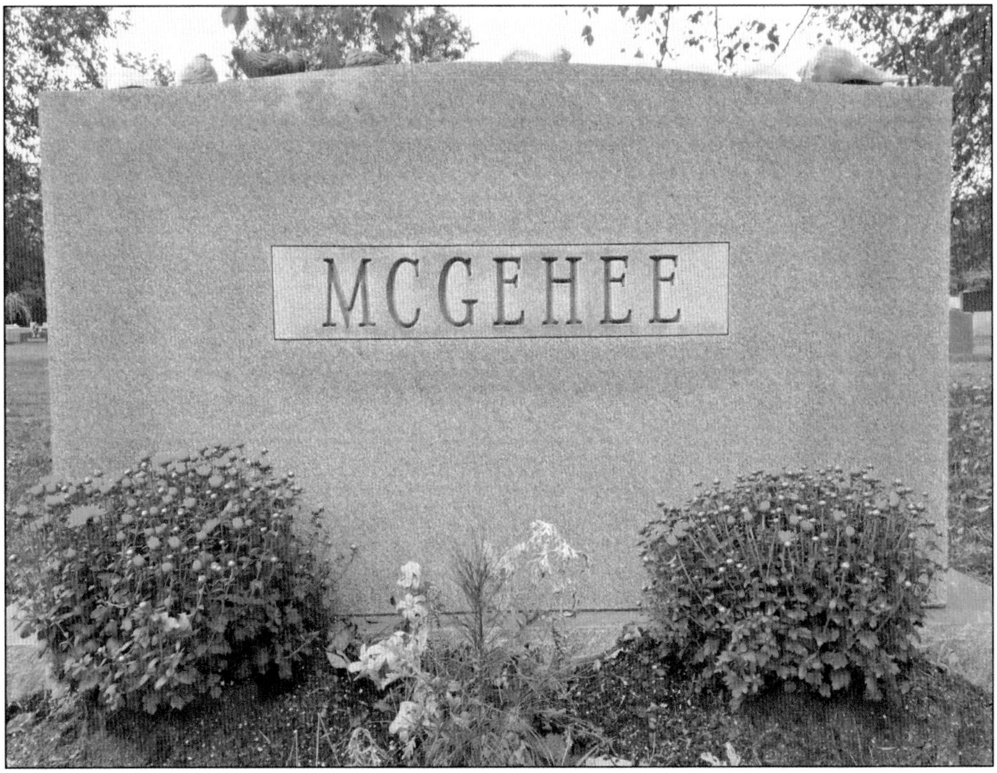

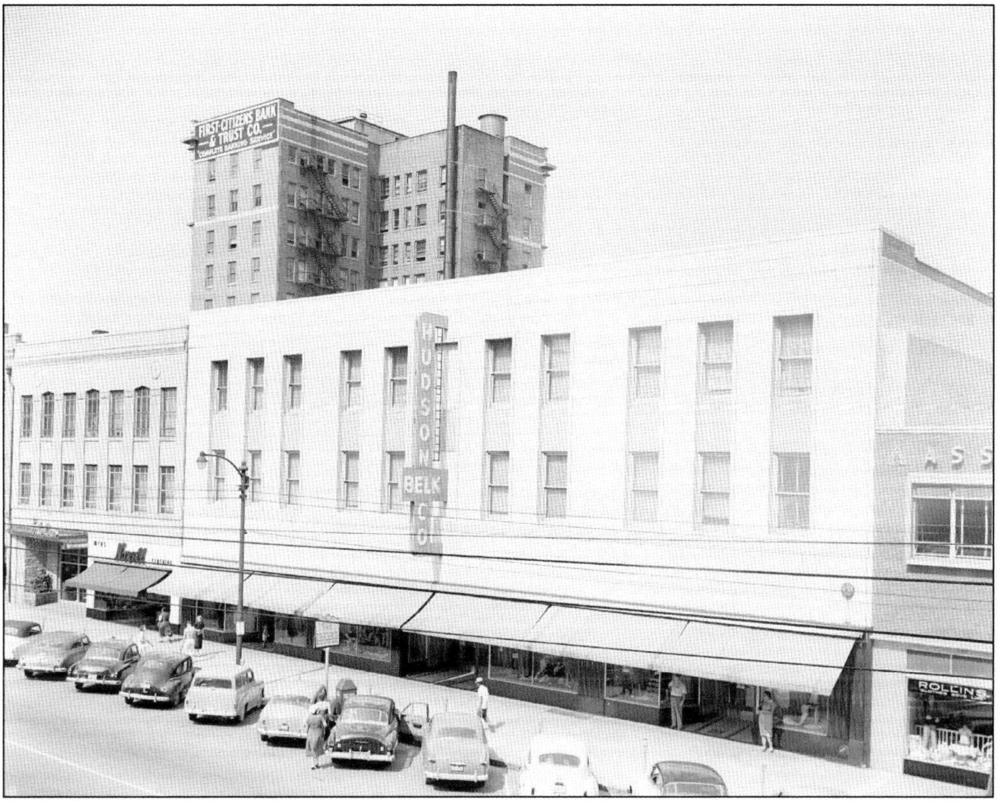

Karl Grier Hudson Sr. (1889–1953) came to Raleigh in 1915 to open the 13th Belk department store, Hudson-Belk, eventually on Fayetteville Street in downtown Raleigh. A popular shopping (and eating) place for decades, by the turn of the century it had moved to the suburbs and the building became condominiums. In 1918, Hudson married Mary White (1892–1978), the daughter of Rev. William McLanahan White (1867–1934), pastor of downtown's First Presbyterian Church. So impressed was Hudson with his father-in-law that he organized White Memorial Presbyterian Church in 1946; the church building was constructed in 1952. In turn, Hudson admirers organized Hudson Memorial Presbyterian Church in 1957. Karl Hudson Jr. (1919–2006), also in Oakwood Cemetery, joined the retail business in 1940 and eventually took over from his father; Karl III also worked at the firm for a time. (Above, SANC; right, Goodwin.)

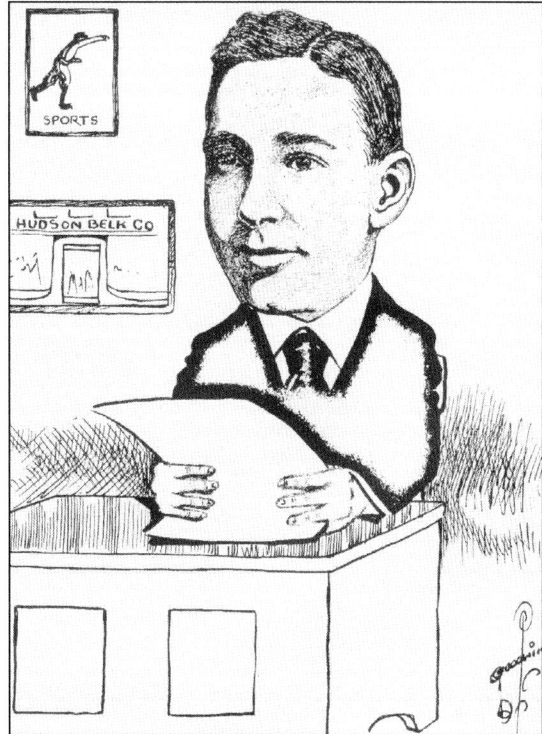

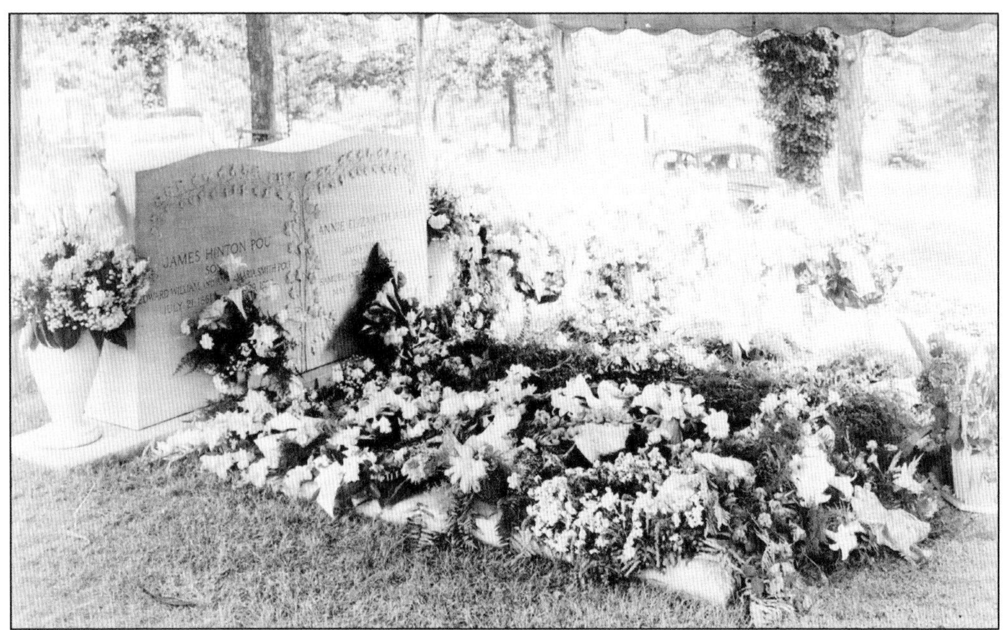

James Hinton Pou (1861–1935), Alabama-born and home-trained in law, became a prominent corporate and criminal attorney and legislator. His creation of the Glenwood Land Company in 1906 led to the development of the city's first planned 20th-century suburb. He later participated in the development of the Hayes-Barton residential area, begun around 1920. (SANC.)

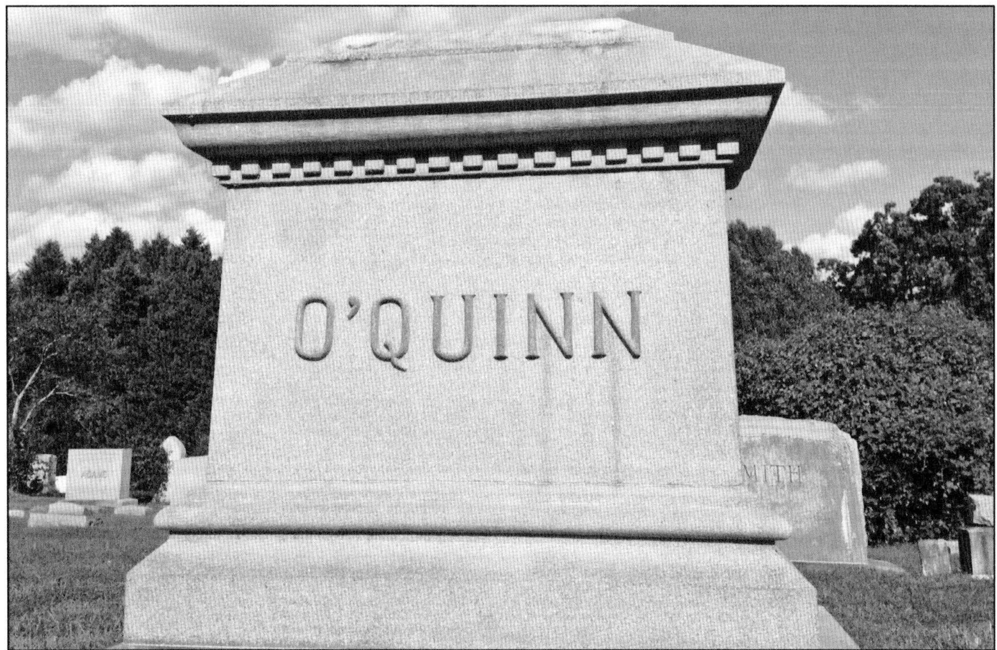

Jesse Lee O'Quinn (1858–1921) also changed the look of the city. A florist, O'Quinn erected a string of greenhouses across Watauga (then Swain) Street from the cemetery between 1900 and 1920; in 1921, the business was sold to J.J. Fallon, and the greenhouses were demolished in the 1980s. In 1888 on that site, the state's first collegiate football game was played; the outcome was Trinity/Duke 16, University of North Carolina 0. (Palko.)

Six

Academics

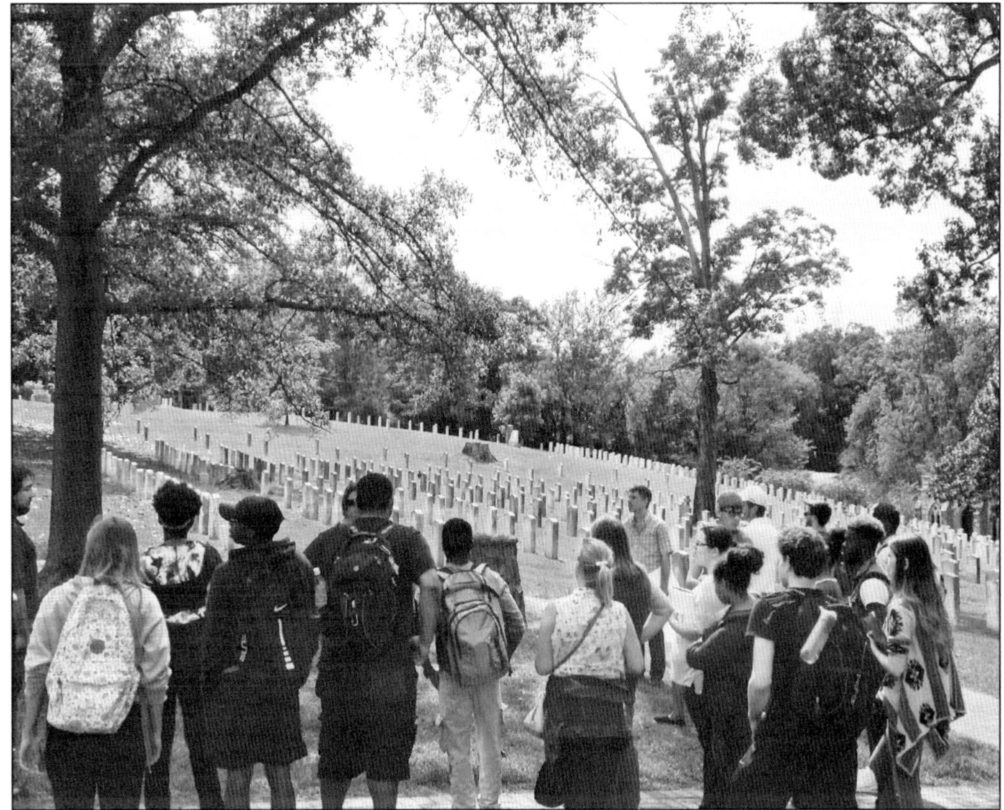

Men and women who promoted and guided education at all levels, from one of the South's first kindergartens through high school and university years, are remembered at Oakwood. Teachers and students from all levels often make use of cemetery grounds for a variety of educational subjects. A class from William Peace University is pictured here. (Palko.)

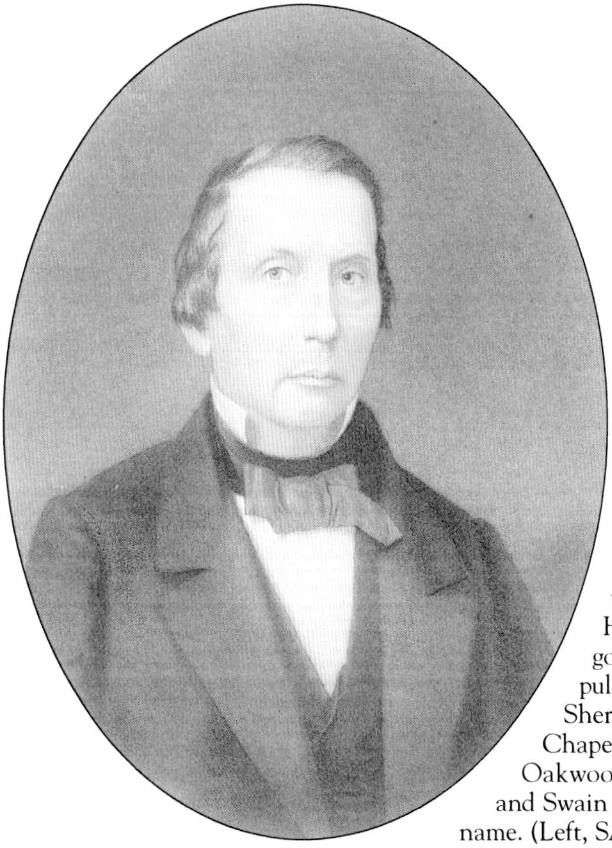

David Lowry Swain (1801–1868), although a legislator, judge, governor (from 1833 to 1835), and the man who turned over the keys of the capitol to one of General Sherman's officers in 1865, may best be remembered as president of the University of North Carolina from 1835 until his death. He worked successfully to keep the Chapel Hill campus open with most students gone to war. Swain died when a buggy pulled by a horse given to him by General Sherman overturned; initially buried in Chapel Hill, Swain was later reinterred in Oakwood. Swain County, North Carolina, and Swain Hall on the UNC campus carry his name. (Left, SANC; below, Palko.)

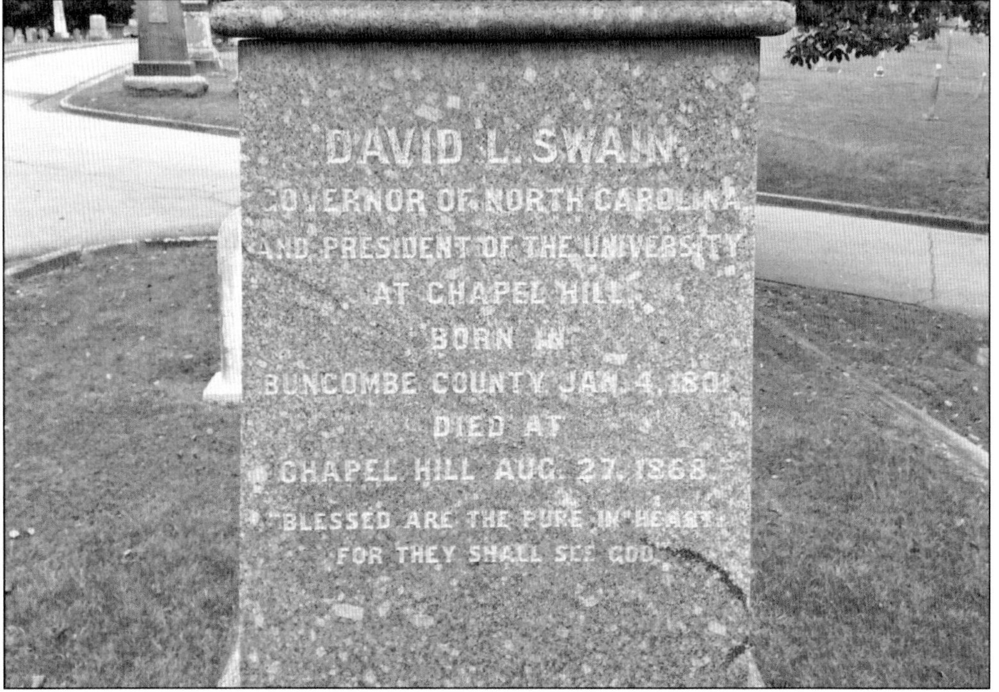

Kemp Plummer Battle (1831–1919) was the son of famed jurist and University of North Carolina professor William Horn Battle (1802–1879; interred in Oakwood), under whom Kemp studied law. Renowned attorney, railroad executive during the Civil War, historian, and also a founder of Oakwood Cemetery, Kemp Battle was the president of the University of North Carolina (1876–1891) when the campus reopened after having been closed in 1871 during Reconstruction. (Palko.)

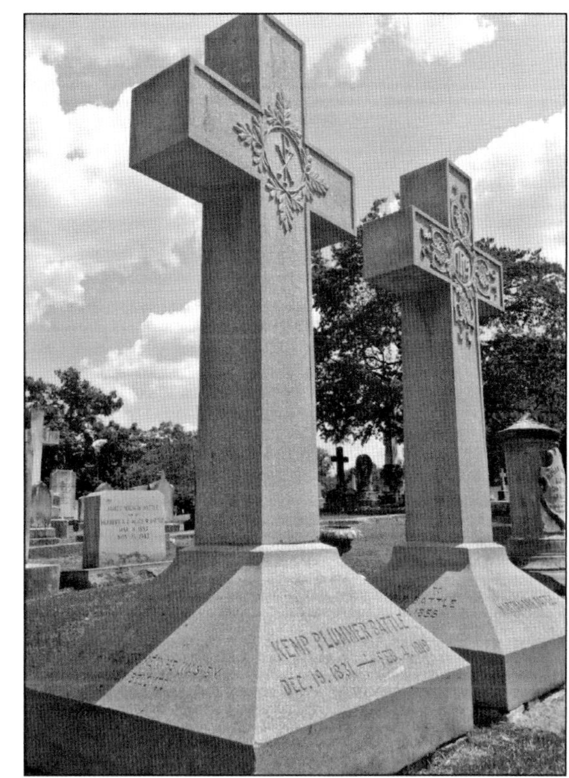

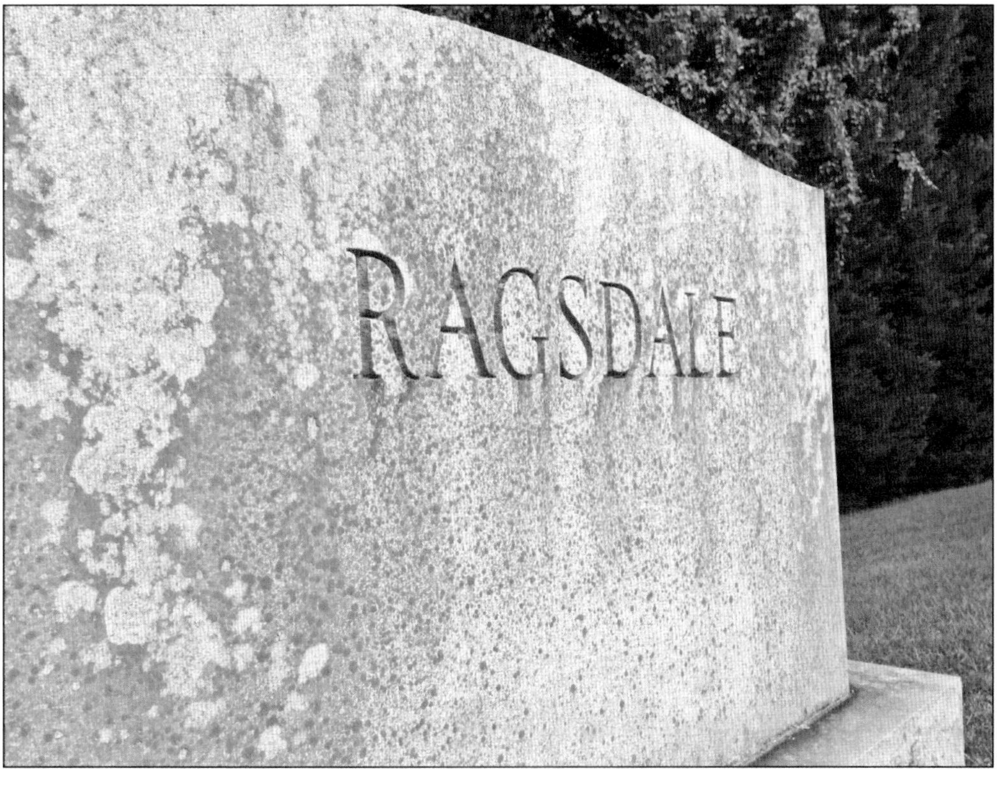

George Young Ragsdale (1903–1990), a Raleigh insurance company executive, will be remembered by many as the creator of the fight song for the University of North Carolina. A member of the class of 1923, he and several fraternity brothers won a campus contest with "Here Comes Carolina-lina," beloved by generations of "born and bred" Tar Heels. Ragsdale's family ran a jewelry store business in Raleigh for many years. (Palko.)

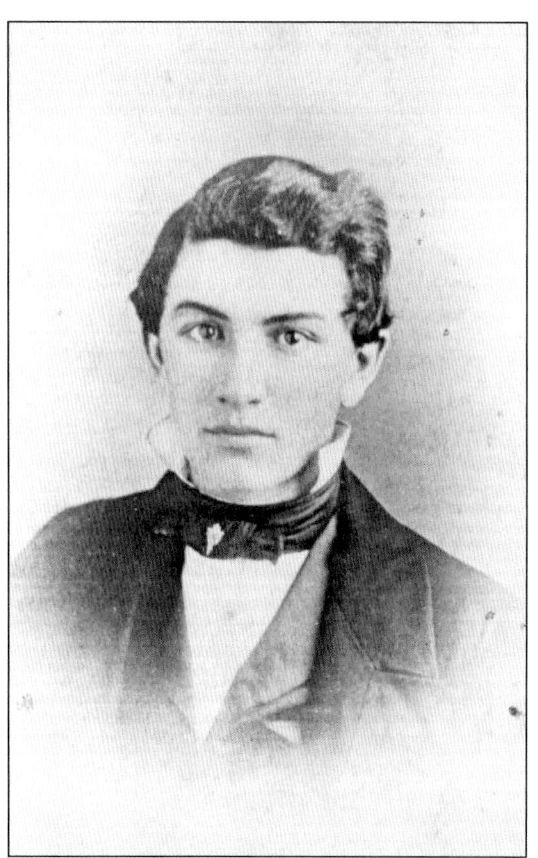

Leonidas Lafayette Polk (1837–1892; pictured around 1857) became a spokesman for agriculture as founder of the *Progressive Farmer* magazine (see page 13), the state's first agriculture commissioner (1877–1880), leader of the Farmer's Alliance and "People's Party," and possible candidate for president in 1892 had he lived. He long advocated a state school of agriculture. Polk's Raleigh home, now on North Blount Street, houses a museum honoring Polk as well as Carolina farmers. (SANC.)

William Joseph Peele (1855–1919) was a Chapel Hill graduate who felt his liberal arts education provided no real skill. He founded the Watauga Club in 1884 to lobby for a technical school as Leonidas Polk lobbied for agriculture training. Together, they were heard: in 1888, Peele was a speaker at the laying of the cornerstone for the North Carolina College of Agriculture and Mechanic Arts, today's North Carolina State University. (Palko.)

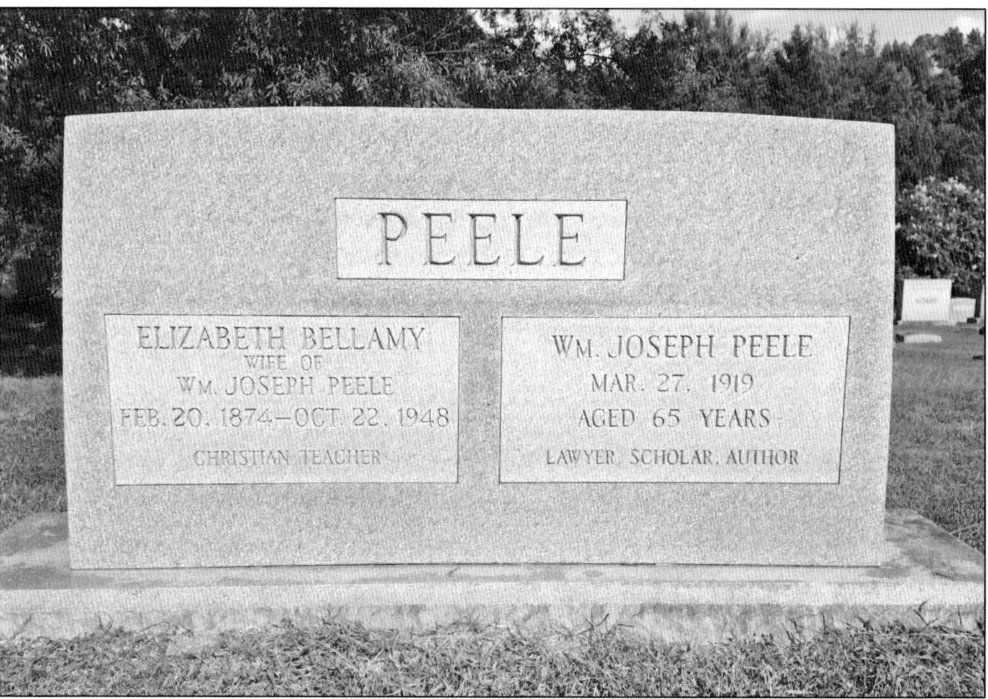

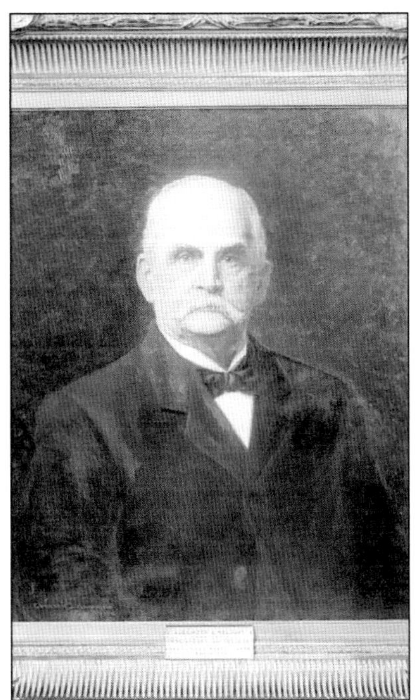

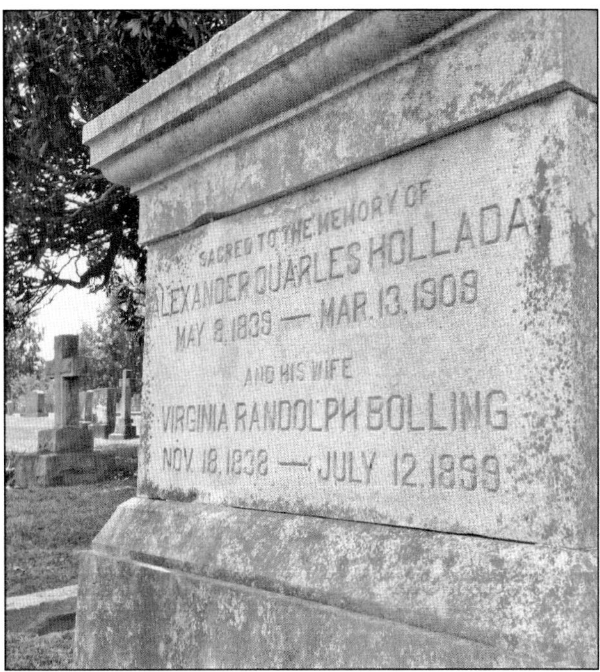

Alexander Quarles Holladay (1839–1909) was the first president (1889–1899) of the North Carolina College of Agriculture and Mechanic Arts (North Carolina State), expanding the new school's "technical" curriculum. The original main building that housed most of the college in the early years is Holladay Hall. (Above left, SANC; above right, Palko; below, SANC.)

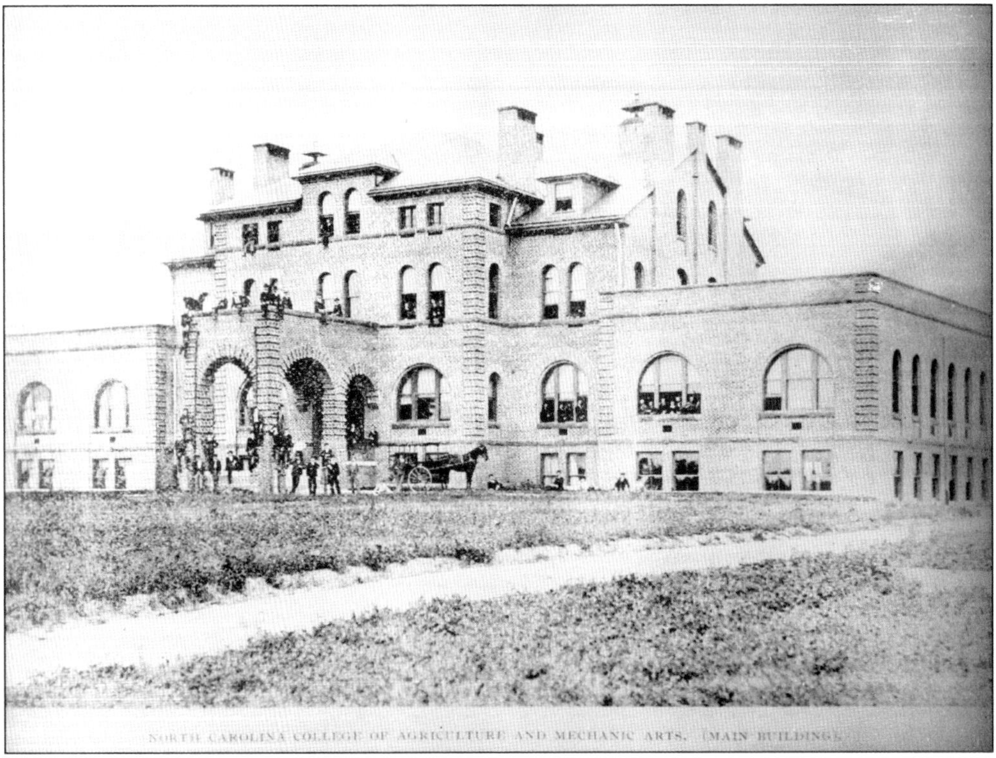

NORTH CAROLINA COLLEGE OF AGRICULTURE AND MECHANIC ARTS. (MAIN BUILDING.)

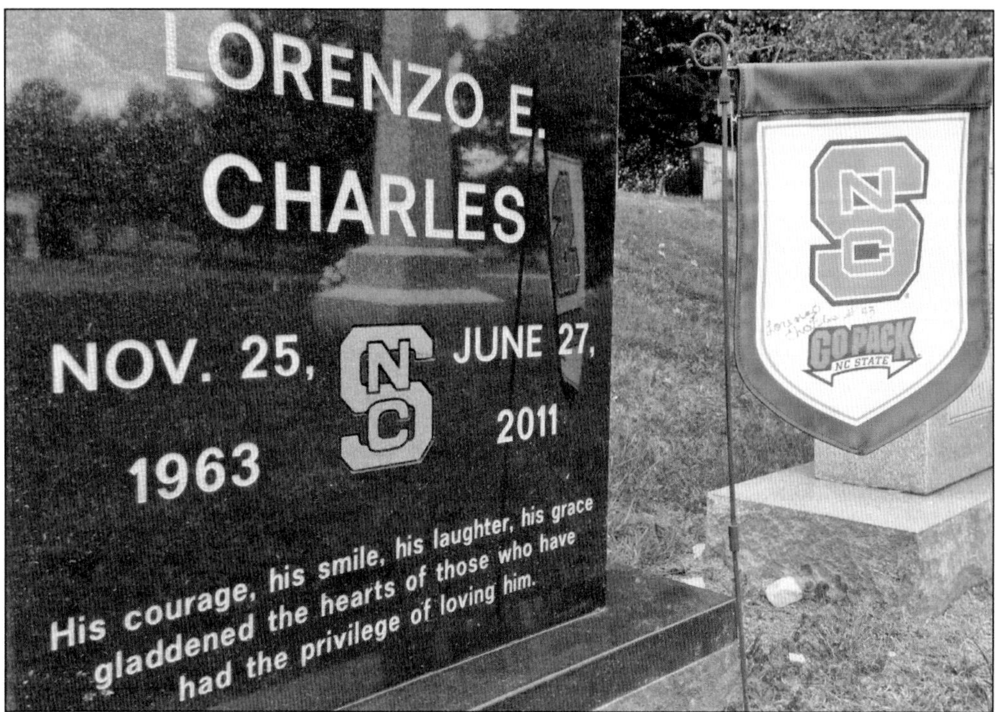

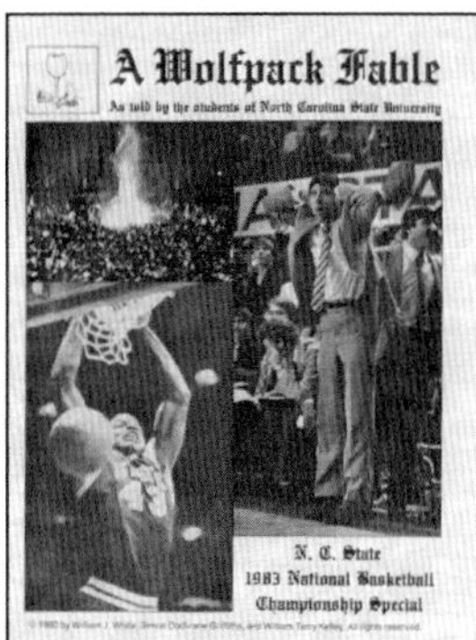

Basketball coach James Thomas Valvano (1946–1993) compiled a 209-110 record at North Carolina State between 1980 and 1990, but he may best be remembered for his team's 1983 national championship and his inspirational speeches. "Jimmy V's" handsome black granite stone is often covered with visitors' mementos. Near his grave is that of Lorenzo Emile Charles (1963–2011), the player who made the final dunk to win that national title. (Above and below, Palko; left, NCSU.)

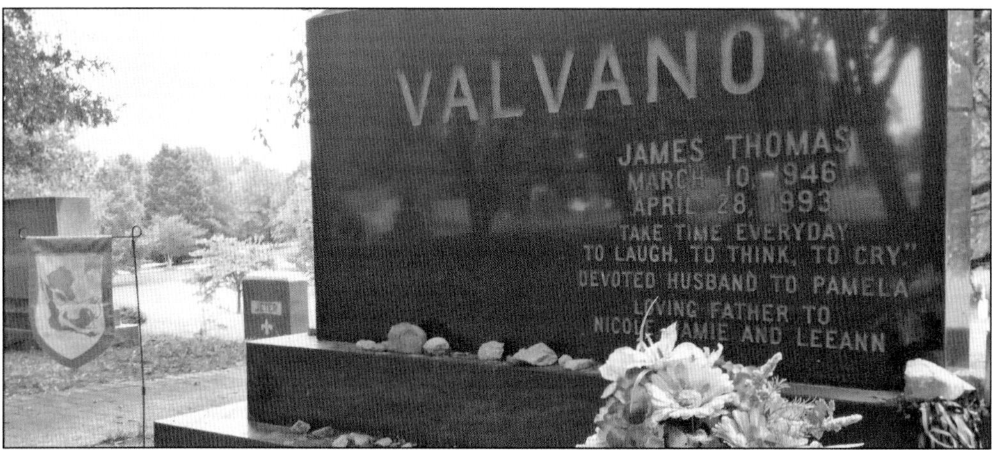

The Reverend Jacob Brinton Smith (1822–1872) was an Episcopal churchman and first head of St. Augustine's Normal School (now St. Augustine's University), founded after the Civil War for former slaves. Smith, an early shareholder in the Raleigh Cemetery Association, was also the first cemetery superintendent and may have created the layout of the original cemetery as a student project. A number of "St. Aug" faculty are interred in Oakwood. (Palko.)

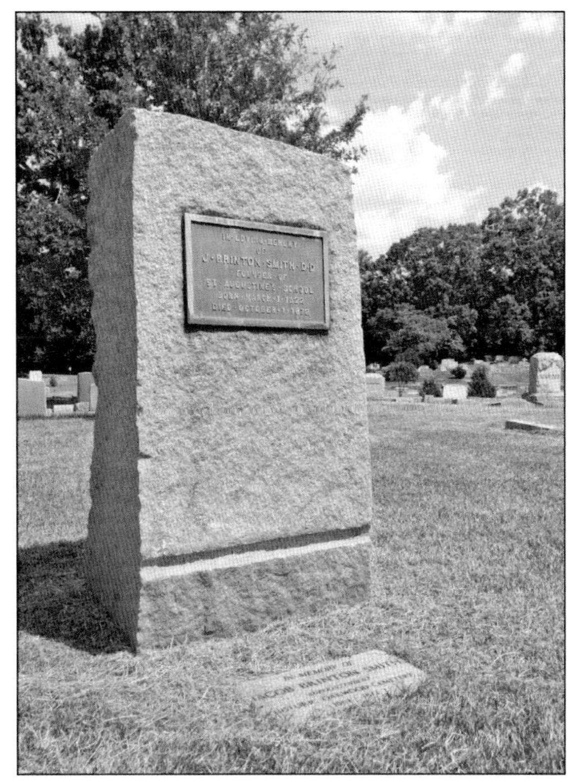

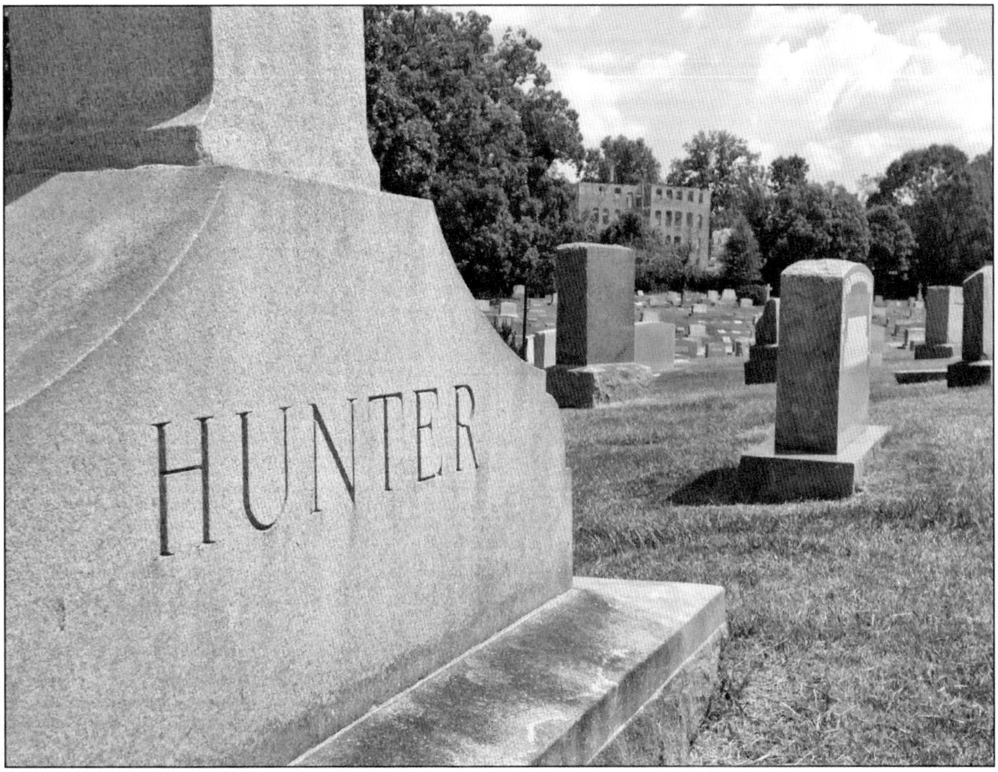

Sarah Lothrop Hunter (1846–1940), the wife of St. Augustine principal Aaron Burtis Hunter (1854–1933), championed the founding of St. Agnes Hospital for African Americans on the college campus in 1896, in the era of Jim Crow. The walls of a later facility of the same name (1909–1965) are visible to the east of her gravesite among the trees, the building no longer used after the desegregation of city hospitals. (Palko.)

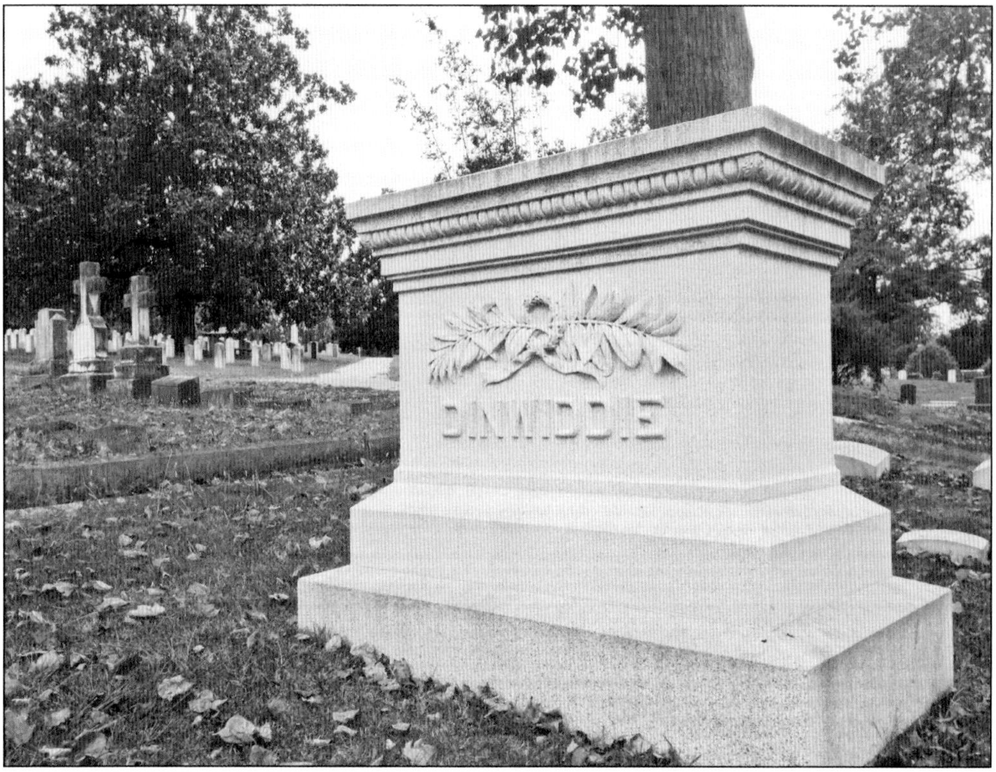

James Dinwiddie (1837–1907) filled educative positions at several institutions before coming to Raleigh's Peace Institute (today William Peace University) in 1890. As the school's owner, he promoted its "progressive evolution" toward a collegiate program and away from a full graded curriculum that had included one of the first kindergartens in the South. Dinwiddie sold his interest in the school just weeks before his death in San Francisco. (Palko.)

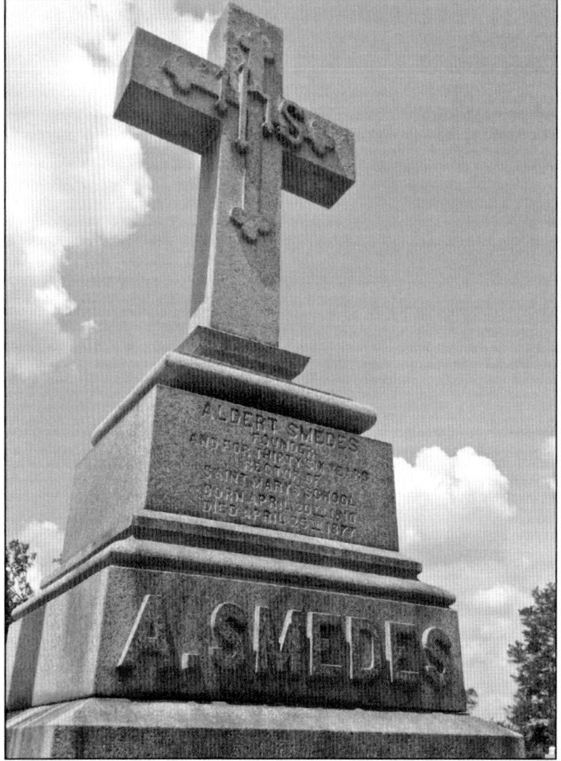

Aldert Smedes (1810–1877), a New York City–born Episcopal priest, founded and successfully headed St. Mary's School for Girls in Raleigh for 35 years, through the Civil War. Robert E. Lee's daughter Mildred went there, and Union soldiers bivouacked on the campus during the occupation of the city in April 1865. A son, Bennett (1837–1899), succeeded his father as head of the school. (Palko.)

In 1899, Elizabeth Delia Dixon Carroll (1872–1934), Raleigh's first female medical doctor and an advocate for many social causes, joined the faculty of the newly opened Baptist Female University (Meredith College as of 1909 and originally downtown). There, she promoted health and taught physiology until her death in an automobile accident. A brother, Thomas Dixon, wrote the 1905 play that inspired Hollywood's first epic film, *The Birth of a Nation* (1914). (SANC.)

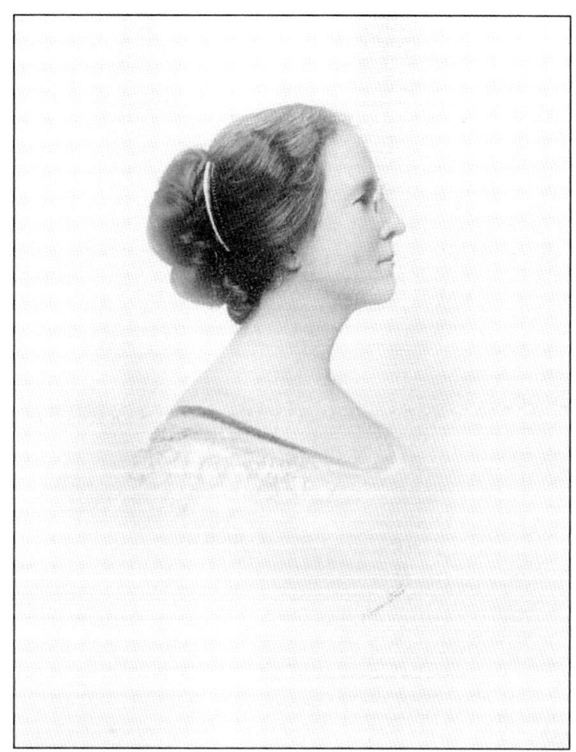

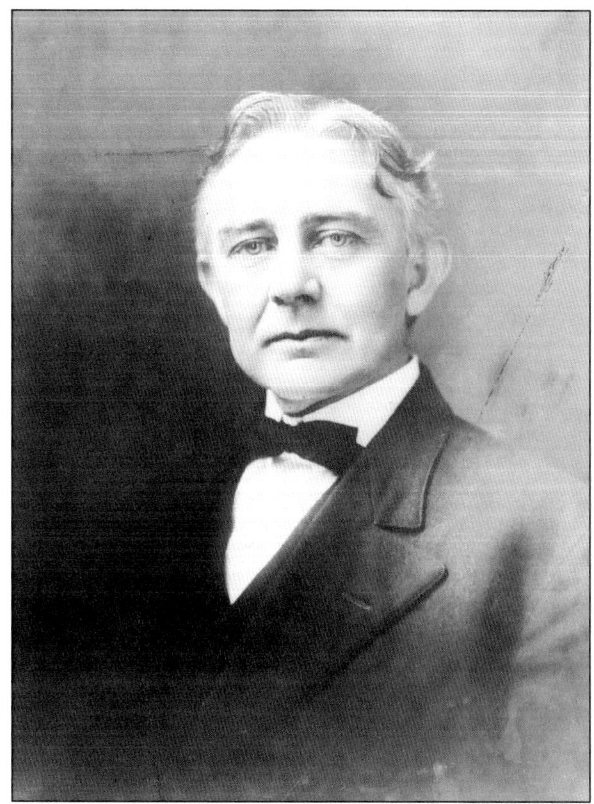

James Yadkin Joyner (1862–1954), a University of North Carolina graduate known as "J.Y.," was appointed state superintendent of public instruction by Gov. Charles Aycock in 1902. During his 17 years in that office, Joyner oversaw major improvements in Tar Heel education, from several thousand new schools to formalized high school instruction to better teacher training and pay. A library at East Carolina University is named for him. (SANC.)

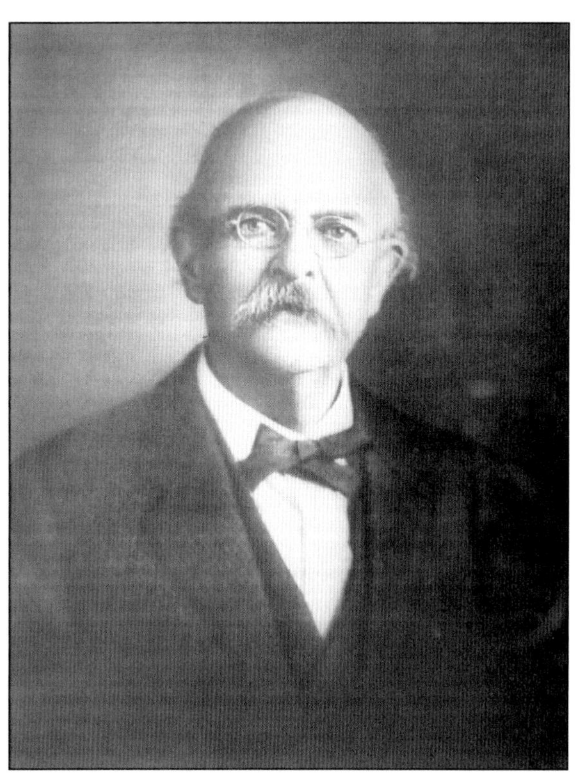

Hugh Morson (1850–1925), a Virginian and a renowned educator, reflects the importance of both private and public schooling in Raleigh's history. From 1877 to 1905, he ran and/or taught in a private Male Academy, closing it when he became the principal of Raleigh's first public high school in 1905. Many prominent Tar Heels, such as Gov. J. Melville Broughton Jr., were schooled by Morson or, like University of North Carolina president Frank Porter Graham, taught under him. A beloved teacher of classical languages, Morson suffered from "melancholia" and took his own life; hundreds of students attended his funeral and his Male Academy graduates purchased his handsome grave monument with its touching epitaph. Morson and his family lived many years near his academy in the Oakwood Historic District. (Left, SANC; below, Palko.)

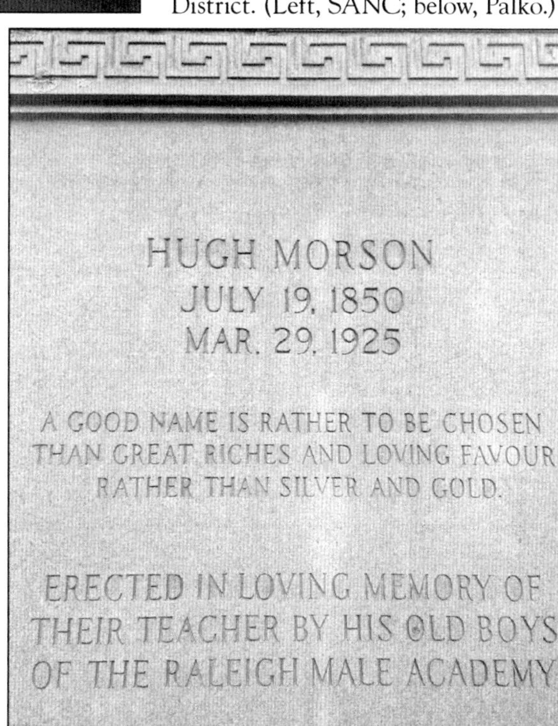

Needham Bryant Broughton (1848–1914), a Wake County–born partner in the respected printing firm of Edwards & Broughton, was a vigorous advocate for education at all levels. Raleigh's downtown high school carries his name. Broughton was an active member of the Baptist Church, a state senator (1901–1903), and a supporter of statewide prohibition. North Carolina governor and US senator Joseph Melville Broughton Jr. was a nephew. (Palko.)

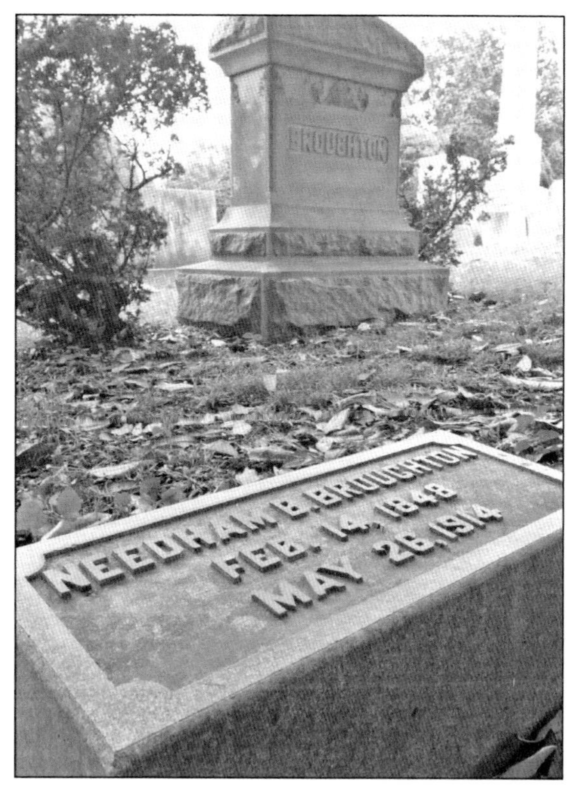

Emma Dowell Conn (1880–1970), a Raleigh-born graduate of Peace Institute, began a public school teaching career in the early 1900s and was for many years a teacher and principal at Murphey School on North Person Street, now the oldest former school building in the city. Like Needham Broughton and Emma Conn, many men and women in Oakwood Cemetery have been honored with public schools named for them. (Palko.)

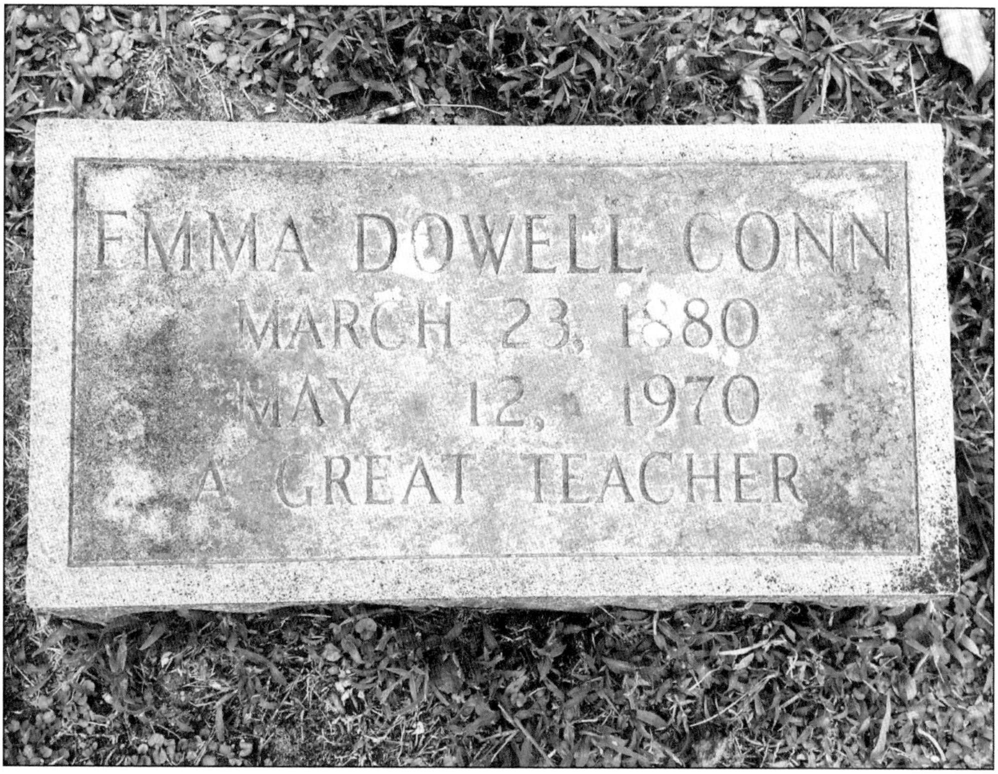

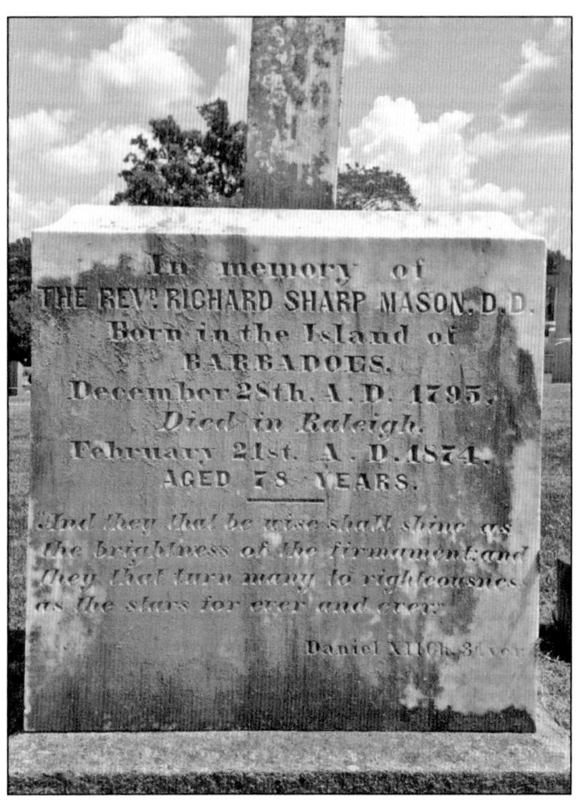

Soon after the Civil War, the Reverend Dr. Richard Sharp(e) Mason (1795–1874), the Barbados-born rector of downtown's Christ Episcopal Church from 1840 until his death, hired the first teacher-principal, Jane Elizabeth Massenburg Henry (c. 1835–1917), for a parish school at the church on Capitol Square. Over the years, this school evolved into Ravenscroft School (1937–present), an independent, college-preparatory school now in north Raleigh. Reverend Mason and "Jennie" Henry rest just yards apart on Oakwood's Chapel Circle. Reflecting her husband's interest in education, Mary Ann Bryan Mason (1802–1881) was the first native Tar Heel to publish a book for children, *A Wreath from the Woods of Carolina* (1859), illustrated by the author and one of several books by her. (Both, Palko.)

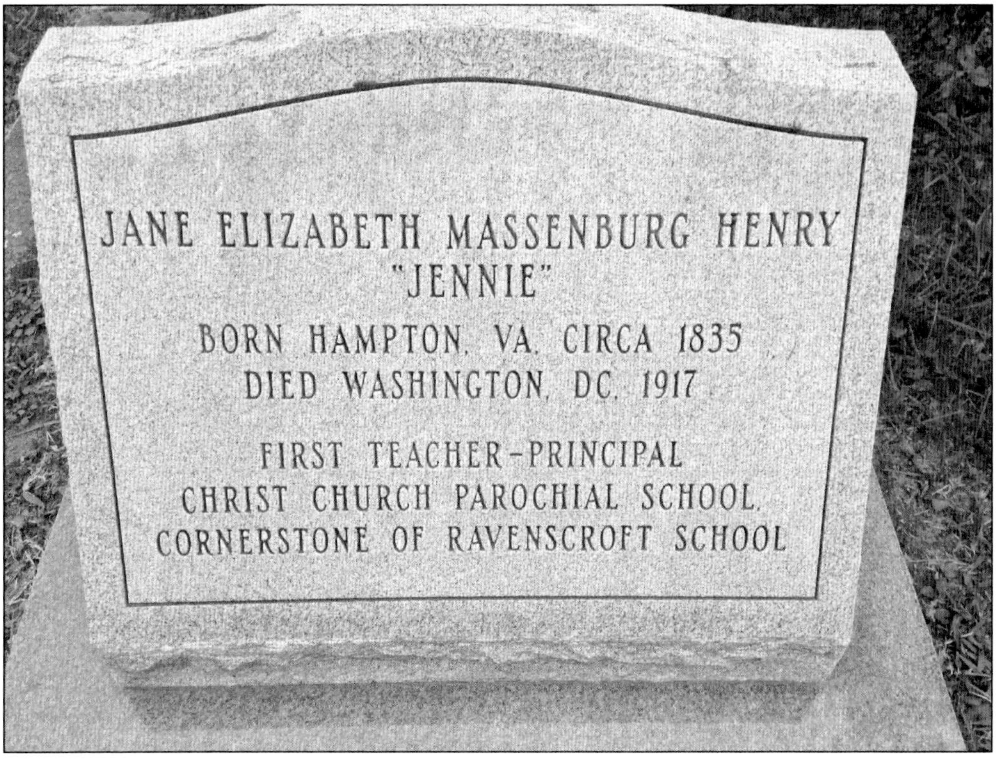

Seven

GREAT ROMANCES

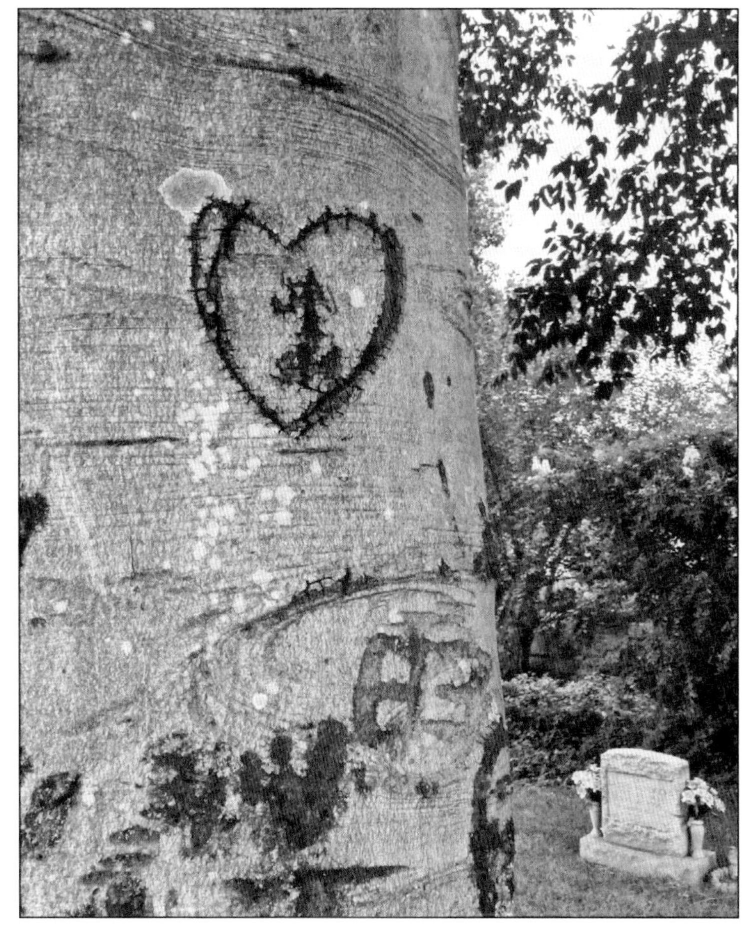

Countless individuals in Oakwood Cemetery enjoyed "great romances." Most of those amours remain forever unknown; some are carved in stone (or on this old cemetery tree) for all to see; some are celebrated, some condemned; and some—like the "Boy Colonel" and Annie Devereux (page 17)—have become legend. (Palko.)

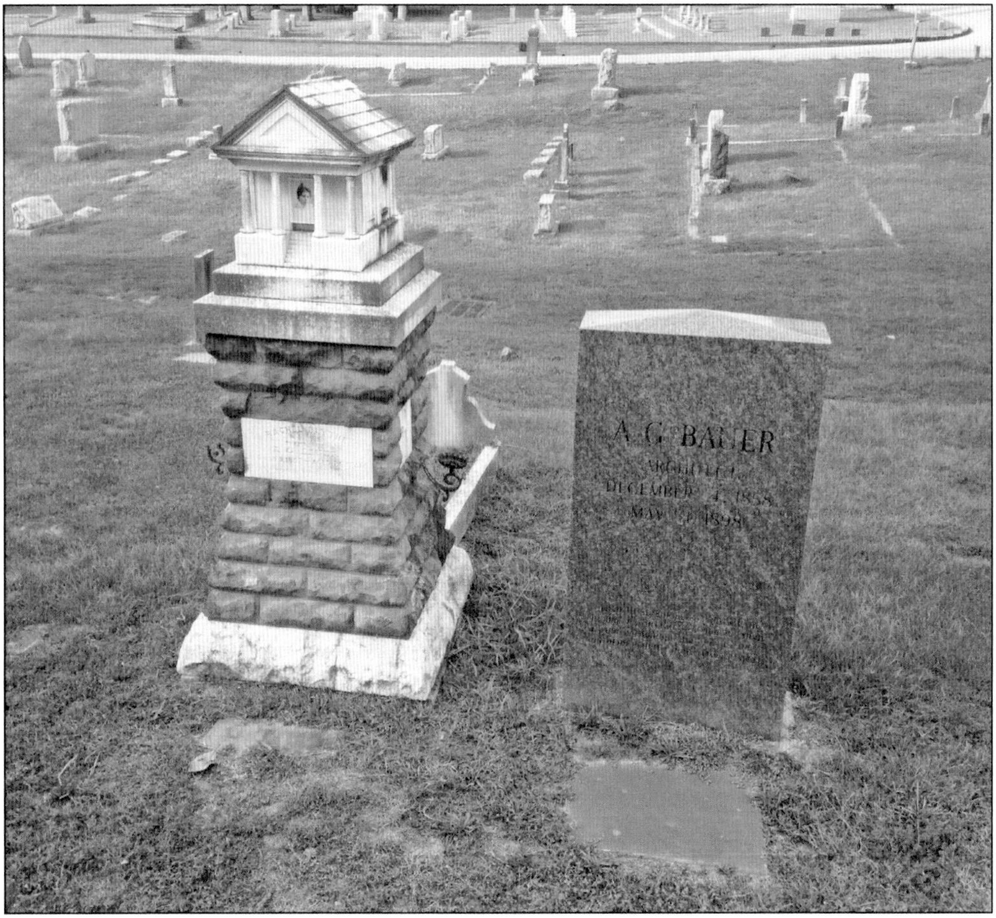

Adolphus Gustavus Bauer (1858–1898), an architect of the Governor's Mansion, and Rachel Blythe (1870–1897), a half Cherokee and a clerk, fell in love in Raleigh around 1891. With interracial marriage then illegal, they married in Washington, DC, "officially" and controversially. Blythe died after the birth of their second child, and in his grief Bauer built her monument, topped by a "temple" with her porcelain photograph in it. Bauer took his own life a year later; and his own monument was erected in 1986, paid for by a fundraising reception held in the mansion he helped to design. Over the years, this has been a favored stopping place for lovers young and old. (Both, Palko.)

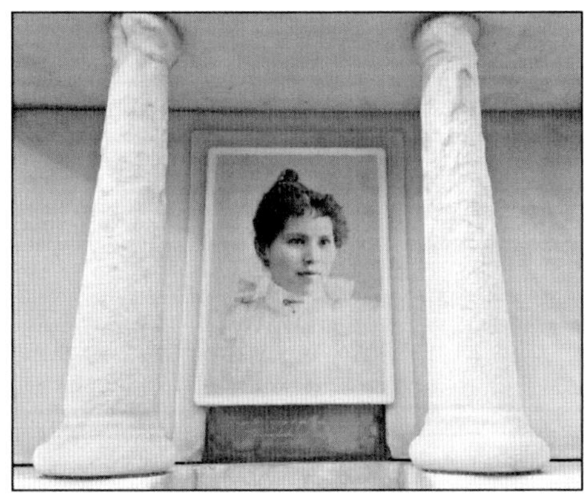

Within days of Sherman's seizure of Raleigh, Union brigadier general Smith Dykins Atkins occupied Chapel Hill. His chance meeting with Eleanor Hope Swain (1842–1881), daughter of University of North Carolina president David Swain (see page 68), was "love at first sight." The general's military band is said to have serenaded Ella, but the students, the town, and even Mrs. Swain condemned the courtship. Nevertheless, Ella and the "Yankee General" were married that August and left soon for his home in Freeport, Illinois, raising a family there. Diagnosed with breast cancer, Ella died visiting Raleigh and lies with her birth family in Oakwood; Atkins lived until 1913 and rests in Freeport. Their story is told in Suzy Barile's 2009 *Undaunted Heart: The True Love Story of a Southern Belle & a Yankee General.* (Right, Suzy Barile; below, Palko.).

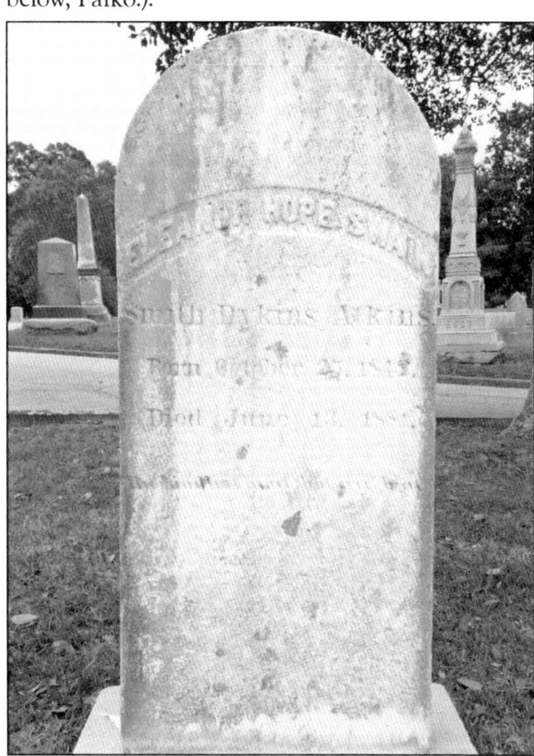

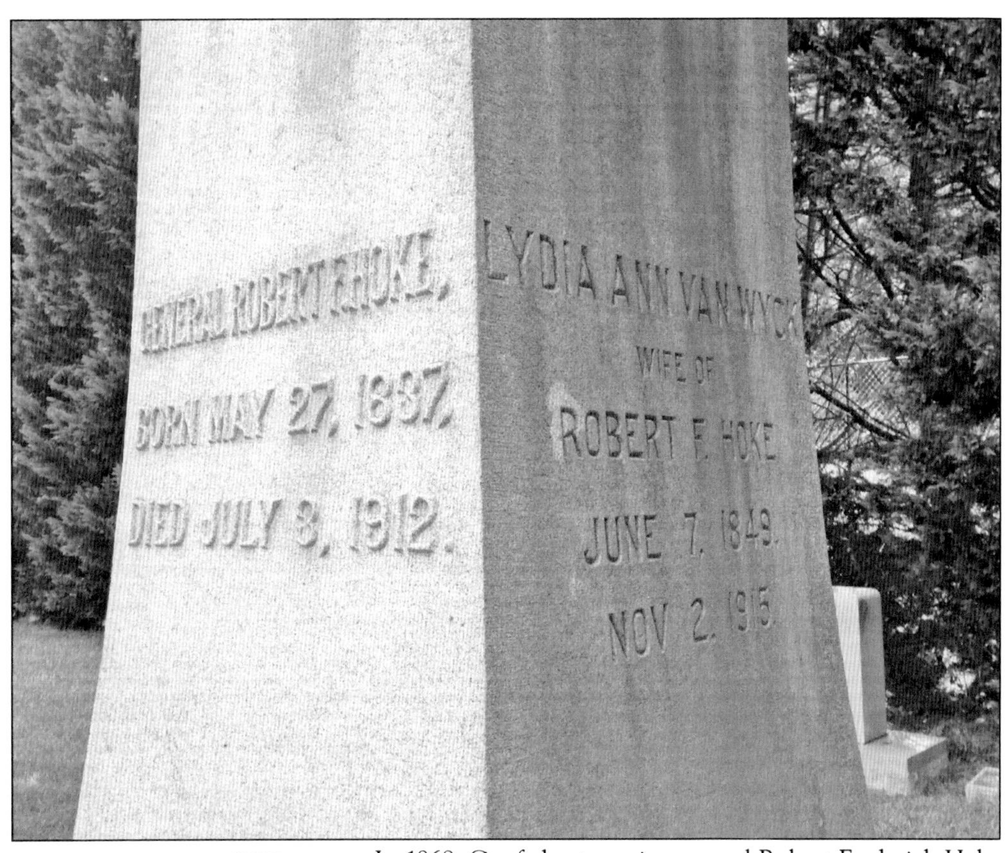

In 1868, Confederate major general Robert Frederick Hoke (1837–1912), a Civil War hero, met Lydia Ann Van Wyck (1849–1915), a southern beauty, sister of the first mayor of a consolidated New York City, and niece of cattleman Samuel Maverick (who gave the English language that word). It was love at first sight, although Hoke was arrested for wearing a Confederate coat in New York while courting her. The couple lived happily for decades in Raleigh, where he became a prominent businessman. A son, Michael Hoke (1874–1944), was a pioneering orthopedist, dealing especially with disabled youngsters. A friend of Pres. Franklin Roosevelt, himself disabled, "Dr. Mike" is interred near his parents. (Above, Palko; left, SANC.)

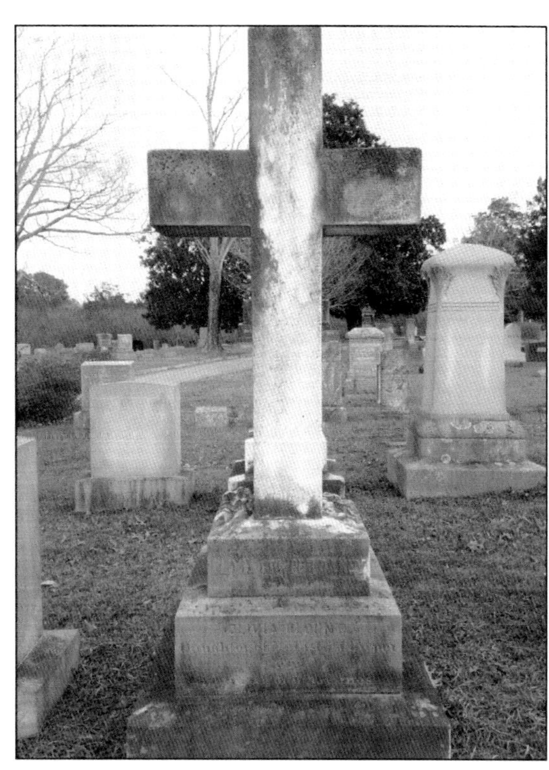

At first friends and pen pals, Christ Church organist Olivia Blount Cowper (1861–1896; pictured) and businessman Richard Beverly Raney (1860–1909) married in 1894; she died in childbirth 17 months later and was buried with the Cowper family. In memory of his beloved bride, a brokenhearted Richard provided construction and endowment funds for Raleigh's first public library, located on Capitol Square from 1901 to 1966; two later libraries in Raleigh also have carried Olivia's name. Richard later married Kate Whiting Denson (1872–1952; interred in Oakwood next to Richard), who designed the flag of the city of Raleigh, but it is the poignant love story of Olivia Raney that the capital remembers so well. (Right, Palko; below, SANC.)

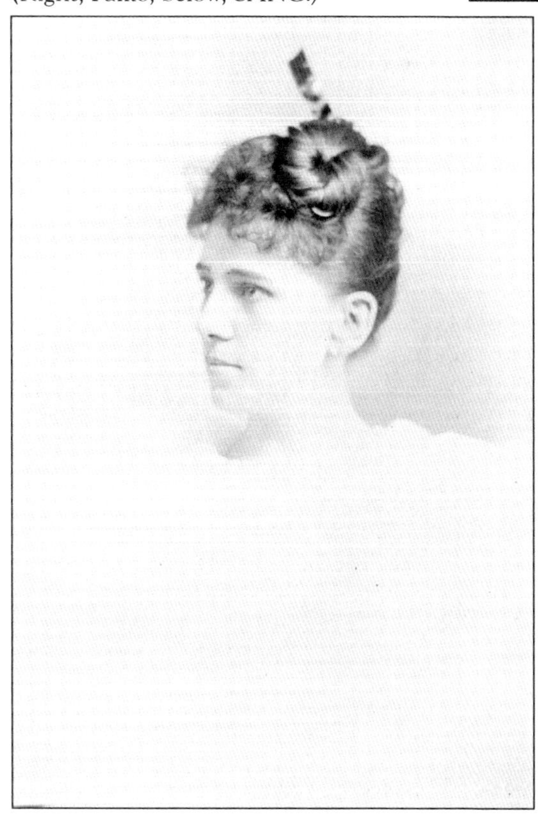

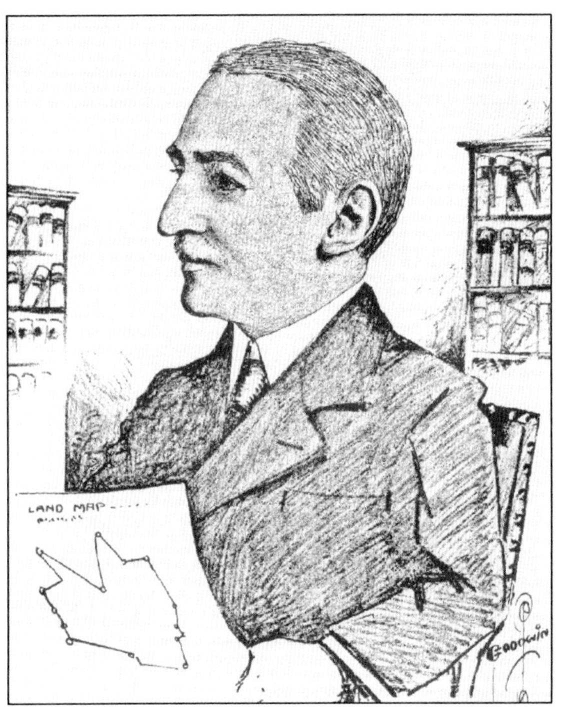

Ernest Haywood (1860–1946) was the grandson of Raleigh's first mayor and a prominent attorney specializing in corporate and estate law. His romantic relationship with an attractive client, widow Gertrude Winder Tucker (shown with son Rufus), became a scandal leading to a downtown confrontation with John Ludlow Skinner (1870–1903; interred in Oakwood), Gertrude's brother-in-law and son of a renowned Baptist clergyman. Haywood killed Skinner with a pistol shot but, in a trial that riveted the city's attention, was found not guilty on the grounds of self-defense. Haywood always denied he had married Gertrude despite her persistent claim; nevertheless, she named a son Ernest and carried Haywood's name for the rest of her life. (Left, Goodwin; below, First Baptist Church.)

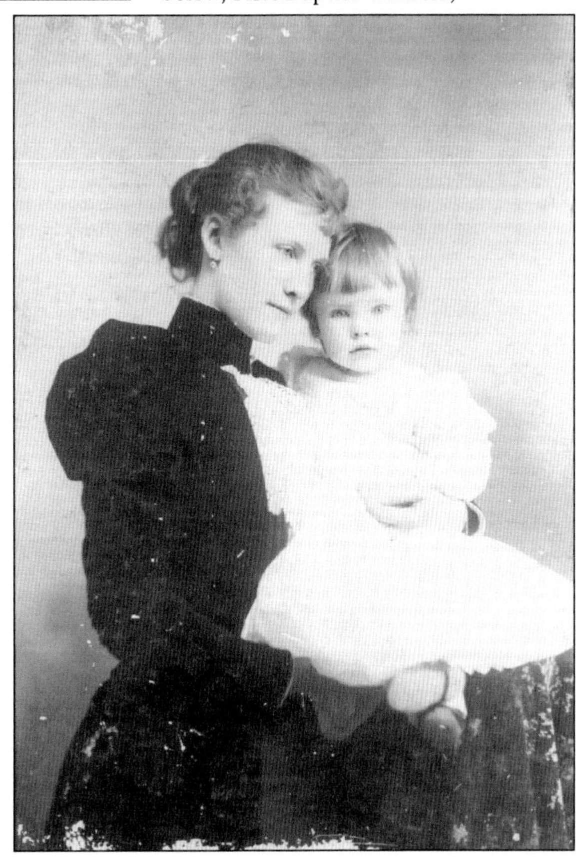

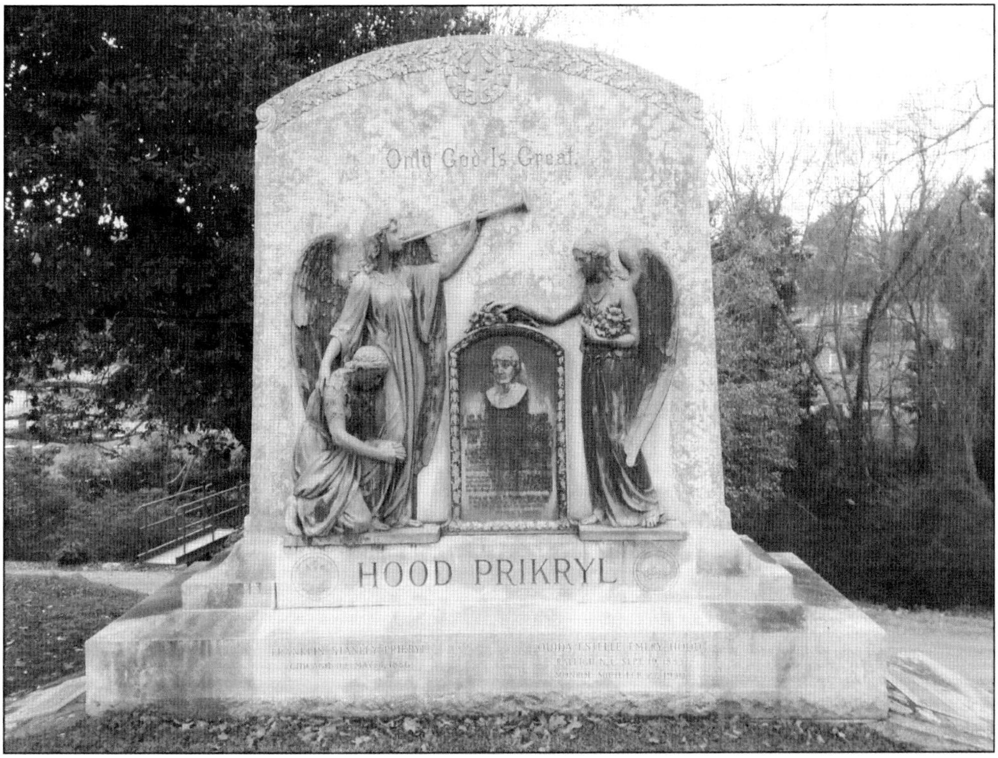

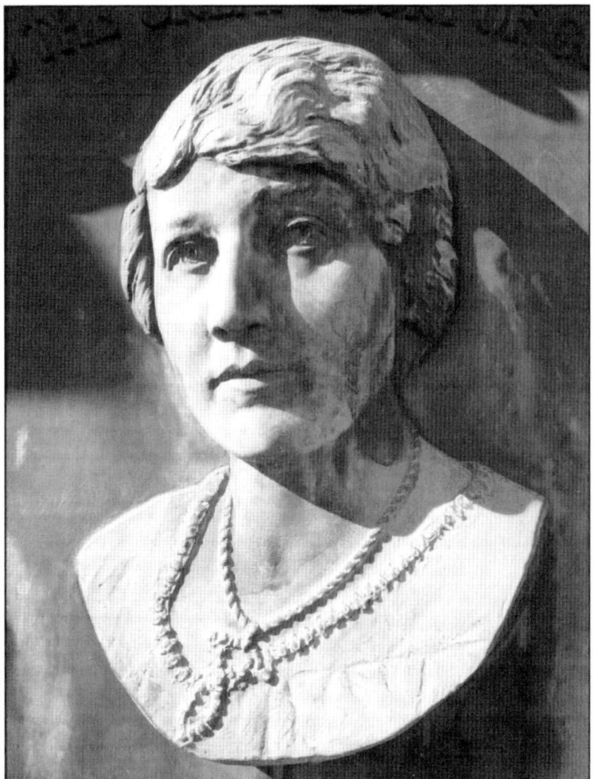

Wealthy Michigander Franklin Stanley Prikryl erected this imposing monument to reflect his devotion to Raleigh's Ouida Estelle Emery Hood (1883–1930). They, along with her husband, prominent auto industry leader Wallace C. Hood, had lived together for a time outside Detroit, where she endeared herself to locals with her civic work. She died unexpectedly at 46 from a sinus hemorrhage likely resulting from anemia. Prikryl arranged to have barrels of Michigan soil shipped to Raleigh for her burial, reuniting her with family in Oakwood and satisfying the community in Michigan, the latter providing a eulogistic plaque in her honor. Prikryl is said to have visited Ouida's gravesite many times, but although his name is on the monument, his death date, 1962, is not. His choice for interment was Forest Lawn Memorial Park in Glendale, California. (Both, Palko.)

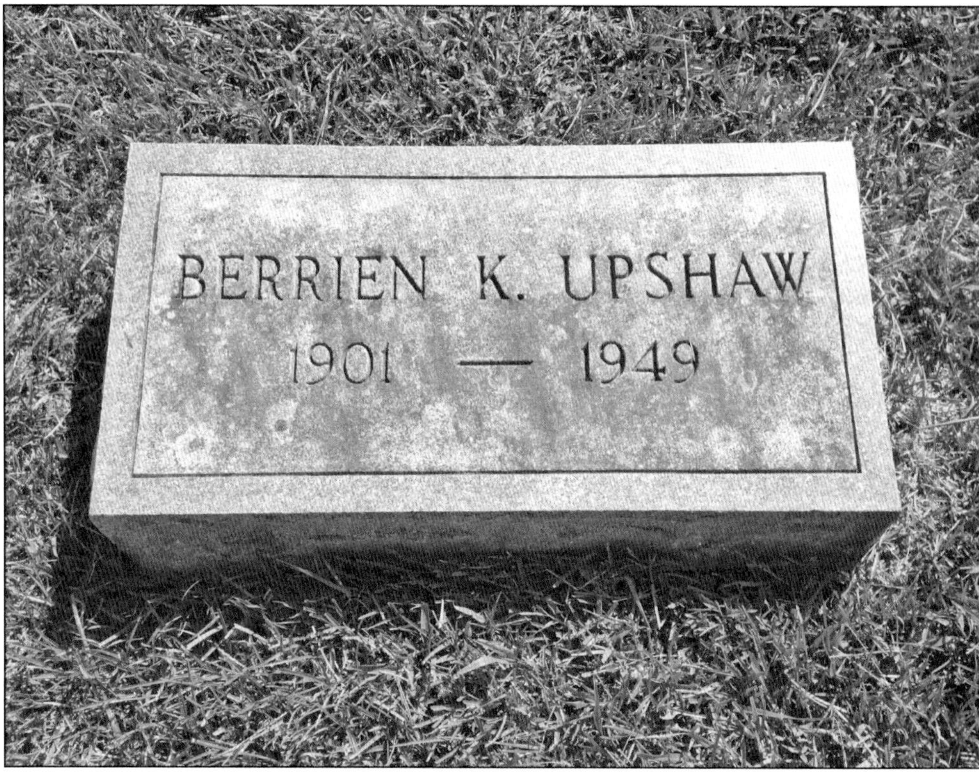

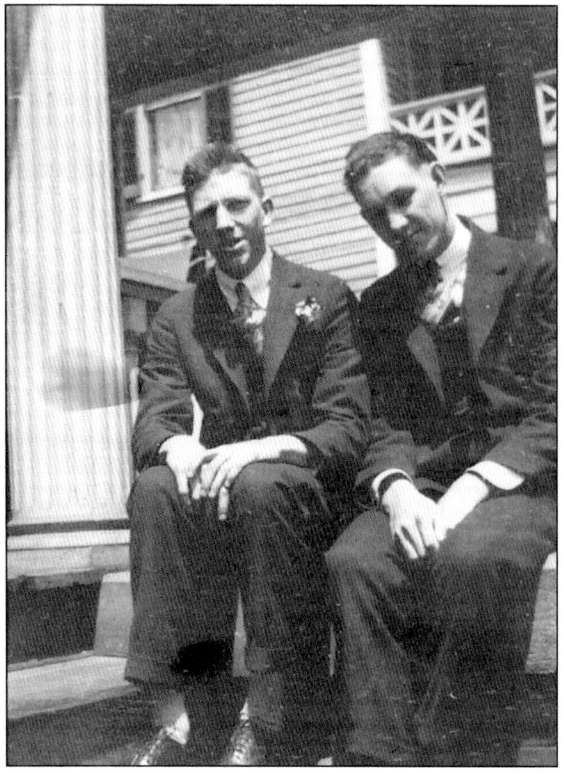

From a solid Raleigh family on Woodburn Road, Berrien Kinnard Upshaw (1901–1949), left, was the first husband of Margaret "Peggy" Mitchell, author of *Gone with the Wind*. Described as "sexy and self-indulgent," he was a gambler and a bootlegger during Prohibition and careless with money when he had it. His stormy, short-lived (1922–1924), and sometimes violent marriage to Peggy was a calamity for her. Nicknamed "Red" for his hair color, Upshaw contributed to the literary persona of Rhett Butler in Mitchell's classic epic of the Civil War. Unlike the man and his story, Upshaw's grave marker is a modest one that nevertheless attracts many visitors. Most of his Raleigh family rest on the far side of the cemetery; Peggy, at Oakland Cemetery in Atlanta. (Above, Palko; left, Atlanta History Center.)

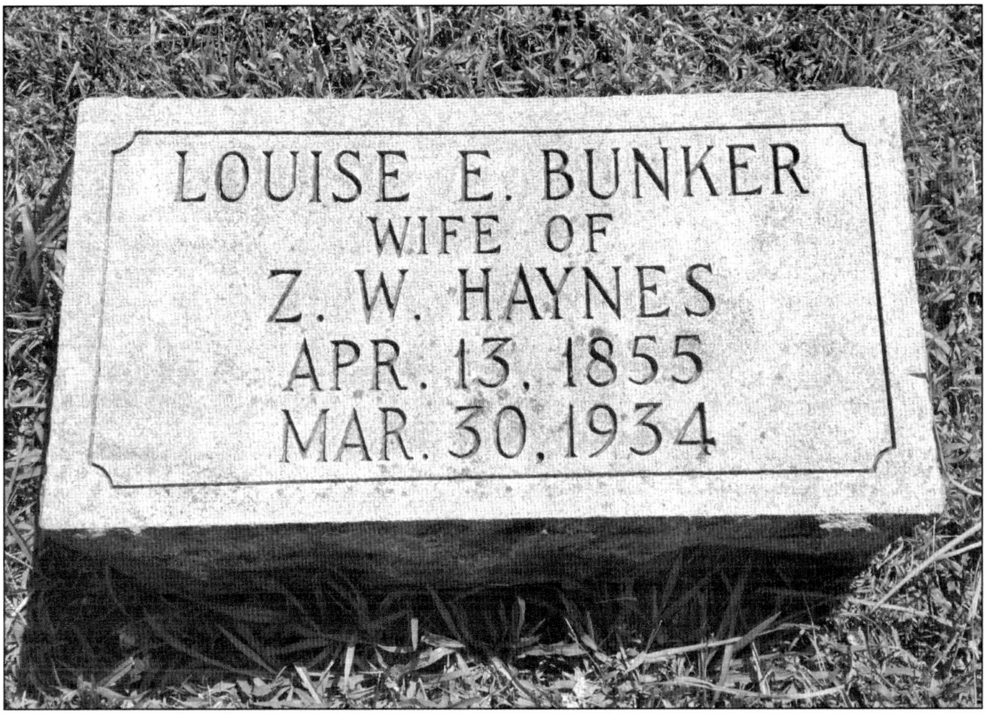

Louise Emeline Bunker Haynes (1855–1934) was one of 21 children fathered by Chang and Eng Bunker, the original "Siamese twins," who married Tar Heel sisters Adelaide (Chang) and Sarah Anne (Eng) Yates. Louise came to Raleigh from the Surry County area of North Carolina to attend the state's school for the deaf, then in downtown Raleigh. Here, she married deaf school instructor Zacharias W. Haynes (1848–1900) and gave birth to 10 children. Over the years, she and her large family lived in several homes (extant) not far from the cemetery and dealt in local property. One young son died in a tragic accident, but the other Haynes children led full lives. (Above, Palko; right, SANC.)

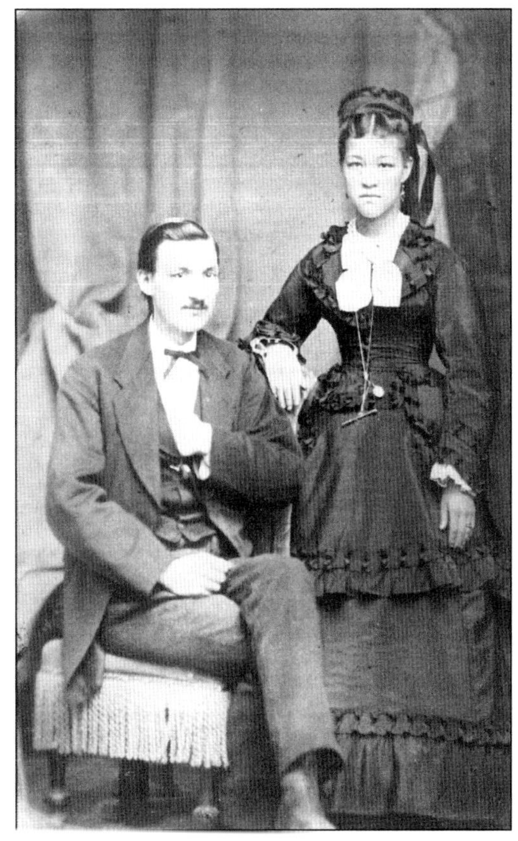

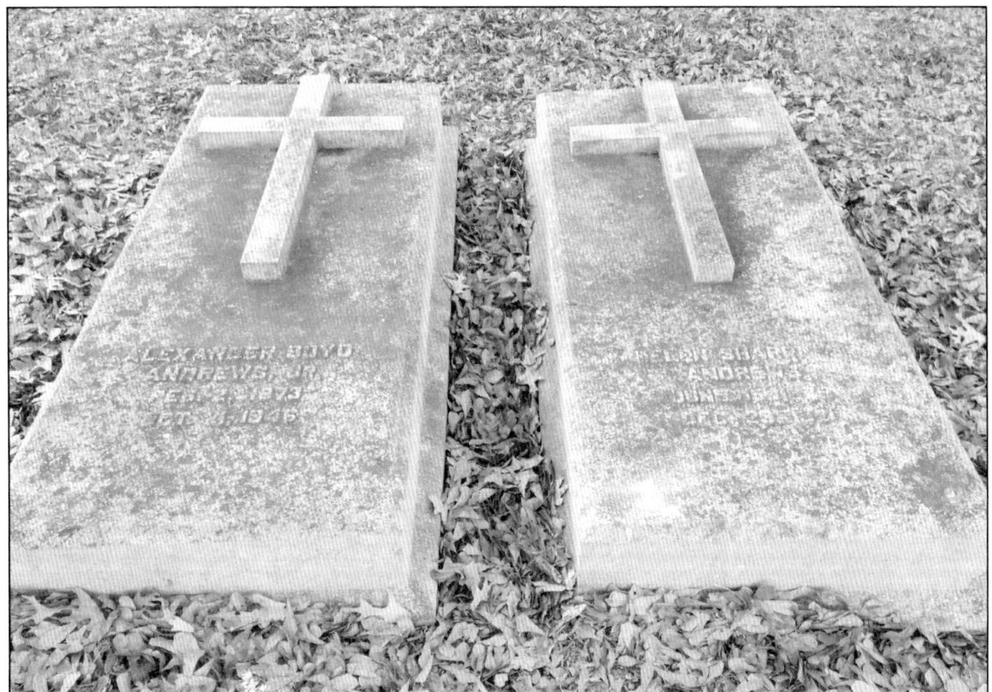

Alexander Boyd Andrews Jr. (1873–1946), the son of a wealthy railroad magnate, married auburn-haired Helen May Sharples (1879–1921), from outside Philadelphia, in 1908. They liked to travel—the photograph shows them in Atlantic City, New Jersey. A decade after their marriage, they purchased the grand house owned by the Heck family (see page 28), across North Street from Alex's boyhood home. While refurbishing the house, Helen died choosing new fabrics; Alex moved into their new home but never permitted curtains on the windows, only shades. The couple had no children, and Alex did not marry again. (Above, Palko; below, SANC.)

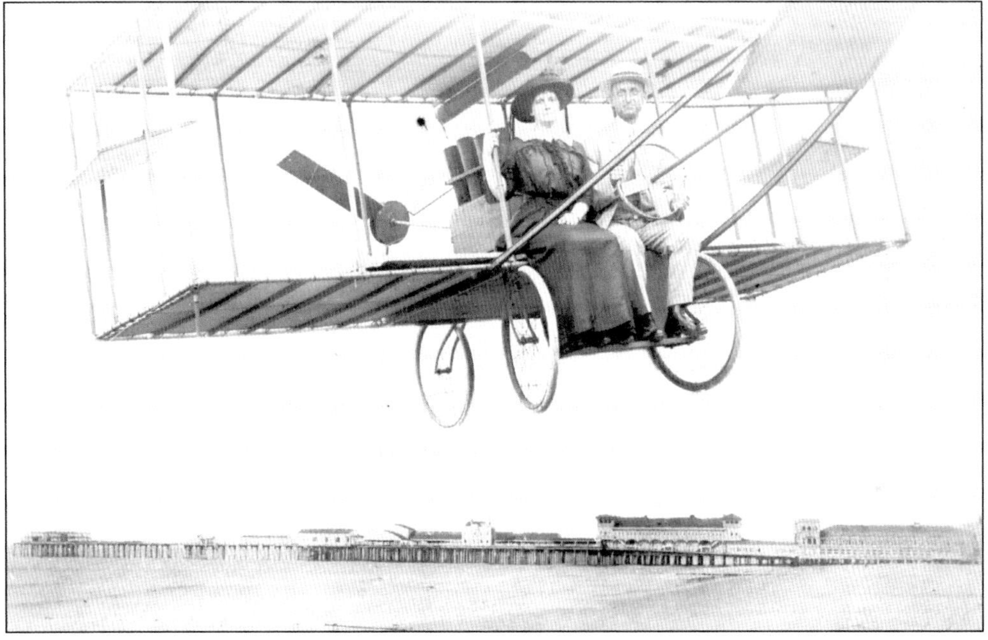

Eight

Their Stories

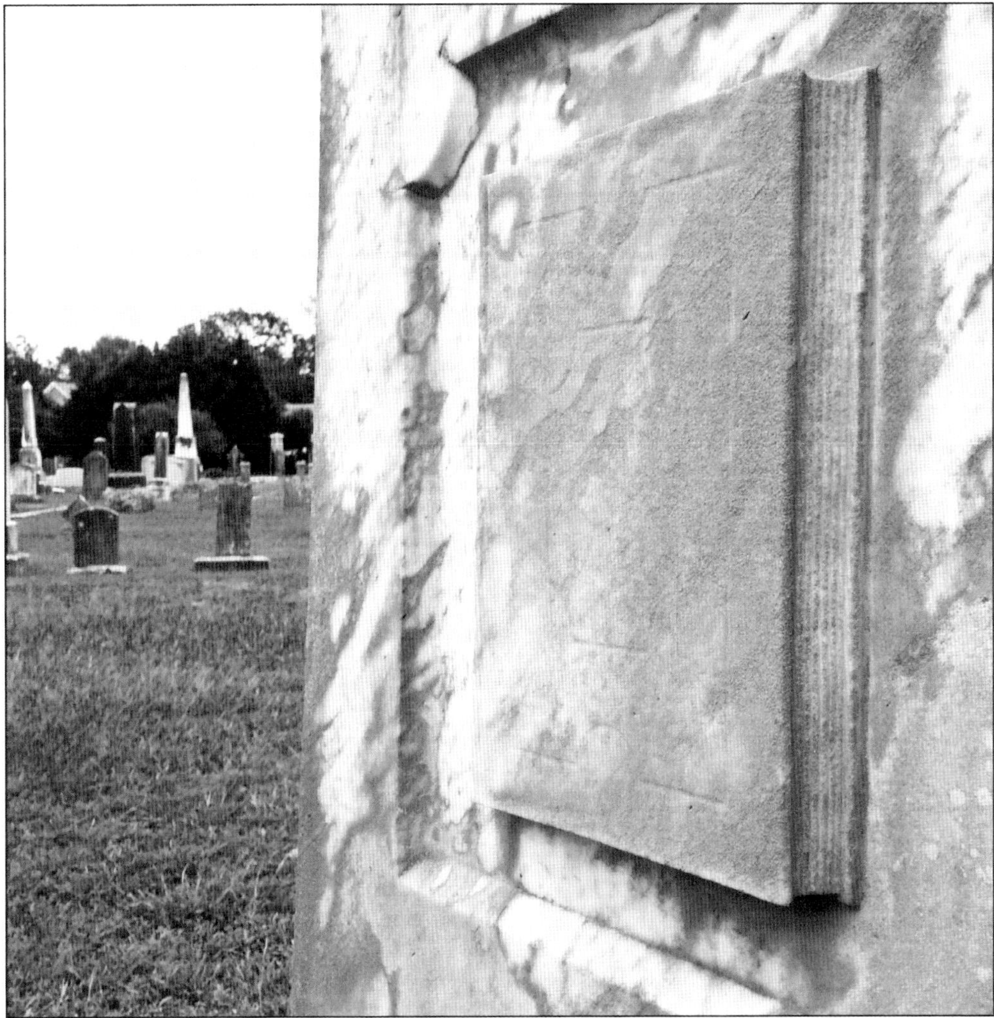

If it is true that every tombstone, like this carved marker, is a book waiting to be opened, then Oakwood Cemetery may have at least 25,000 tales to tell. Here is a sampler of brief biographies of those in Oakwood who, to borrow from Longfellow, are not dead but merely departed. They live today in their stories. (Palko.)

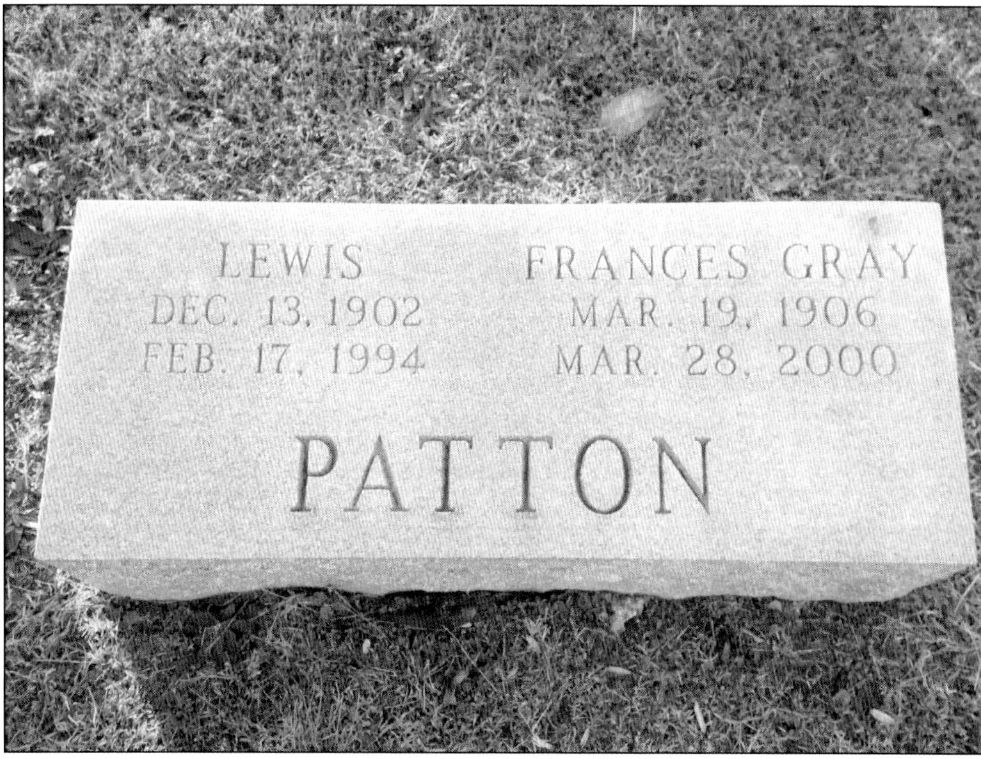

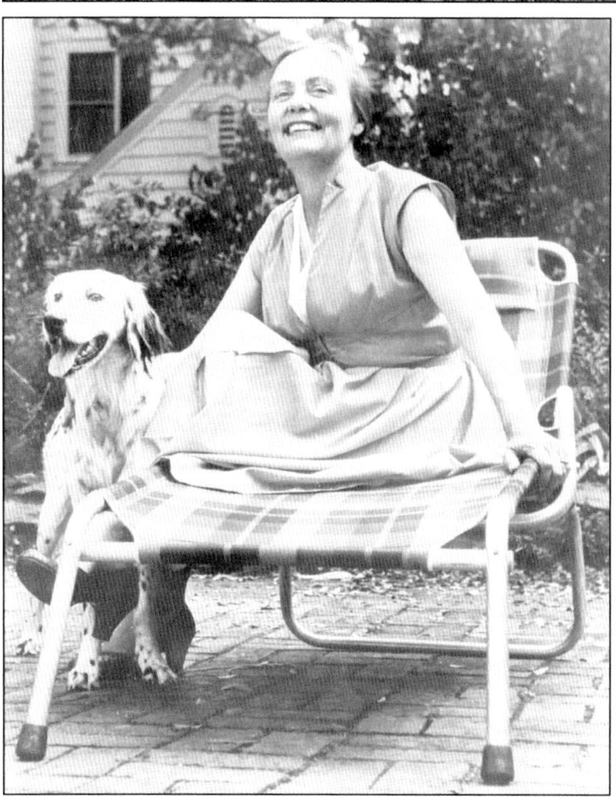

Frances Gray Patton (1906–2000) was an award-winning writer, the so-called Jane Austen of the South. The daughter of a renowned newspaper editor, she grew up not far from the cemetery, and her years in Raleigh became a basis for many of her numerous short stories published in *Ladies' Home Journal*, *Collier's*, *Harper's*, and other national magazines, especially the *New Yorker*. Patton was best-known for the sentimental best seller *Good Morning, Miss Dove* (1954), made into a major motion picture. A graduate of Trinity/Duke (1926), she married Duke English professor Lewis Patton and was the mother of one son and twin daughters. (Above, Palko; left, SANC.)

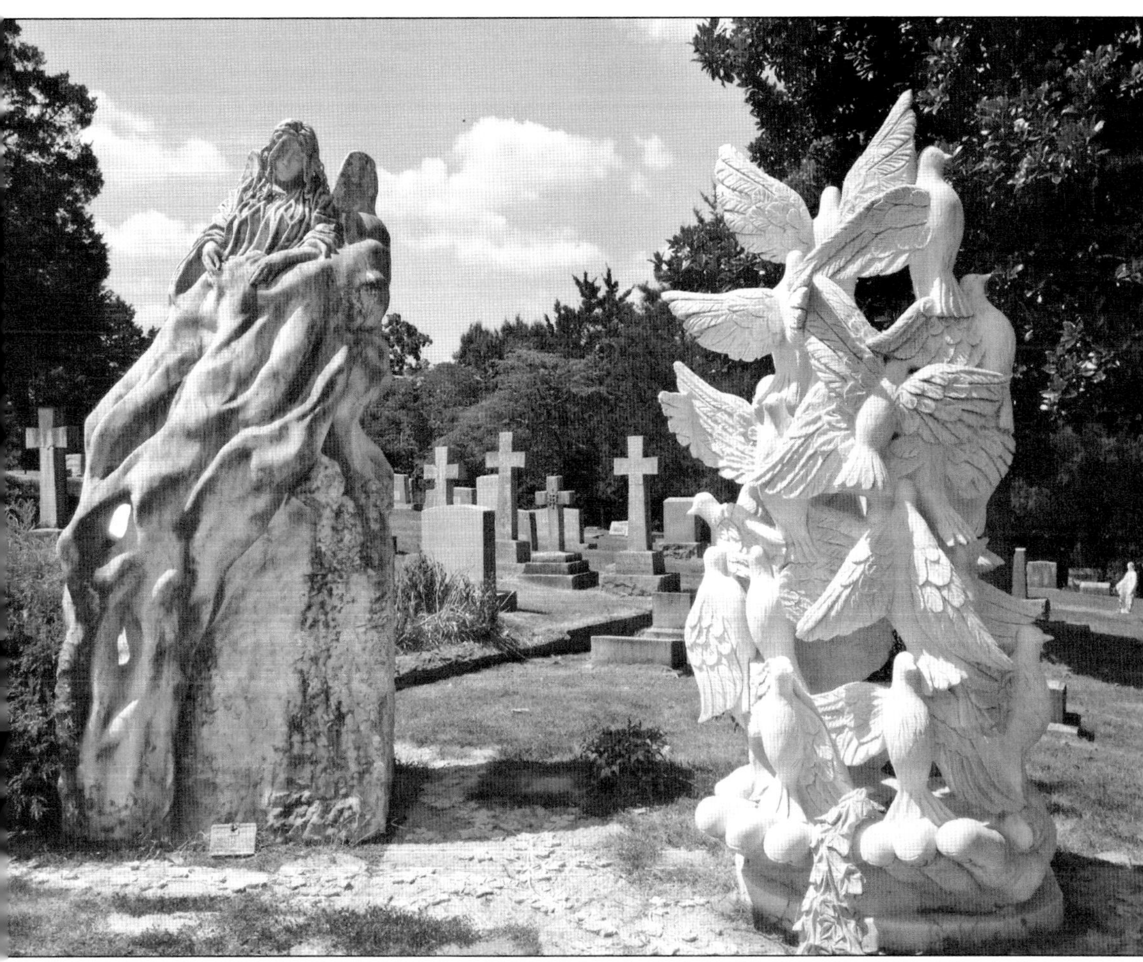

The graves of Lucius Wade Edwards (1979–1996), on the left, and his mother, Mary Elizabeth Anania Edwards (1949–2010) are among the most visited in the cemetery. A student at Raleigh's Broughton High School, Wade died in a car accident between the capital and Wilmington. Sculptor Robert Mihaly created Wade's memorial, a mourning angel cradling the young man's image. Elizabeth Edwards, wife of attorney, US senator, and presidential aspirant John Edwards, died after a brave battle with breast cancer. She was also an attorney and the author of two books that drew on her personal experience, *Saving Graces* and *Resilience*. Elizabeth and her son are joined by a carved vine, symbolizing loyalty, at the bases of their monuments. Her memorial, also created by Mihaly, depicts 27 doves released from two hands. (Palko.)

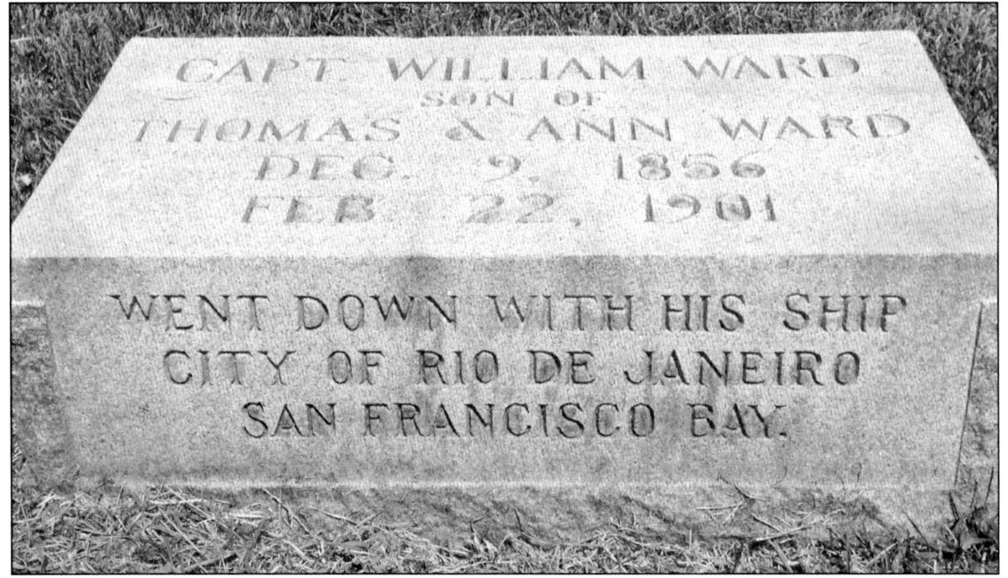

William Charles Ward (1856–1901), born in England, was the captain of the steamship *City of Rio de Janeiro* when it went down in the fog near the mouth of San Francisco Bay. Some 120 lives, mostly Chinese immigrants, were lost, including Ward's. Over a year later, his decomposed body was found on a California beach and sent to Raleigh for interment with family. (Palko.)

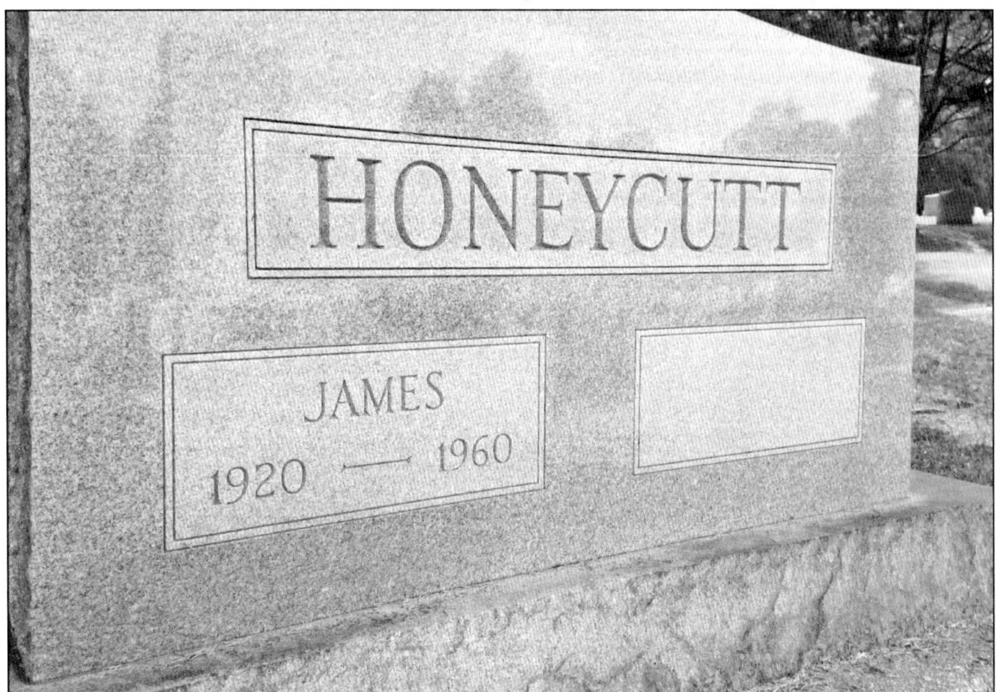

James D. "Jim" Honeycutt (1920–1960), a Raleigh native, worked in Niagara Falls, New York. On July 9, 1960, he took Roger Woodward, age 7, and his sister Deanna, 17, boating above the falls. The boat capsized, and Deanna was saved, but Honeycutt and Roger went over the falls. Honeycutt perished; but Roger, pulled aboard *Maid of the Mist,* is one of the few people to have gone over Niagara Falls unprotected and survive. (Palko.)

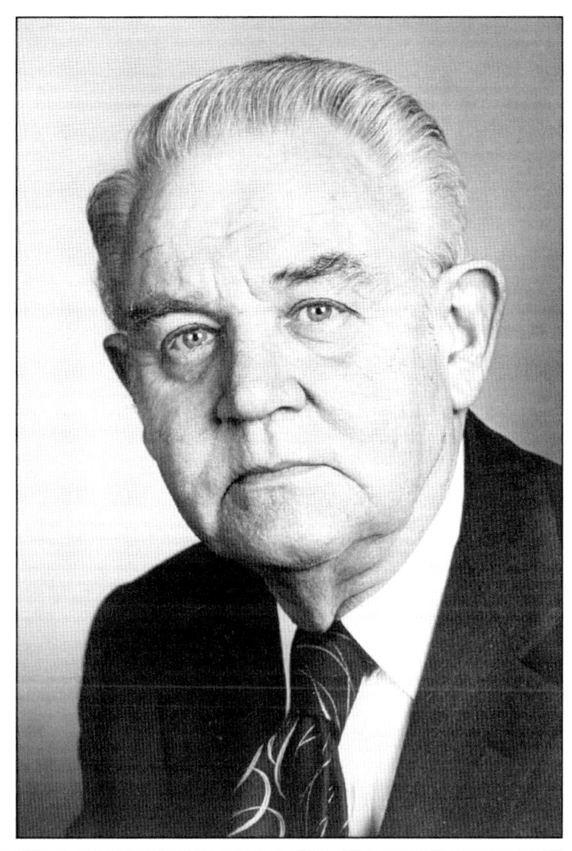

Vermont Connecticut Royster (1914–1996), born into the candy-making Raleigh family known for their state names and schooled at the University of North Carolina, made journalism a career, nearly all of it with the *Wall Street Journal*. A US Navy officer during World War II, he later rose through the ranks at the *Journal*, to editor (1958–1971) and director of Dow Jones & Company, the publisher. Vermont Royster wrote a column for the *Journal* after formal "retirement"; his oft-published Christmas editorial from 1949 is a favorite. Among his numerous awards were two Pulitzer Prizes. He spent his final years in Raleigh. (Right, SANC; below, Palko.)

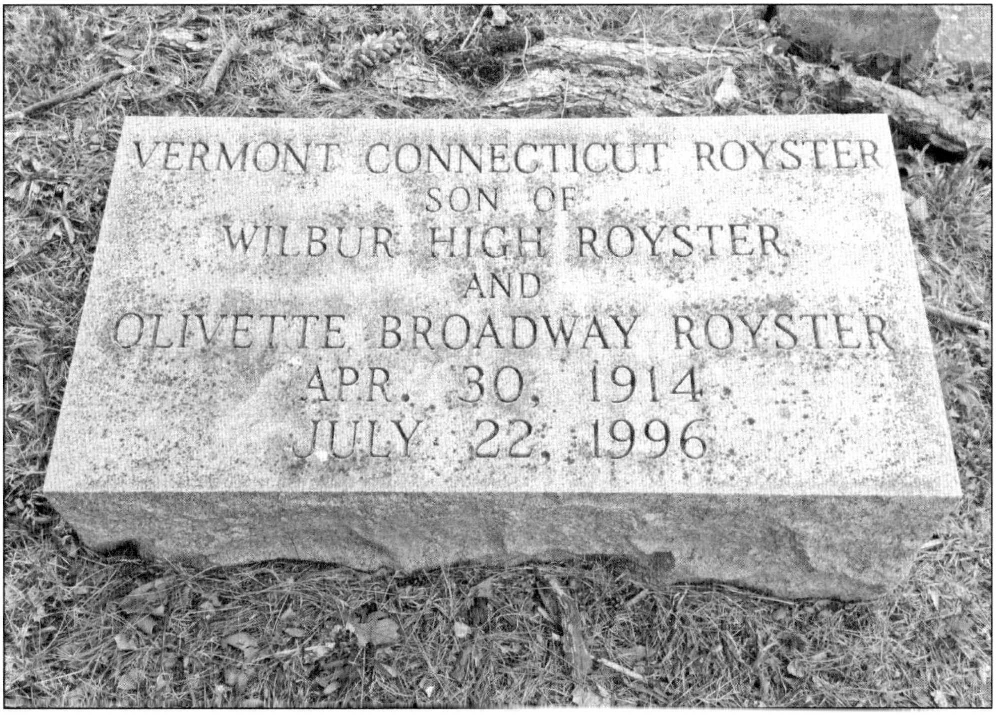

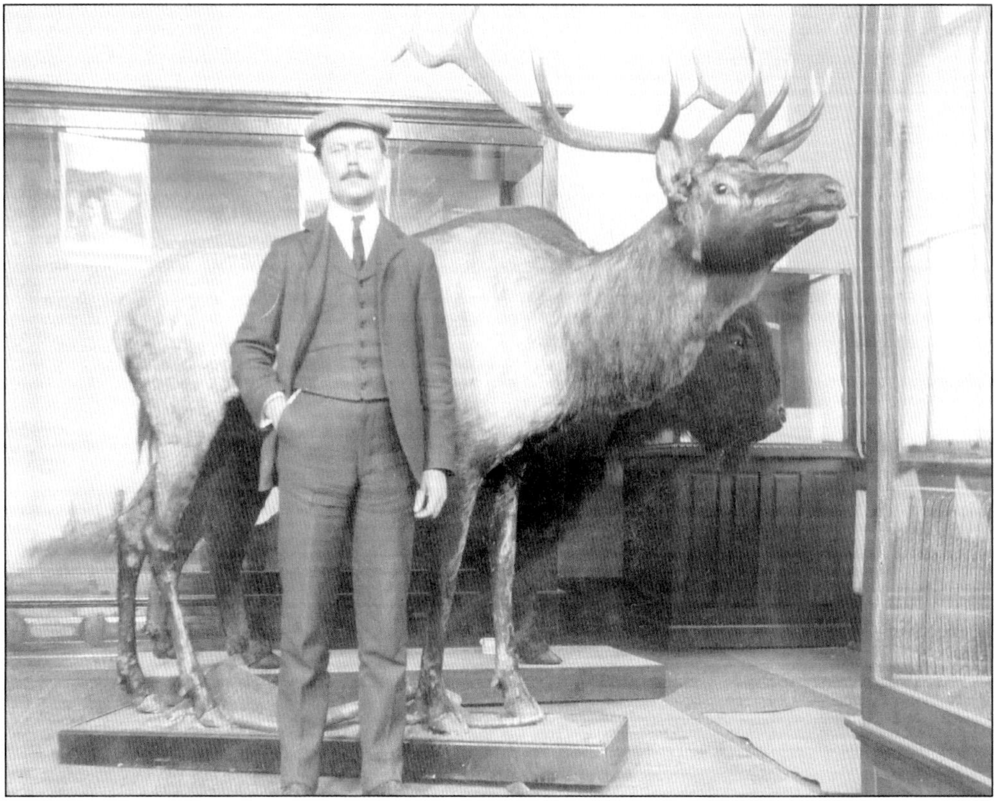

Herbert Hutchinson Brimley (1861–1946), with his brother Clement Samuel (1863–1946), immigrated to the United States from England in 1880, opening a taxidermy and biology supply business in Raleigh. Recognized as brilliant naturalists, they were hired by the state for various scientific projects, including the reconstruction of a 50-foot right whale skeleton in 1894. The next year, "Herb" (pictured) was appointed head of the North Carolina State Museum, a position he held for over 40 years. He and Clement, also interred at Oakwood Cemetery, died within months of each other. Their right whale is still on exhibit at the museum. (Above, SANC; below, Palko.)

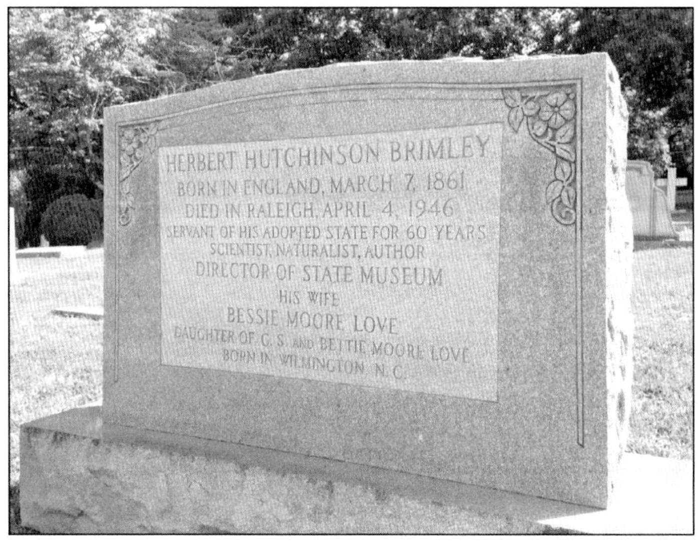

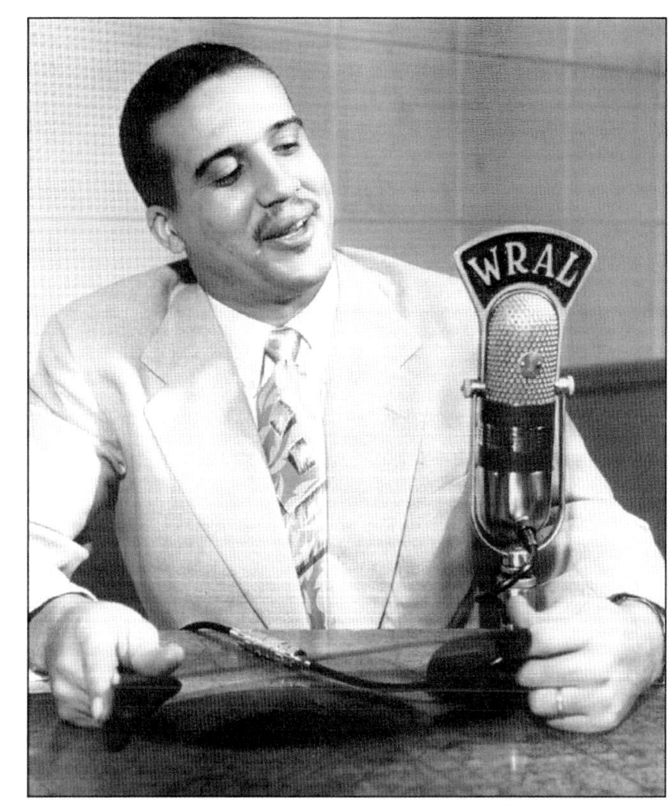

John Davis "J.D." Lewis Jr. (1919–2007) grew up in Raleigh and became a pioneering broadcaster and civic leader. Morehouse College–educated, JD has a number of firsts to his name: one of the first 200 blacks to serve in the Marine Corps; the state's first African American radio announcer (for WRAL radio); and the first black host in America with a regularly scheduled television show (*Teenage Frolics*, a dance show on WRAL-TV in 1958). Davis also hosted minority affairs and consumer advocacy shows at Capitol Broadcasting Company, one of the nation's most innovative media firms; he participated in numerous civic organizations and is a 2010 member of the Raleigh Hall of Fame. (Right, Capitol Broadcasting; below, Palko.)

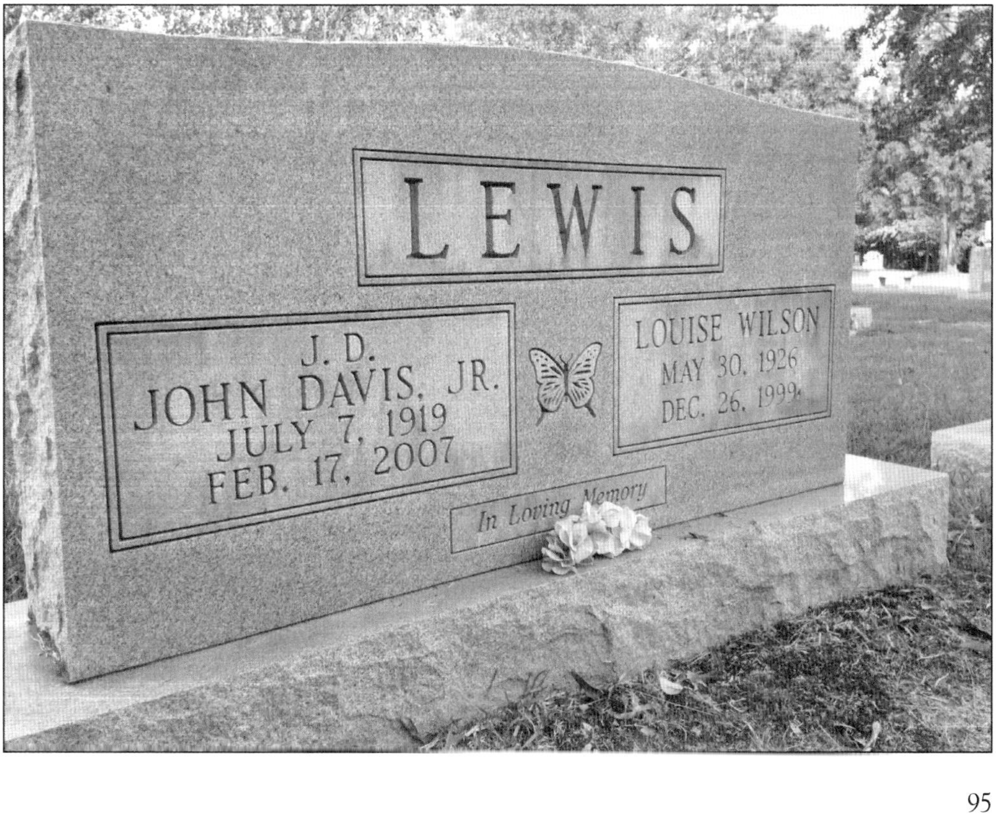

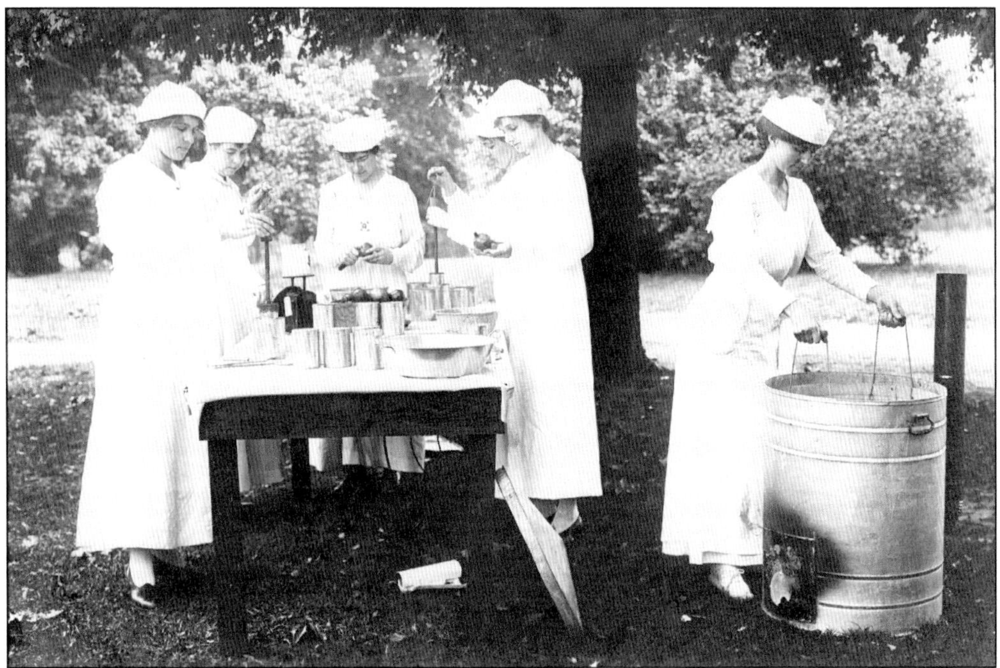

Jane Simpson McKimmon (1867–1957), a pioneer in home education and administration, attended Peace Institute and at 59 was the first woman to get a degree from North Carolina State College. She became internationally known for her "home demonstration" method, developing "clubs" (shown) and a cadre of instructors to bring to rural Tar Heel families training in all aspects of home economy. She won countless awards for her service and an honorary doctor of laws from the University of North Carolina (1934). Before retiring at 80, McKimmon wrote *When We're Green We Grow* (1945), a look back at her extraordinary career. North Carolina State's McKimmon Center for Extension and Continuing Education carries her name. (Above, SANC; below, Palko.)

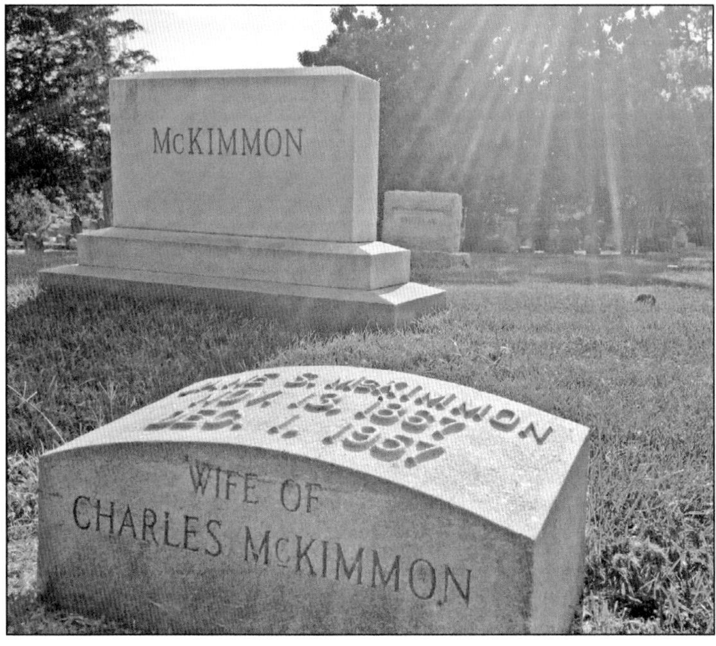

William Andrew "Will" Wynne (1869–1951), a competitive bicyclist, one of the state's first major-league baseball players (Washington), and developer of the city's first telephone system, also established Raleigh's first commercial radio station, WRCO (Wynne Radio Company) in 1924; it was sold in 1929 to Durham Life Insurance Company, when it became WPTF ("We Protect the Family"). (Palko.)

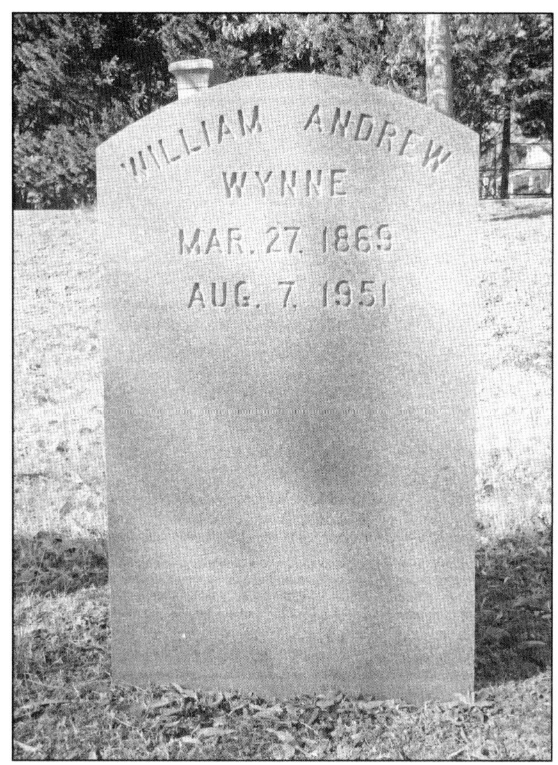

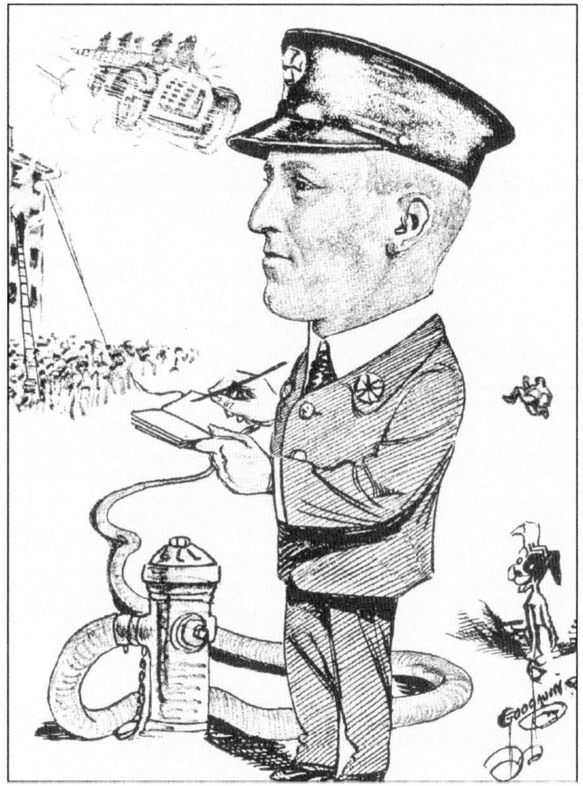

Charles D. Farmer (1882–1949), a Raleigh boy trained in mechanical trades, went from fire chief (pictured) to the first commander of the new North Carolina State Highway Patrol in 1929. At that time, 27 patrolmen rode Harley-Davidsons, 10 officers drove Ford Model As, and Farmer had a Buick. After leaving command, Farmer stayed with the force as communications director. (Goodwin.)

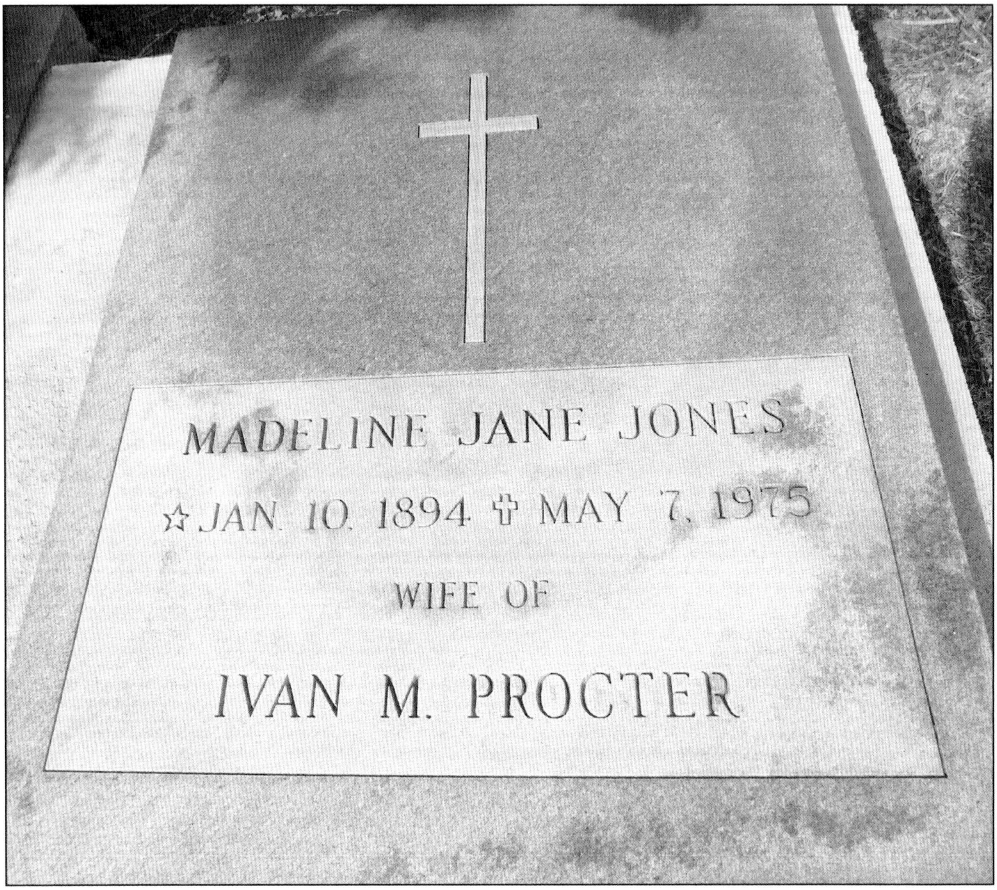

Madeline Jane Jones Procter (1894–1975), as a teen in Philadelphia, joined Anna Jarvis in promoting a national day of recognition for the mothers of America. The women wrote letters and distributed carnations as part of their nationwide campaign. In 1914, Woodrow Wilson signed the enabling legislation for Mother's Day. Madeline, a mother of four, died just four days shy of "her" day. (Palko.)

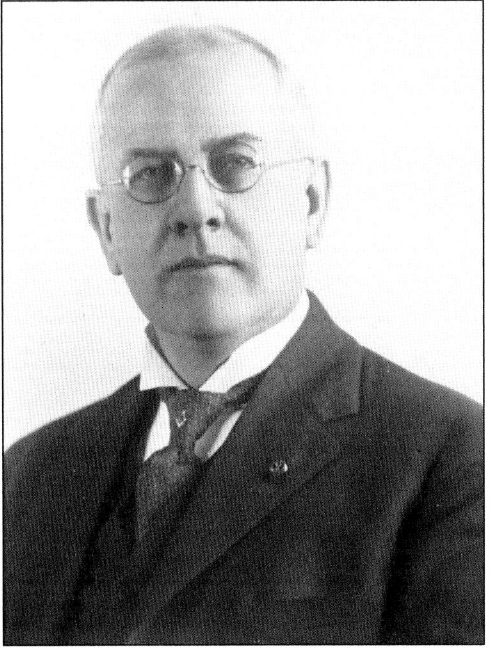

Marshall DeLancey Haywood (1871–1933), descended from a prominent North Carolina family and a Johns Hopkins graduate, was a scholar of remarkable achievement: historian of the US War and Navy Departments, the Sons of the American Revolution, the Episcopal Diocese of North Carolina, and others, and author of numerous books on American history. He lived much of his life in Raleigh's Richard Haywood House (1854), his father's home and a local landmark. (SANC.)

Dr. Alexander Boyd Hawkins (1825–1921), a physician by training and an investor in fact, may be best known for his grand house. It was his brother, William Joseph Hawkins (1819–1894), who built "AB's" house around 1885 at the corner of North and Blount Streets as a (somewhat unwelcome) "surprise" for Hawkins and his wife, wealthy Floridian Martha Bailey (1838–1910), while the couple was away. The huge brick mansion, with its crafted walnut woodwork and marble fittings, became a meeting place for "Old Raleigh" gentry when Blount Street was synonymous with postwar high society. The house, within yards of the Governor's Mansion, is now (2017) the office of North Carolina's lieutenant governor. (Right, SANC; below, Palko.)

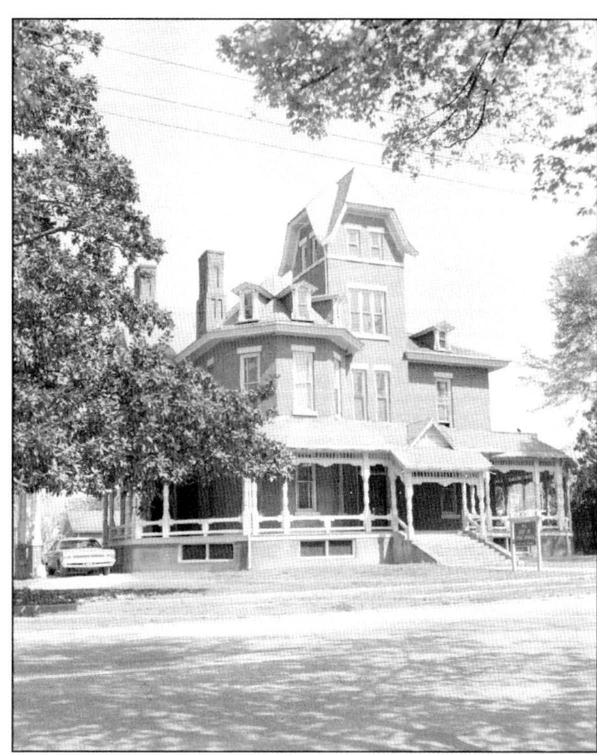

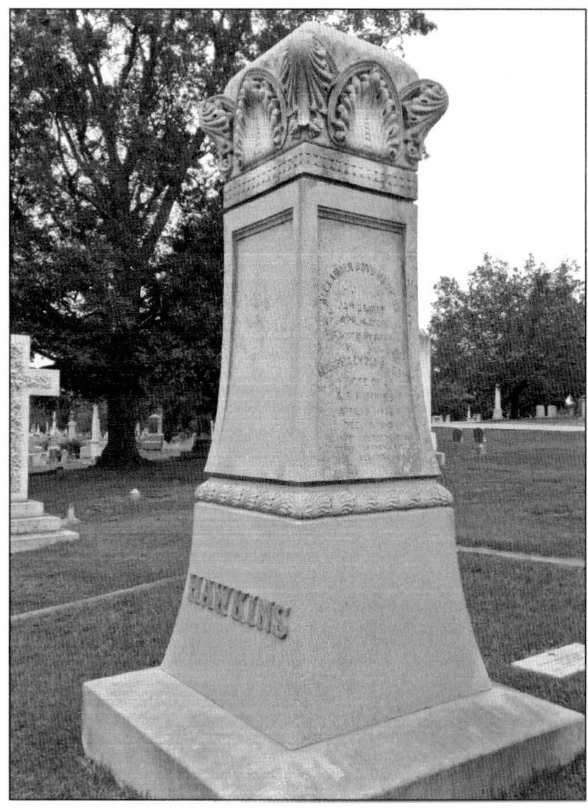

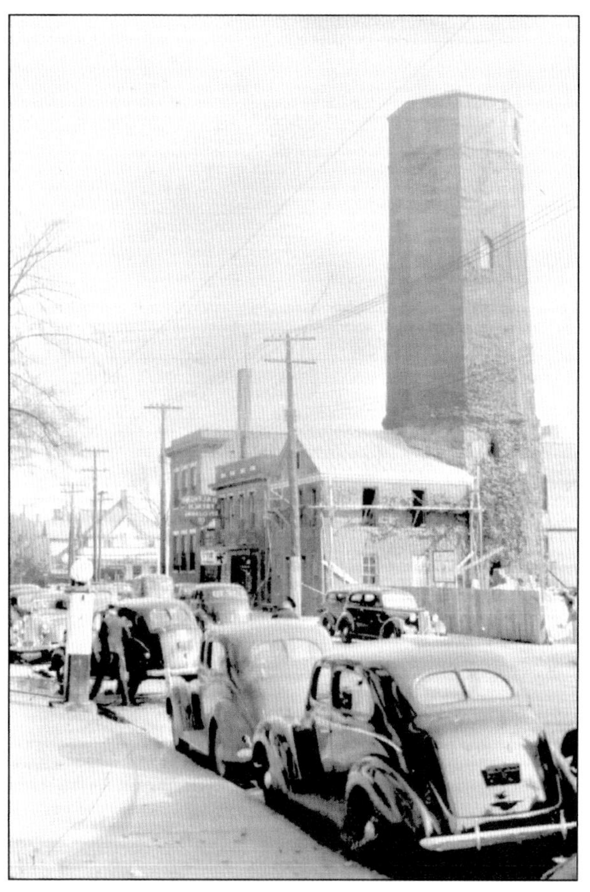

William Henley Deitrick (1895–1974), one of the state's esteemed 20th-century architects, was a Virginian and a Wake Forest graduate whose career became centered in Raleigh. While many of his buildings suggest traditional styles (such as the Italianate-style Broughton High School, 1929), he is known as a pioneering Modernist, especially as a partner in the construction of the famous J.S. Dorton Arena (1952). In 1938, Deitrick restored Raleigh's 1887 water tower (extant; pictured) and put his office there, reflecting his respect for historic preservation. Many of his buildings—public and private, commercial and residential—still stand in Raleigh and throughout the state. (Left, SANC; below, Palko.)

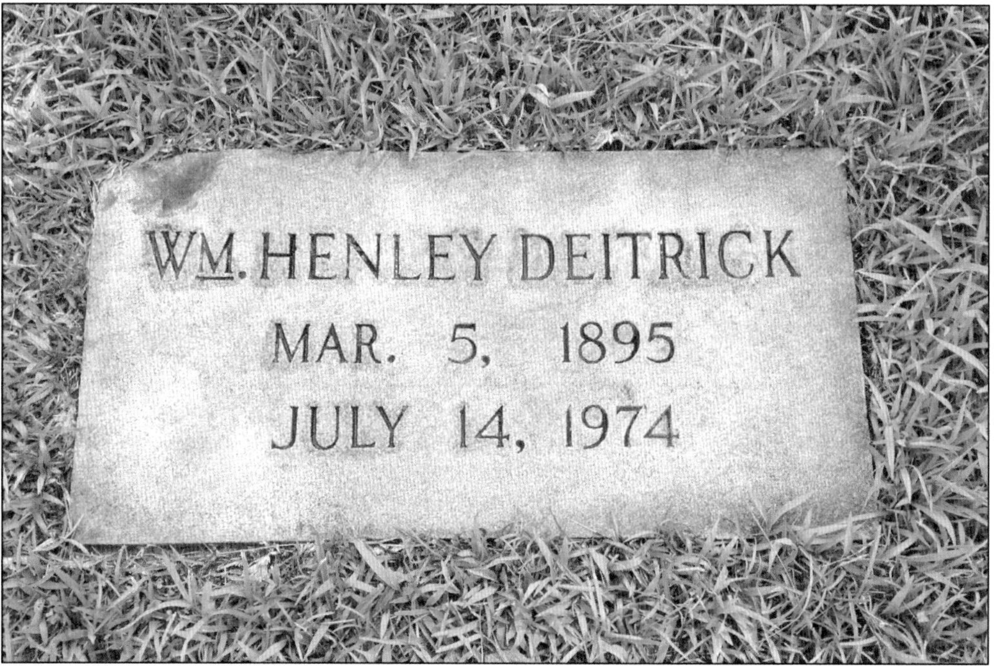

Annie Louise Wilkerson (1914–2005) was a pioneering female doctor in Raleigh. She began early, traveling with her physician father as he made house calls in his horse and buggy. After study at Duke, and later the University of North Carolina, Annie went to medical school in Virginia (as a female, she was inadmissible to UNC's medical school). She became an ob-gyn, headed the staffs at Rex and, later, Wake Hospitals, and delivered thousands of babies through the years. Despite association with the eugenics movement, her reputation is unsullied and her legacy as a skilled, compassionate physician lives on. At her death, she gave her valuable, rural retreat, ALW Haven, to Wake County for a nature preserve. (Right, Palko; below, *Raleigh News & Observer*.)

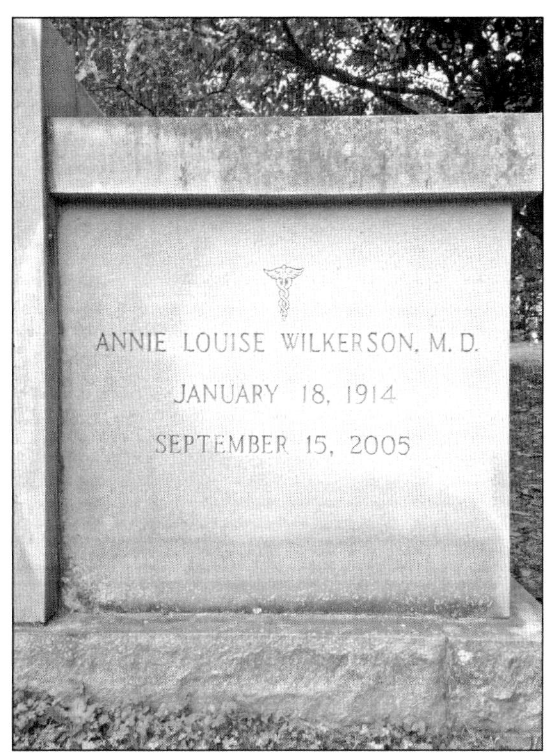

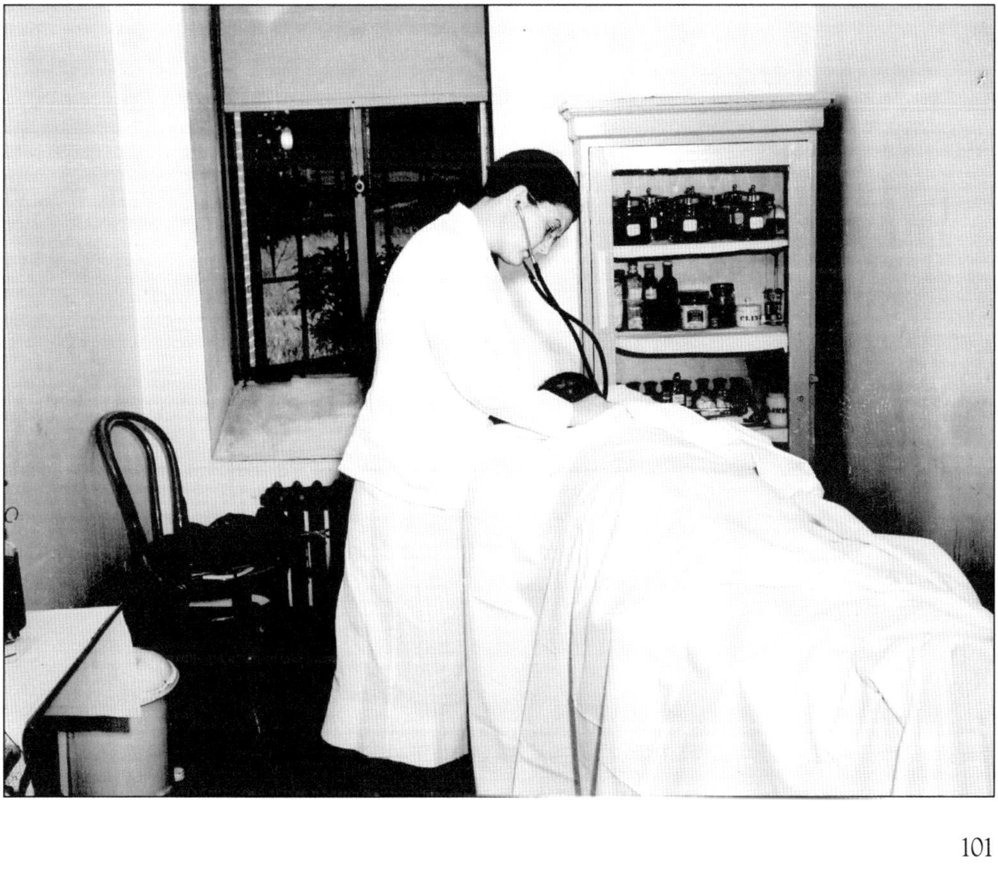

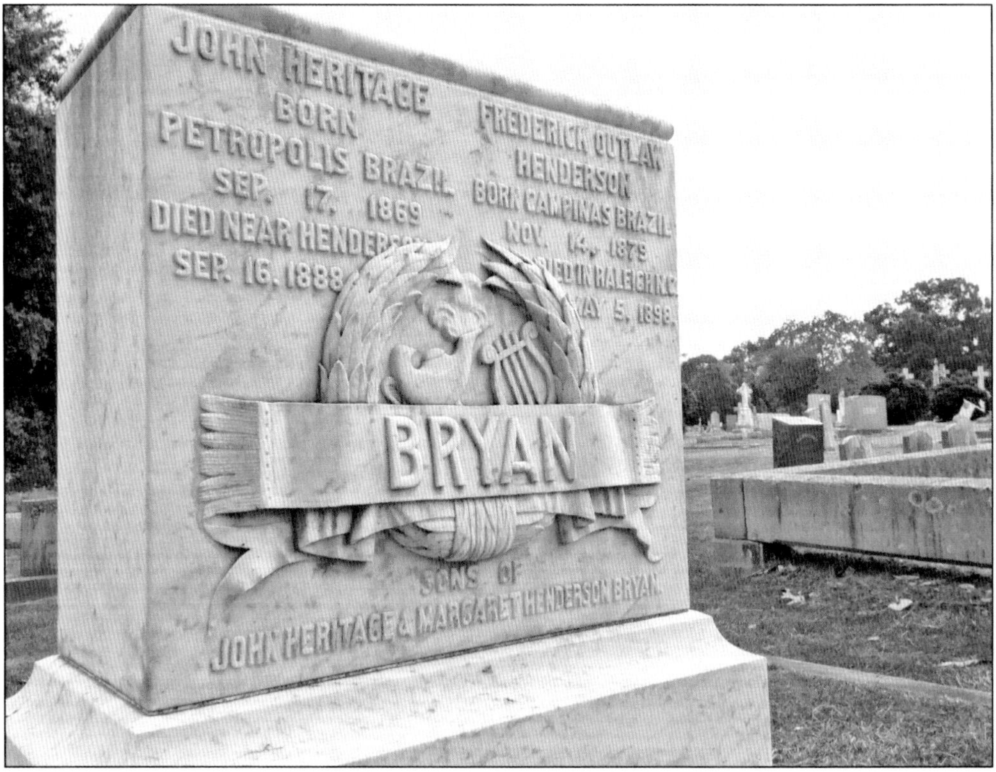

John Heritage Bryan III (1869–1888) and his brother, Frederick Outlaw Henderson Bryan (1879–1898), were part of a family of Confederados, Southerners who emigrated to Brazil from the United States after the Civil War. Surviving members of the Bryan family—these boys, their mother, and several sisters (Minnie was one)—eventually returned to Raleigh and are buried in scattered locations; husband and father John Heritage Jr. and several children are interred in Brazil. The descendants of many former Americans from Dixie still live "south of the border" and take pride in their Confederate heritage. (Both, Palko.)

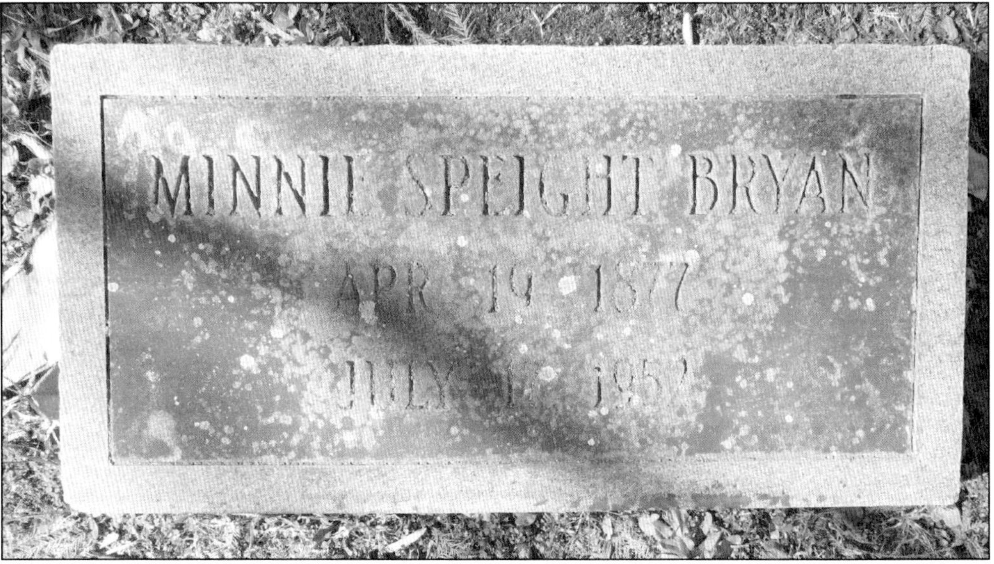

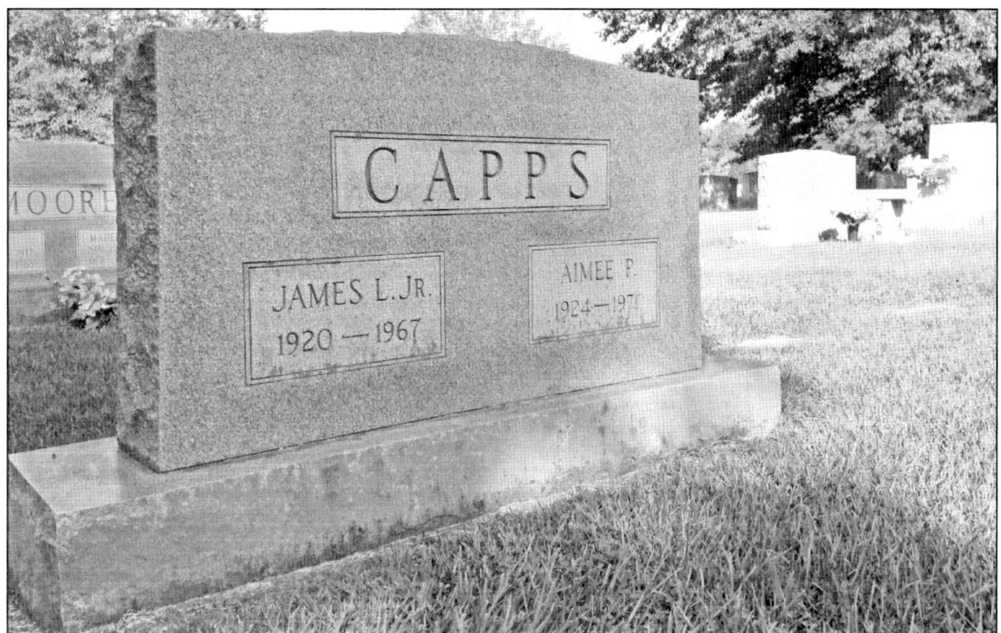

James Lee Capps Jr. (1920–1967), a radio disk jockey, was known as "Jimmy" to a generation of Tar Heels who heard him evenings on 27 stations, in Raleigh on WPTF. His show was *Our Best to You* and his music, like his voice and poetry reading, tended to the soft and gentle. Popular on college campuses, Capps also ran a recording business that produced records by local artists. (Palko.)

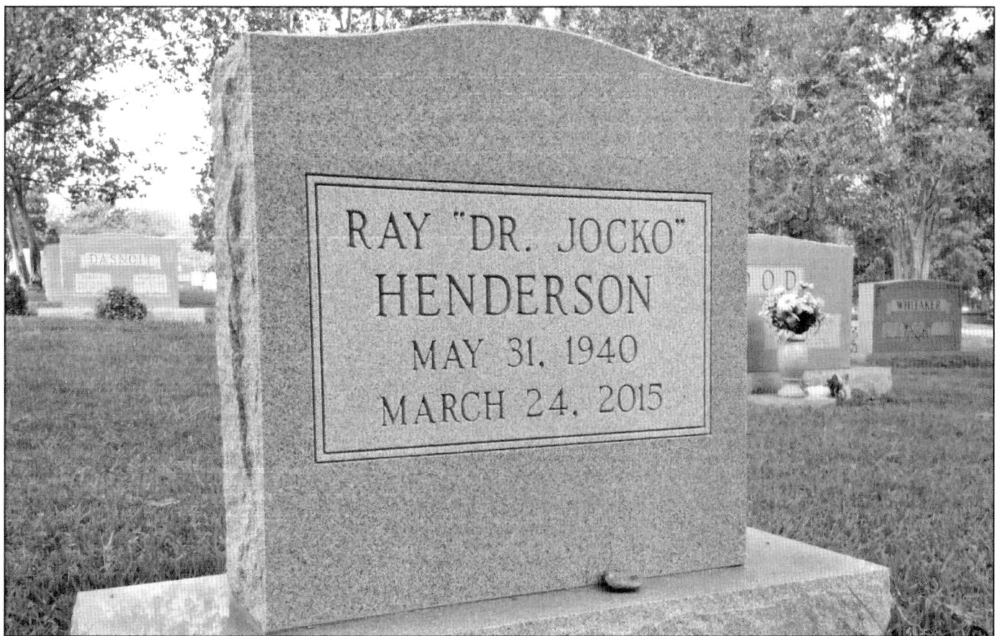

Raymond Henderson Sr. (1940–2015), a Raleigh high school and college student (St. Augustine's), made his mark as Dr. Jocko, a disk jockey playing blues hits on Detroit AM stations. An executive for Motown Records, he toured as emcee for musician James Brown. A very public figure during the civil rights era, Henderson is remembered as one who promoted calm in both black and white communities. (Palko.)

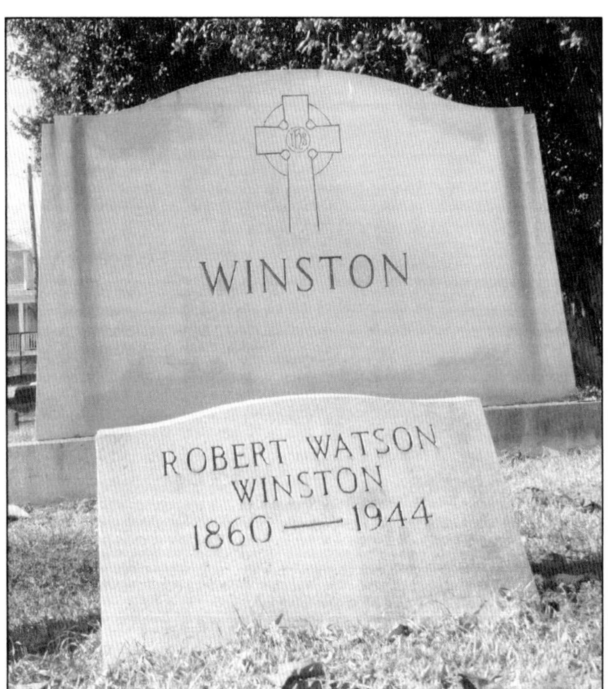

Robert Watson Winston (1860–1944), often referred to as "Judge Winston" from his superior court years (1889–1895), is also remembered for his "second" career as a historian. He had graduated from the University of North Carolina in 1879 and its law school in 1881 but at age 60 returned to Chapel Hill for an undergraduate course of study. Winston later won acclaim as a biographer of Andrew Johnson, Jefferson Davis, and Robert E. Lee, while his autobiography, *It's a Far Cry* (1937), takes a look back at an older South. Winston's home (not extant) stood on Blount Street in the heart of Raleigh's high society district. He attributed his long life of accomplishment to "Doctors Quiet, Diet and Merryman." (Left, HOC; below, SANC.)

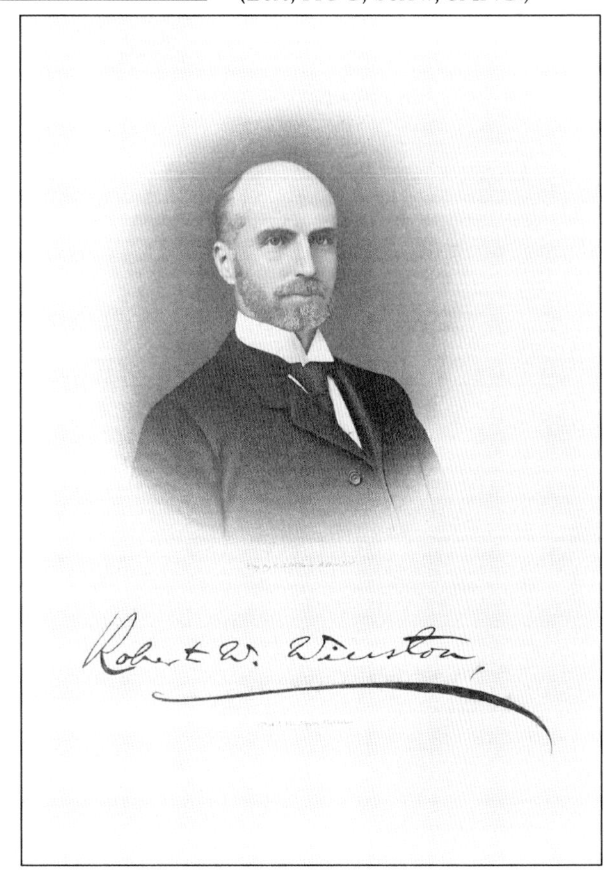

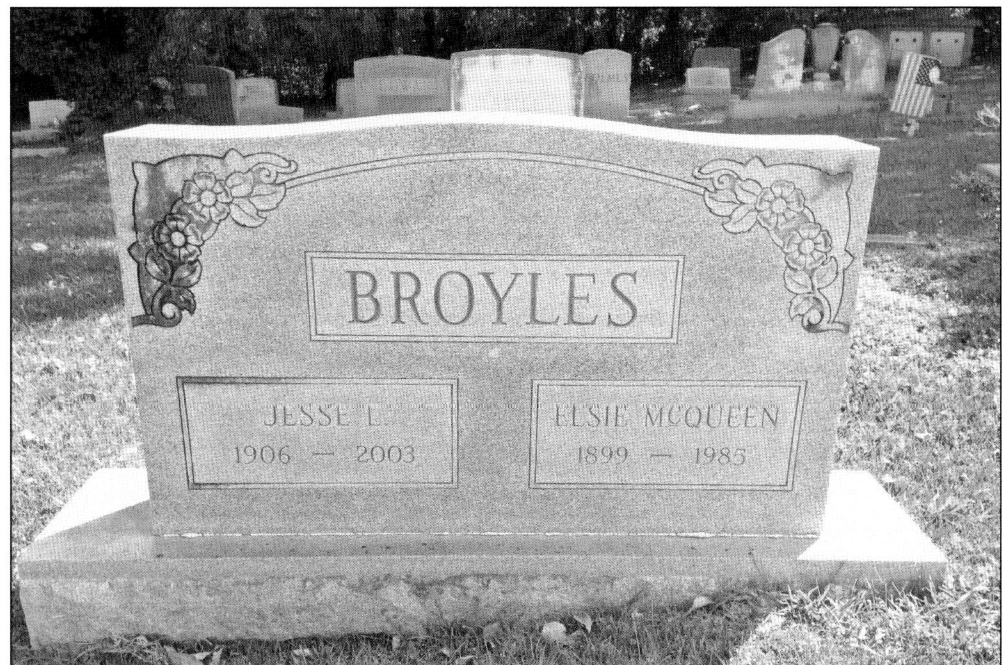

Jesse Littleton Broyles (1906–2003) is fondly remembered by old-timers as "the Peanut Man." Shell-shocked as a marine on Iwo Jima, he "retired" to Raleigh, living in the Oakwood District with his wife. Broyles later sold peanuts from a charcoal heater on Capitol Square (1963–1981), earning him his nickname, a story in *Life* magazine, and the love of countless hungry pigeons, often perched on his head and shoulders. (Palko.)

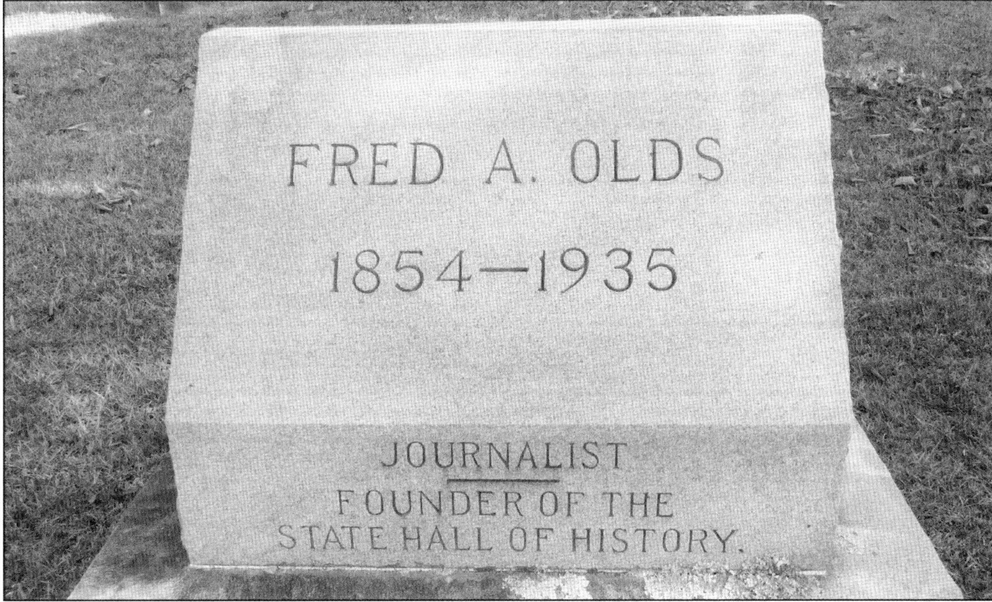

Frederick Augustus Olds (1854–1935) is remembered as a journalist, historian, tour giver, entertainer of children, and collector; it was his accumulation of thousands of Tar Heel documents and artifacts that made up the original displays of the North Carolina Museum of History in Raleigh, where his statue now greets visitors. (HOC.)

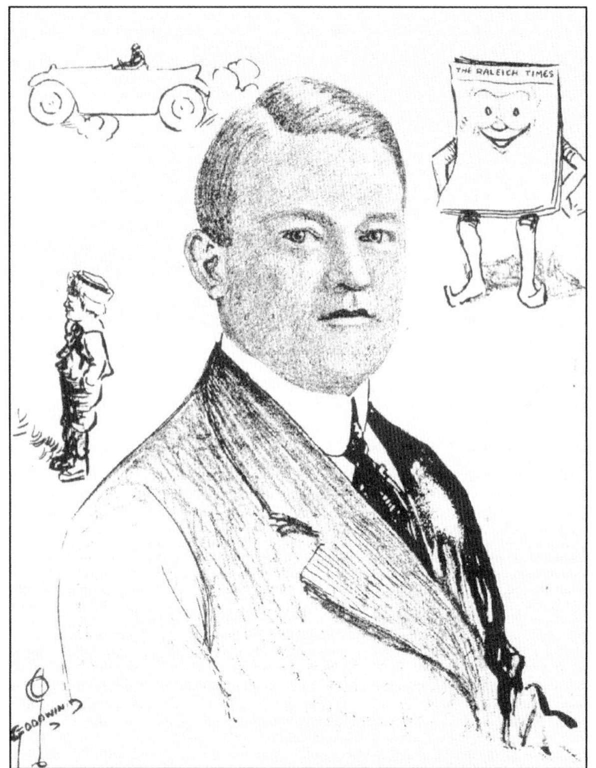

John Alsey Park (1885–1956), something of a Raleigh "character," became one of the city's first automobile owners and car dealers after graduating from State College; as such, he designed his own license tag (#100) and helped to develop North Carolina's early driving rules. In 1911, Park purchased the *Times* newspaper and made the paper a conservative rival of the *News & Observer*, which eventually bought his paper in 1955. A world traveler who wrote of his journeys abroad, Park promoted "Books for Berlin," a program that sent millions of books and magazines to Germany after World War II. An active member of the Raleigh Rotary Club, he entertained members each birthday by standing on his head on a piano. (Left, Goodwin; below, HOC.)

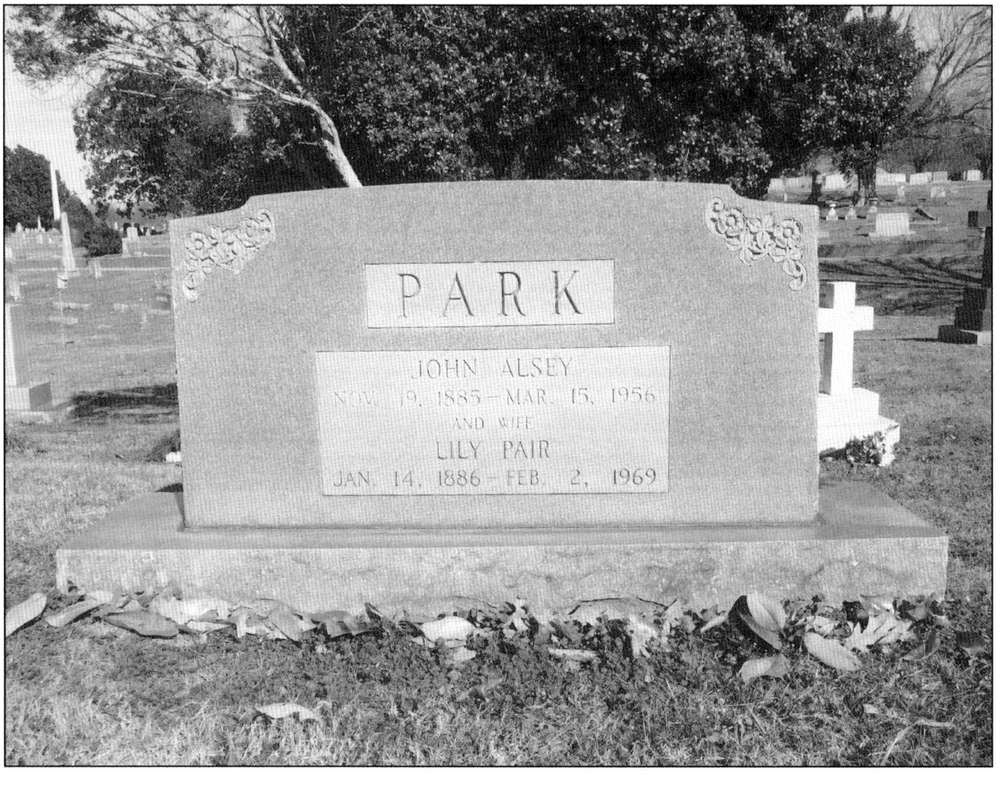

Nine

Symbols in Stone

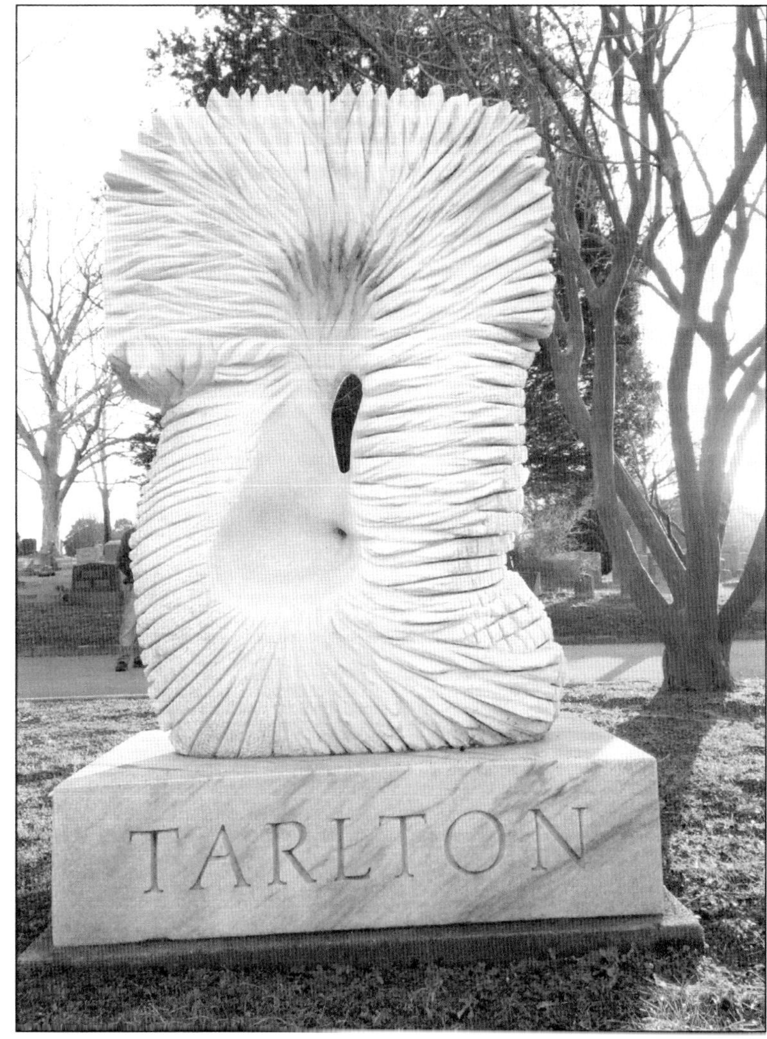

Cemetery art has always mirrored the passage of time. Stones often become symbols of specific eras, reflecting the tastes, resources, whimsy of the deceased or his or her family, and/or even the skill of the stonecutter. This modernist monument by Paris Alexander for art dealer William Samuel Tarlton (1921–2009) is called *Rubicon*—after the river in Italy that one could not cross with a standing army, and doing so, as Julius Caesar famously did, symbolized a point of no return. (Palko.)

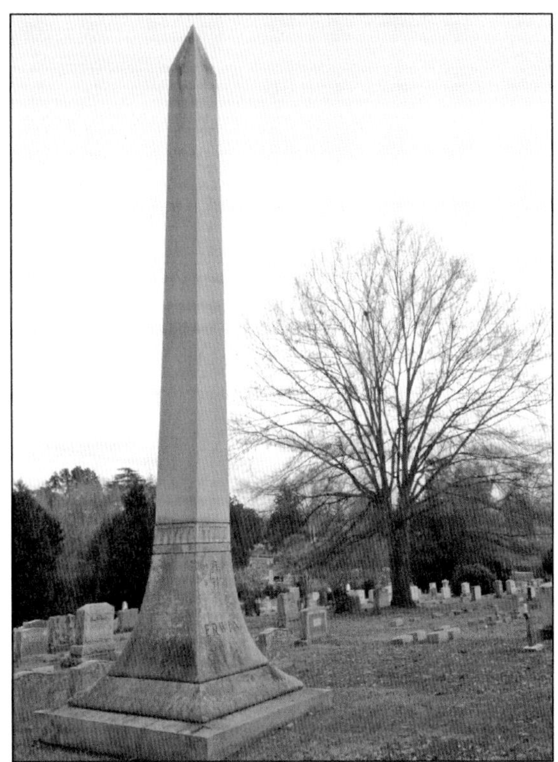

Obelisks, or as schoolchildren call them, "Washington Monuments," show the Victorian era's interest in ancient civilizations, including Egyptian symbols (obelisks stood outside of temple doors in ancient Egypt). This is the Erwin obelisk, the tallest in the cemetery. William Allen Erwin (1856–1932) ran the textile mills for the Duke family, including one in Harnett County in a town that used to be called Duke, now Erwin, North Carolina. (Palko.)

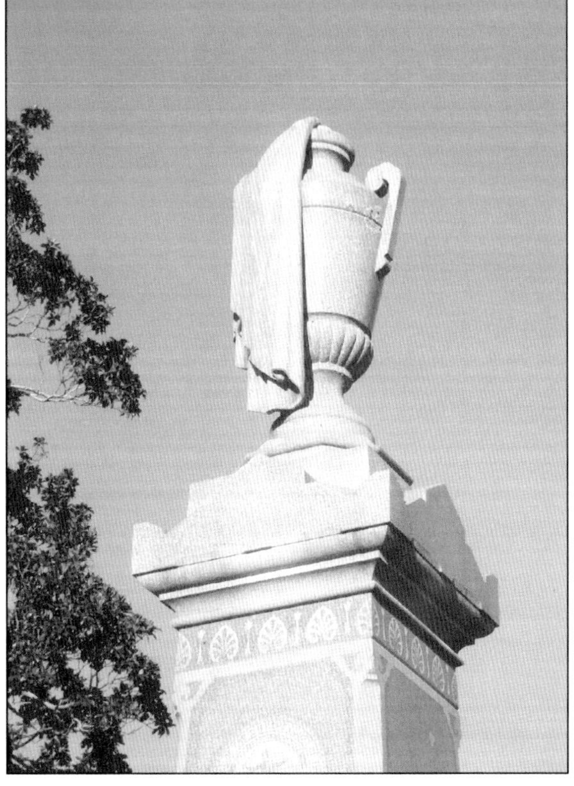

When people think of urns today, they often think of cremation vessels, but an urn at Oakwood Cemetery can be another symbolic reference to ancient Egypt. During the mummification process, organs were put into ossuaries or urns. An example at Oakwood is the draped urn of jurist Richmond Mumford Pearson (1805–1878), chief justice of the North Carolina Supreme Court for many years. (HOC.)

Cemeteries are places of rest, peaceful gardens of reflection, with intentional landscape and monuments like that of Mollie Little (1843–1879), which graphically equates death with "At Rest." If one looks closely, he or she will see the carving of a woman, presumably Mollie, sleeping. Cemetery records do not explain much about her, but it is likely that her monument provided comfort to the family. (Palko.)

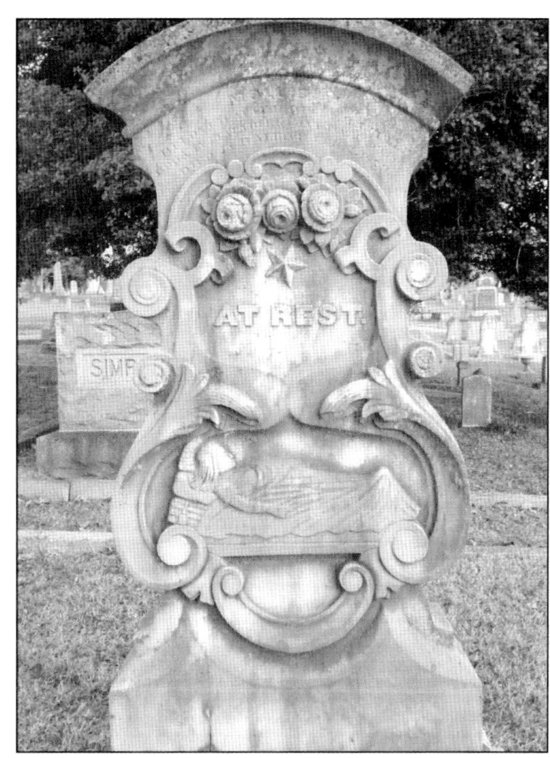

Another example of "at rest" in Oakwood is the monument of Sylvester Brown Shepherd (1906–1940). It is the only example of pillows in the cemetery. Such a peaceful image associated with a loved one asleep helps families say goodbye even today. This monument also may represent the empty pillow at home. (SANC.)

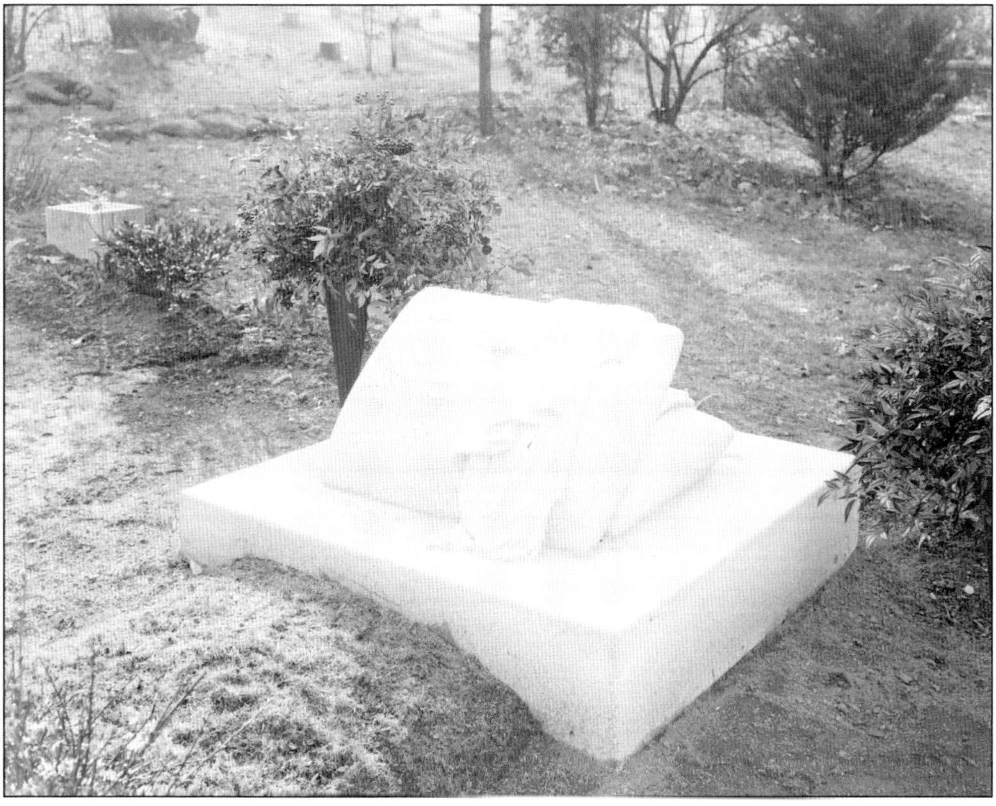

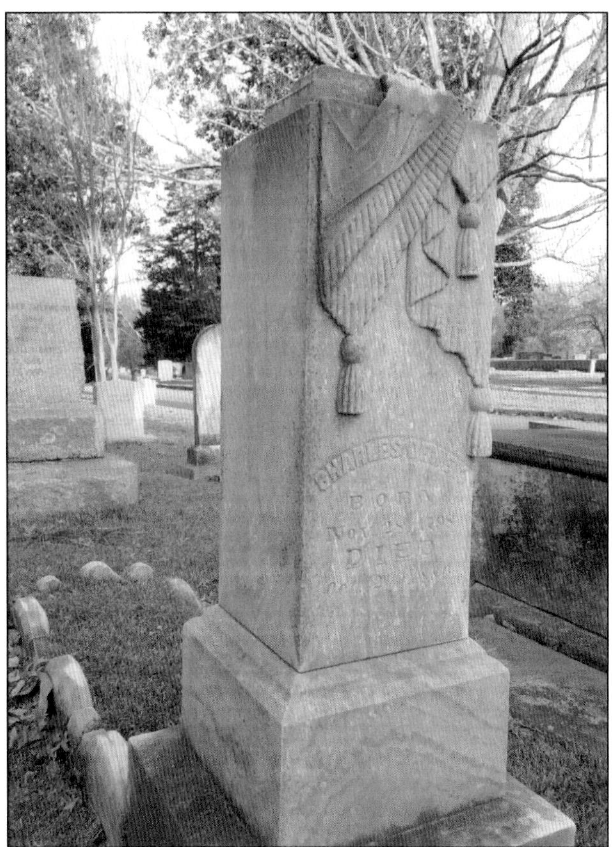

At the time of someone's death in the 1800s, the clocks in the home would be stopped and the windows and mirrors covered with dark bunting or blankets to show mourning; if the blankets had tassels, it was a sign of wealth. This monument to Charles Dewey (1798–1880) demonstrates how families subtly displayed their wealth, in life and in death. Note the "empty bed" behind the monument, a symbol of loss. (Palko.)

Symbols appear not only on headstones but also at the time of the burial. Flowers, while beautiful in their own right, are also an outward expression of grief. Note the broken spoke on the flower wheel to the left, a symbol of lost family member Mattie J. Hood (1876–1921). Palm fronds lie about the grave as a symbol of victory over death or resurrection. (Janice Thompson.)

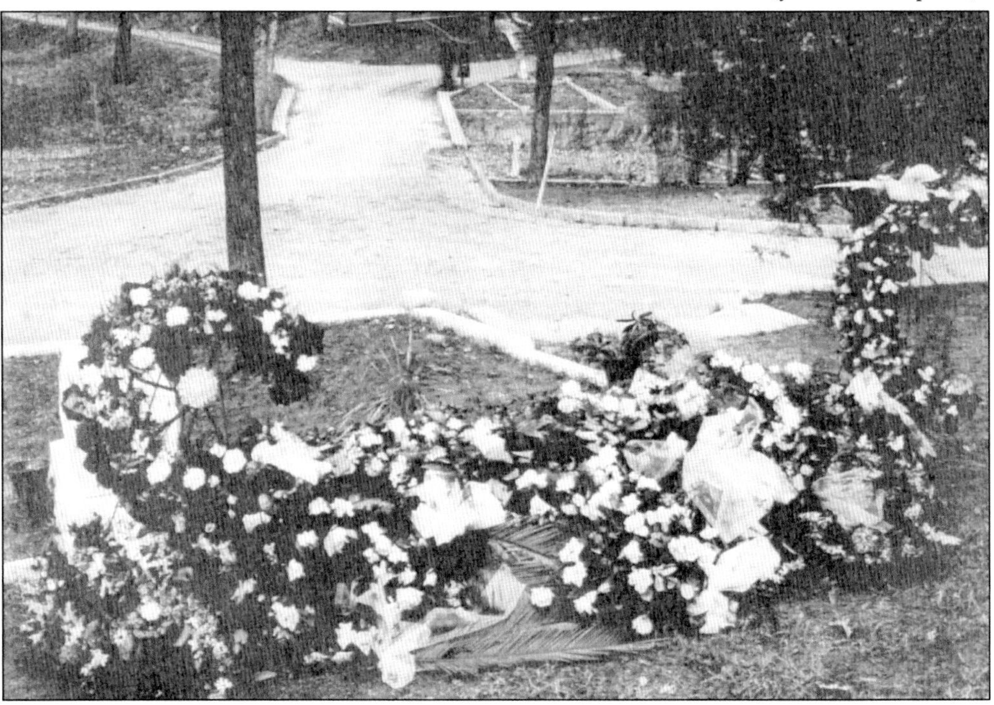

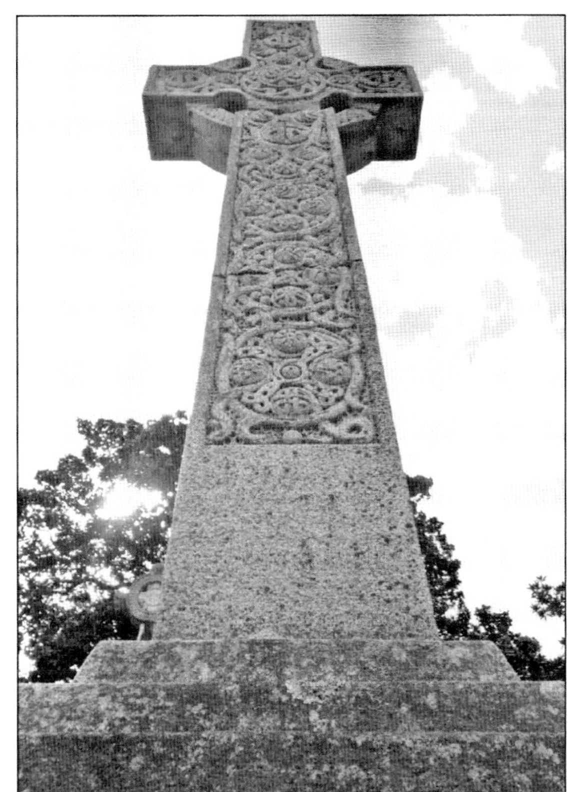

Not all monuments are peaceful or well received. This Celtic cross, a monument to William Holt Willamson (see page 63), is different than it originally appeared, when the intricate braiding represented snakes with open, fanged-tooth mouths. At the time, cemetery managers did not approve of what they considered an "offensive" design, and the snakes' heads were ground down so that they are no longer visible, the curves now suggesting intertwined vines. (Palko.)

Early monument carvers often made themselves known. The monument of Martha Allen (1815–1897) displays the name of the stone carver as a "signature," in this case that of William Oliver Wolfe. Formerly Martha's son-in-law, "W.O." later was the father of author Thomas Wolfe and the basis for the character W.O. Gant in Wolfe's books. Wolfe lived in Raleigh from 1870 to 1880, leaving at least eight identifiable carved monuments in Oakwood Cemetery. (Palko.)

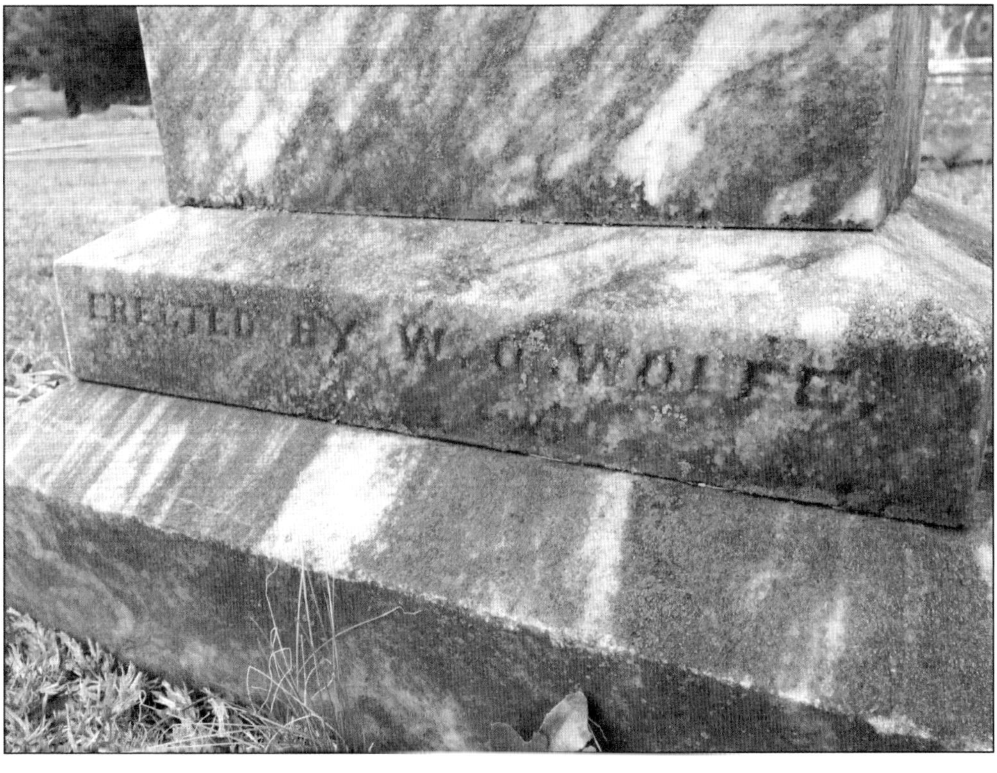

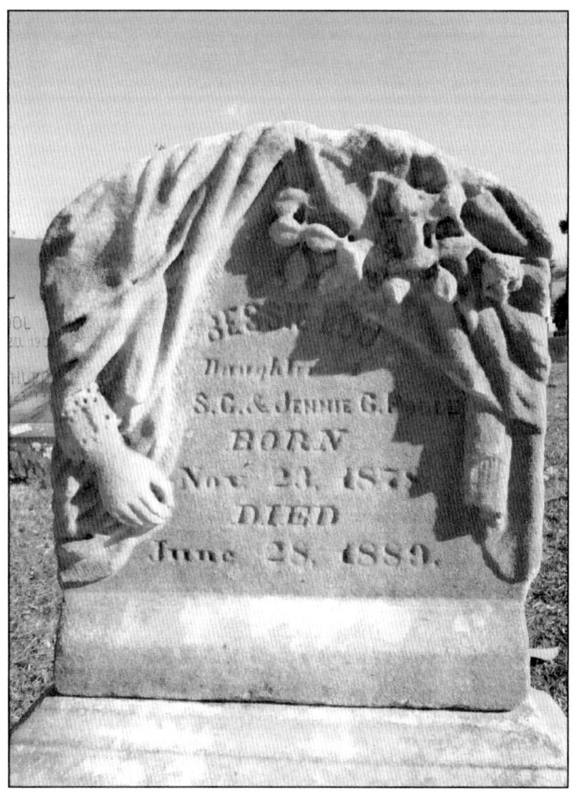

Monuments for deceased children are poignant regardless of the era. In this monument, the veil between life and death is slowly being pulled back by the hand of the child. It shows the viewer that a high childhood mortality rate often left families grieving the loss of multiple children, with each loss felt strongly. (HOC.)

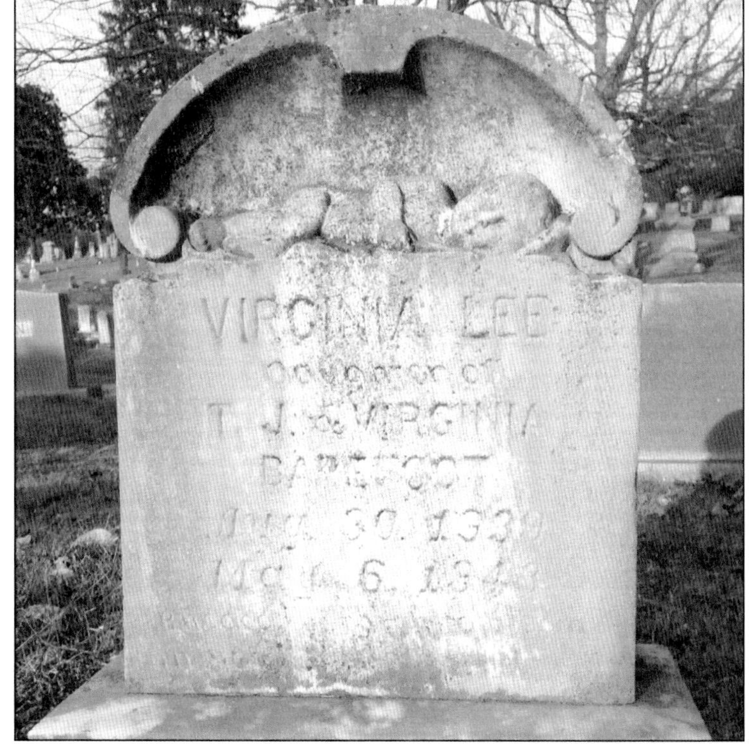

A favorite monument of local photographers is that of Virginia Lee Barefoot (1939–1943). Known as the "baby in the half shell," Virginia's monument is reminiscent of Venus and her shell, a symbol not only of fertility but also of love. The baby resting in the scalloped shell is another symbol of grief. Perhaps the symbol of fertility was a hope for more children after a heartbreaking loss. (Palko.)

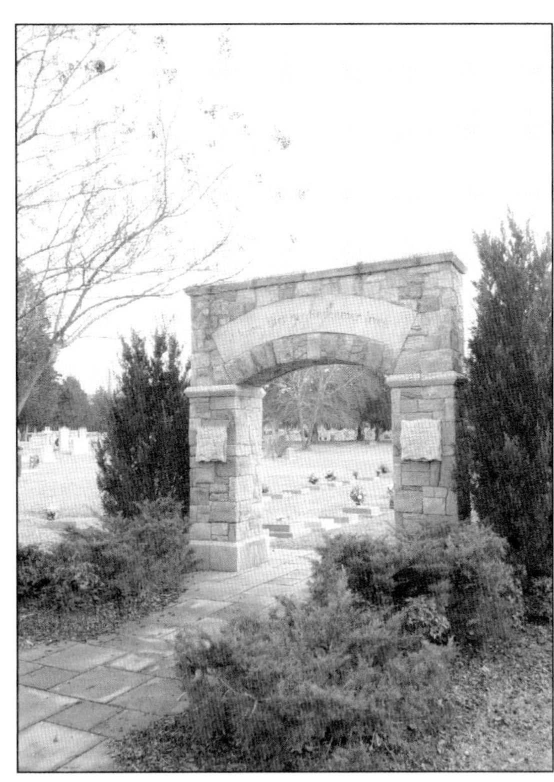

Oakwood serves people of all religions, and some churches have established sections of their own. The first church to have its own section was Christ Episcopal Church; an area of the cemetery is named for it, although church members are buried throughout the grounds. Next, the Greek Orthodox Church created what became three sections, with many monuments in Greek. Finally, the Raleigh Moravian Church created God's Acre, a Moravian Cemetery within Oakwood's grounds. This section is highlighted by the beautifully carved archway at its entrance and the consistent, uniform flat markers in order of death, although consecutive spaces are reserved when the first spouse dies. (Both, Palko.)

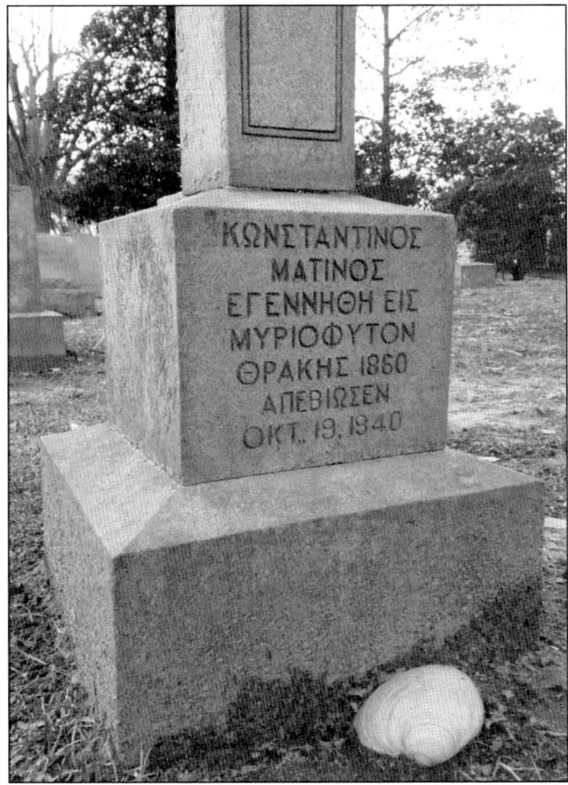

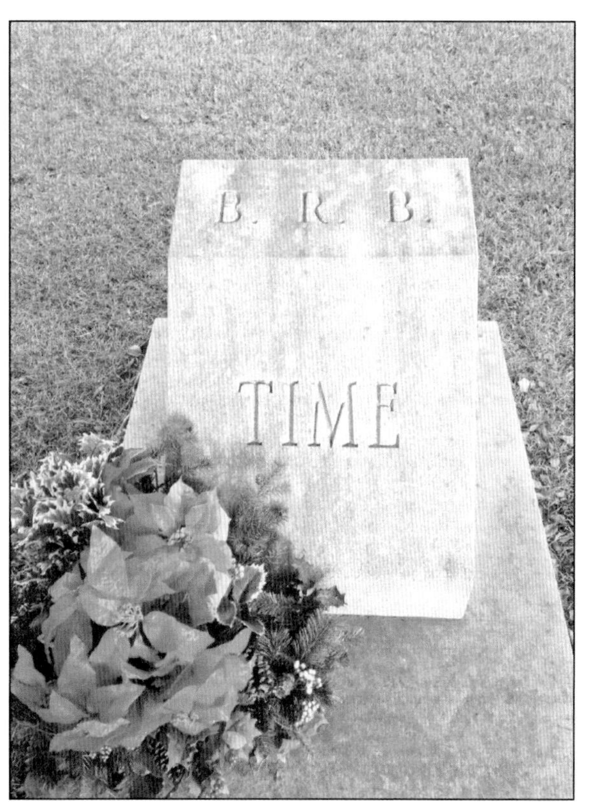

Cemetery art is nothing if not a marker of the passage of time. No better headstone in Oakwood conveys that than the face of the Bradsher family monument, marked as it is simply with the word "Time." Designed by the patriarch of the family, Billy Ray Bradsher (1935–2014), the stone indicates what he came to feel is the most valuable possession people have. (Palko.)

Another reminder of the passage of time is the stone of much-loved Rev. Isaac McKendree Pittenger (1843–1923), pastor of the Episcopal Church of the Good Shepherd in downtown Raleigh. His headstone puts the days of his life at 29,212 and urges all "to number our days." (Palko.)

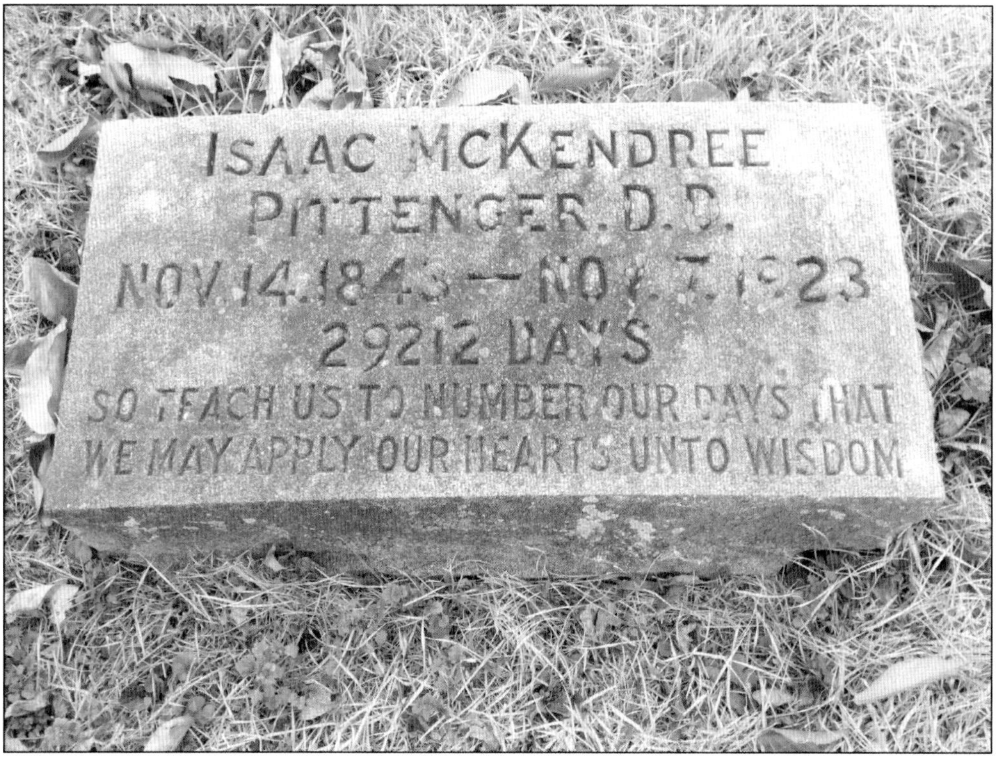

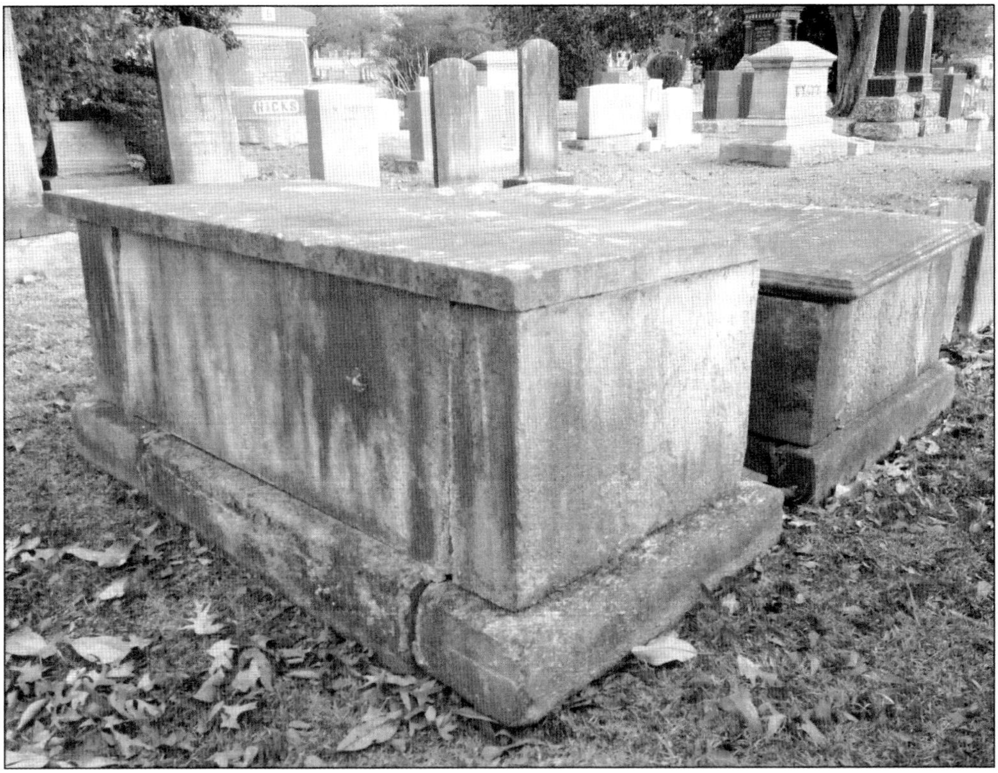

A chest tomb, a hollow box that rests on top of a grave, was a popular marker in the 18th and 19th centuries. The box reflects the sarcophagi of previous generations but contains no remains. This particular chest tomb honors Gavin Hogg (1788–1835), a prominent Raleigh attorney whose remains were moved to Oakwood from City Cemetery; his family home stood where the State Archives of North Carolina building is today. (Palko.)

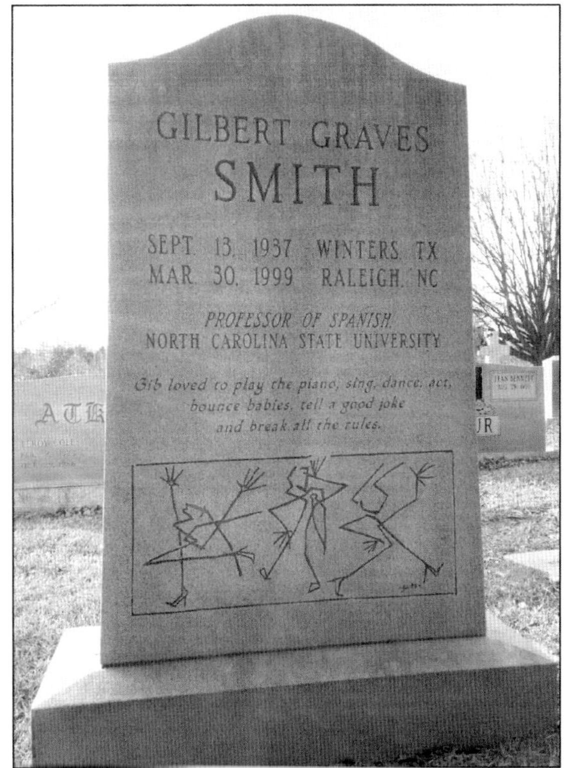

Early gravestones were designed with symbols that all would understand. However, personalization reigns supreme in modern cemeteries. This monument of Gilbert Graves Smith (1937–1999) not only features stick figures dancing but also states the parts of life he loved the most. The stone carries more than a name, for it introduces to the visitor a person who lived well and loved life—as all can now see. (Palko.)

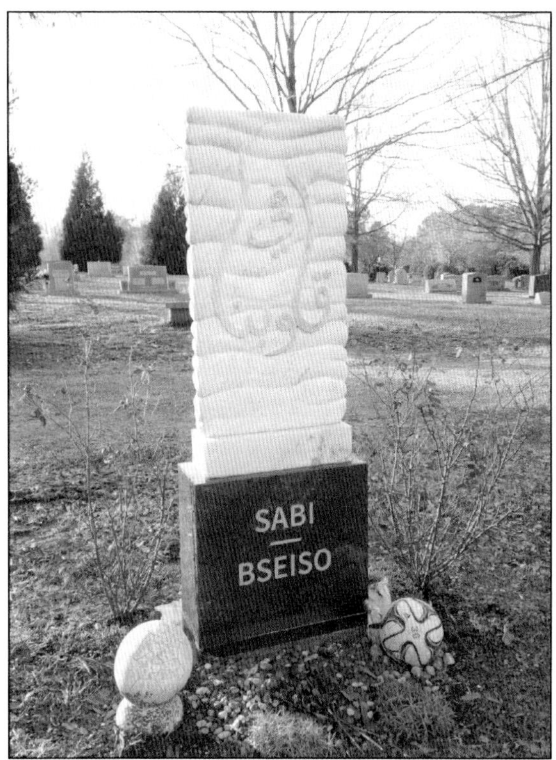

Cemeteries have always reflected popular styles of art. These two monuments were done by local Raleigh artist Paris Alexander. One is for famed soccer player Farouk Bseiso (1989–2014), who died in a tragic accident in the Czech Republic; he played for North Carolina State University, the former Carolina RailHawks, and in Europe. His monument, *Stone Poem*, displays the Arabic for "mother," which was tattooed on his wrist. A more recent Alexander monument with a modernist motif, entitled *Gates of Parnassus*, is that honoring James Leonard Cresimore (1928–2014), a food industry executive, art collector, and restorer of historic Mary Elizabeth Hospital. (Left, Palko; below, ©Simon Griffiths Photography 2017.)

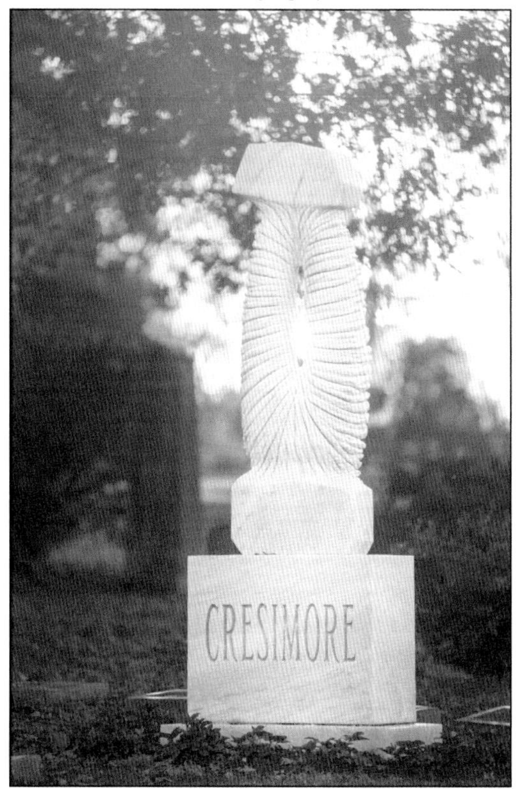

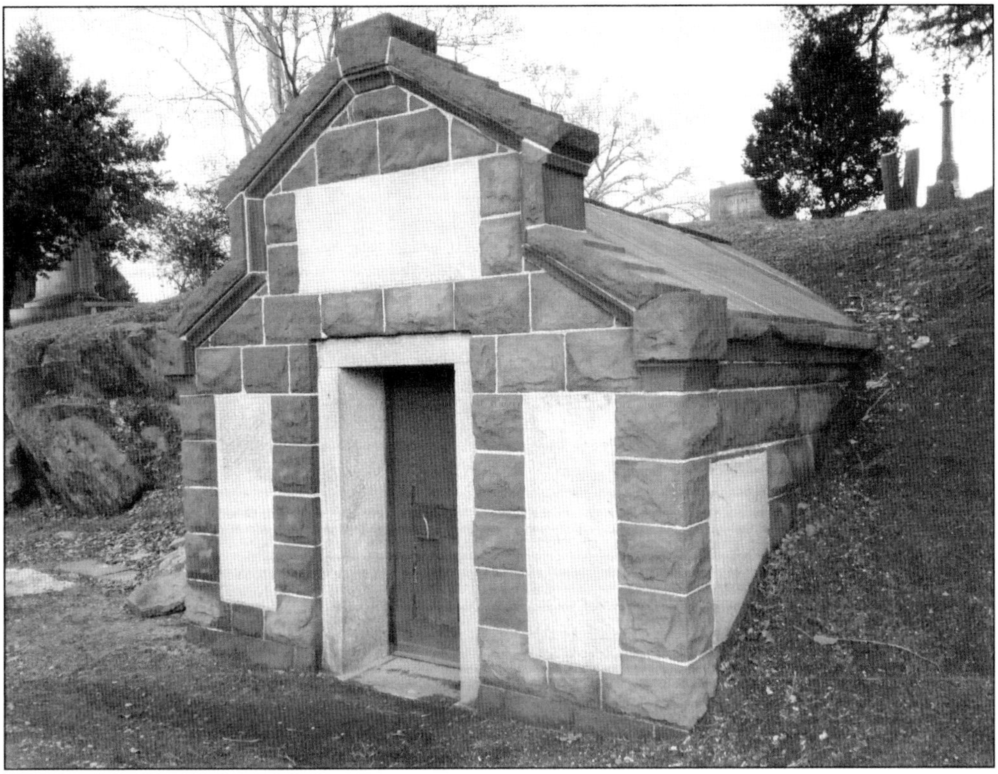

The Raleigh Cemetery Association met the demand of a growing business with the construction of new buildings, the first of which was a Romanesque-style "receiving vault," around 1896. At the time, local papers reported the cemetery in "urgent" need of such a vault to hold caskets until graves were prepared. Restored in 2016 –2017, the vault is clad in the same brownstone as the Governor's Mansion. (Palko.)

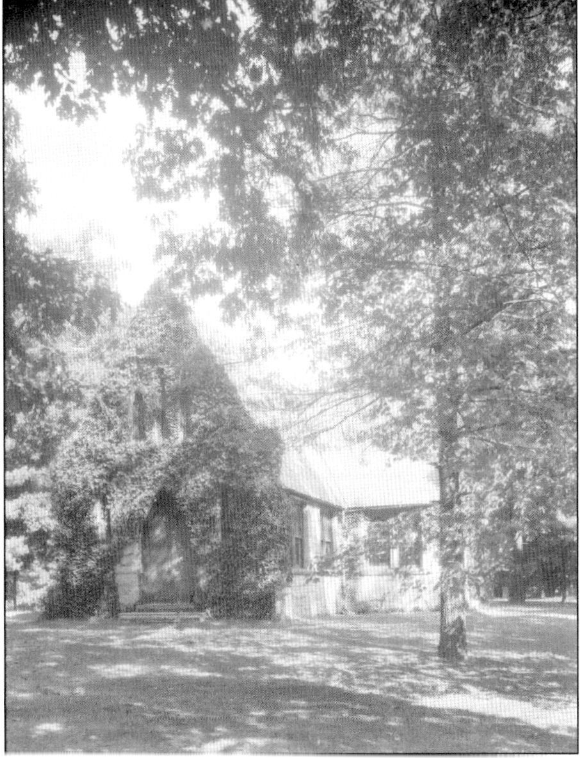

Early cemetery incorporators envisioned "when it was deemed necessary a chapel where desired services might be held." This vision was realized in the 1890s when, on the brow of the second hill, a Gothic chapel was erected, designed by architect Thomas Martin Ashe (1876–1900). Cross-shaped, constructed of natural stone, and covered with a blue slate roof, the chapel was razed in the 1960s. Its location is today called Chapel Circle. (SANC.)

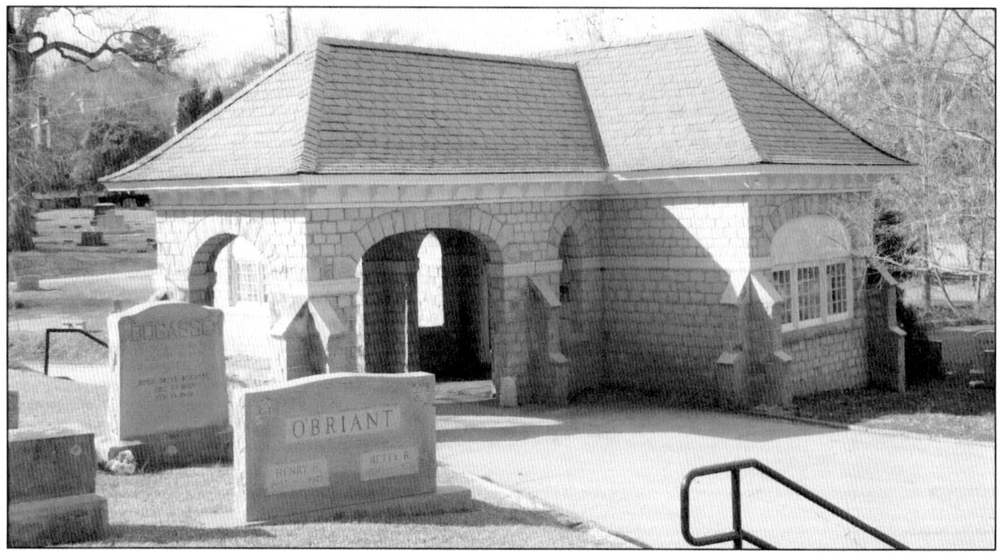

In its early years, cemetery business may have been conducted in the keeper's house near the current main gate, from private homes, or even in offices downtown. Around 1910, Oakwood built the current office building, enlarged in 2002. Constructed at the same time and with the same stone as the main gate, the office boasts a heart of pine groin ceiling. The Raleigh Cemetery Association meets quarterly in the office boardroom. (HOC.)

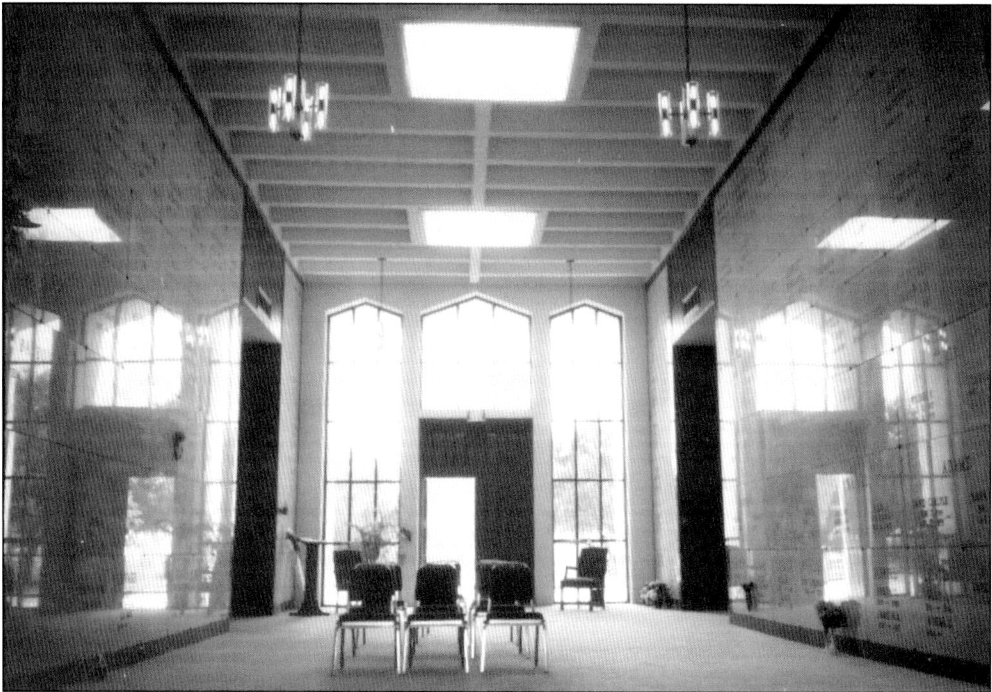

Meeting the needs of a growing Raleigh, Oakwood Cemetery built the city's first community mausoleum in 1970, with an addition in 1990. Constructed of Mount Airy granite, the mausoleum accommodates 600 entombments, with both interior and exterior access. The enclosed mausoleum center hall, heated and air-conditioned, hosts community events, including classes, programs, competitions, and funeral services. (HOC.)

Ten

A Cemetery Full of Life

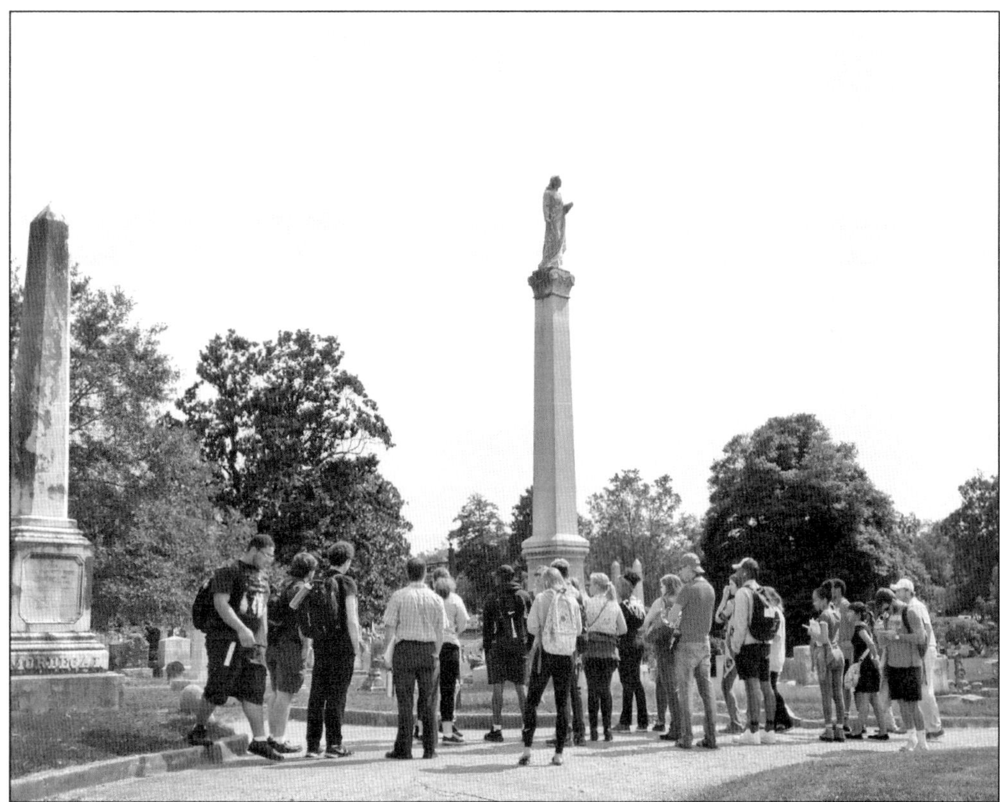

Oakwood is patterned after 19th-century "garden cemeteries" in Europe and America that offered gravesites in green surroundings—and often a great deal more. They were also places for community gatherings, frequently with refreshment stands, shows, artists, picnicking, and so forth; some charged admission. Oakwood, too, offers a variety of activities, from drama and classes to marathons and wildlife appreciation. (Palko.)

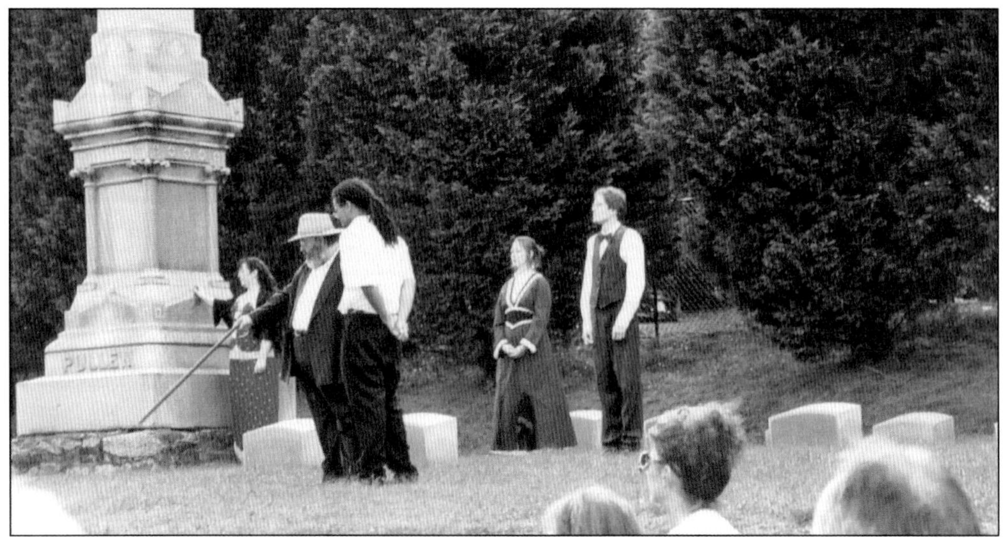

For over 10 years, Oakwood Cemetery has partnered with Burning Coal, a local professional theater group, to perform *Oakwood Lives*, performances in the cemetery that directly relate to the individuals interred here. Audiences "see the people behind the stones" and learn about what they were like when they walked among the living. (HOC.)

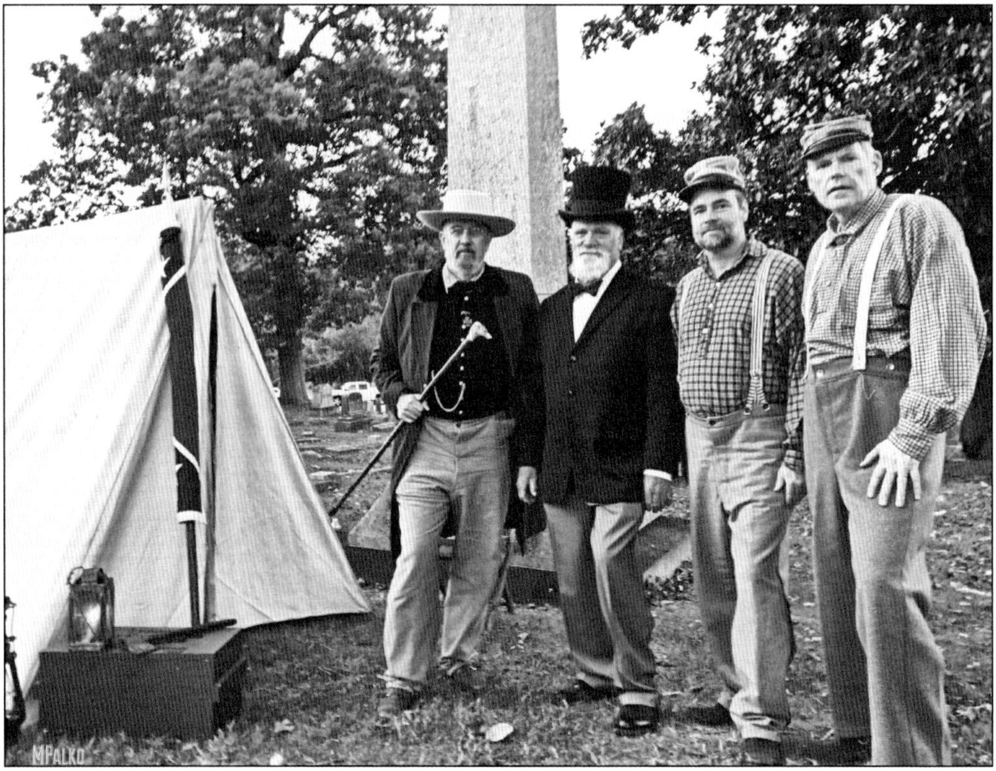

Oakwood's oldest graves are those of Confederate soldiers, and that section remains an active memorial. An annual October tradition of 30 years is the *Lantern Walk*, during which Civil War "reenactors" appear in vignettes that touch on topics regarding the war years. This community favorite raises funds for restoration work in the Confederate Cemetery. (Palko.)

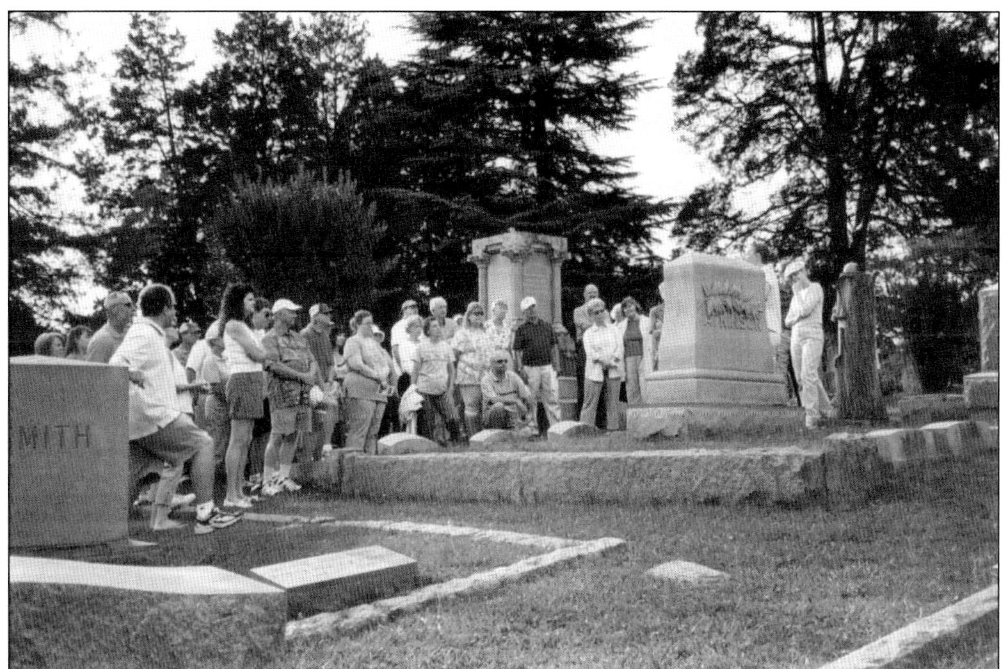

Oakwood Cemetery welcomes tour groups on a regular basis. School and college students, docents from area museums, book clubs, Scout troops, civic groups, and others come through the gate day and night to study North Carolina's history, art, and more. Local groups also provide valuable community service hours by weeding flowerbeds, planting bulbs, and cleaning headstones safely. (HOC.)

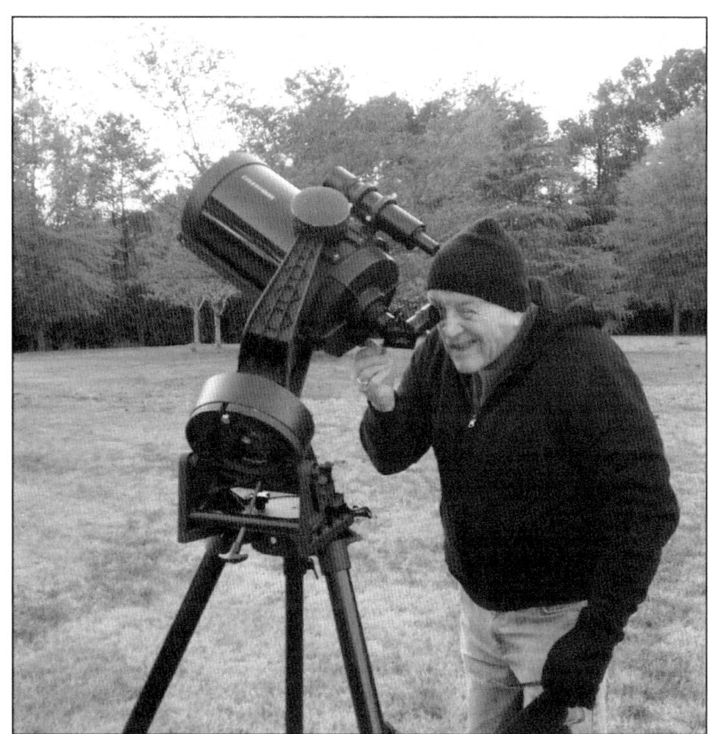

Oakwood Cemetery participates in the North Carolina Science Festival. In 2016, members of the North Carolina State University Astronomy Club came with their telescopes for the Star Party portion of the festival. Community members received a unique opportunity to gaze at the constellations from the cemetery grounds and participate in hands-on science activities at this popular event. (Palko.)

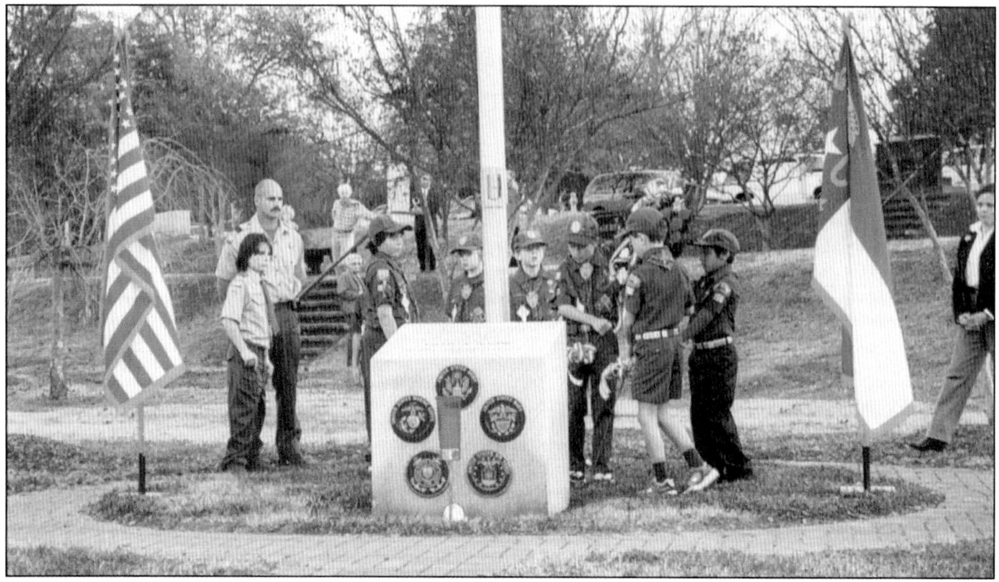

The Field of Honor for veterans and their spouses was created in the early 1990s (see page 46). Active duty personnel, veterans, Boy Scouts, and community members participated in the Field of Honor Dedication Service. The memorial honoring all branches of the military was placed at the base of the flag in 1997. (HOC.)

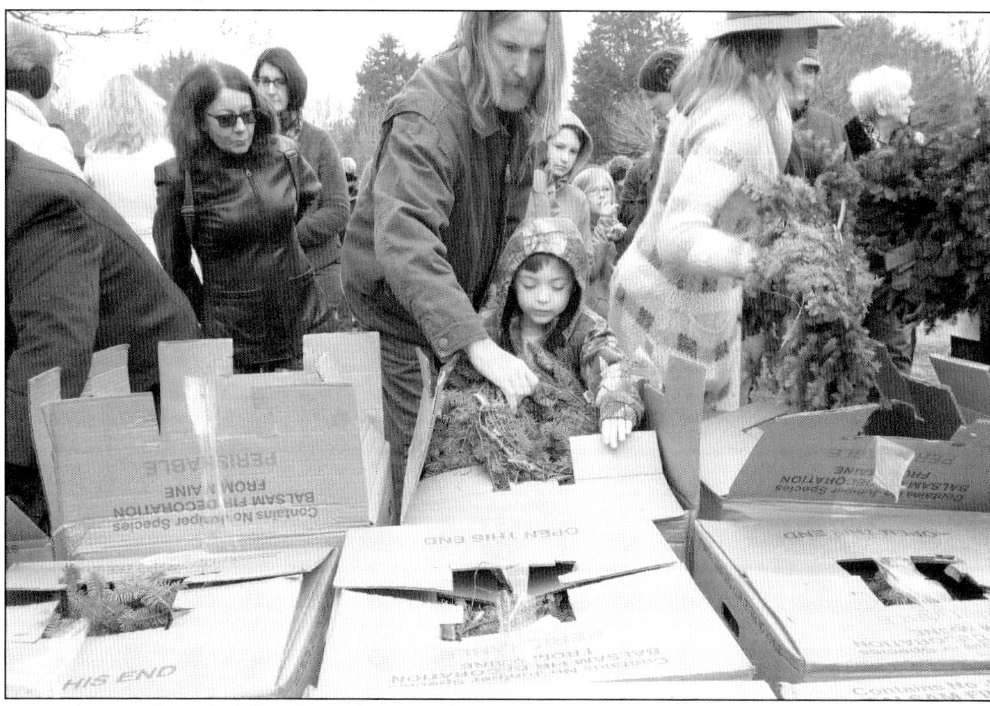

Beyond funerals with full military honors, the veterans section is also the location of important events throughout the year, including the annual Memorial Day service, the placing of wreaths for Wreaths Across America (shown here), and flag retirement ceremonies. The sounds of "Echo Taps" and bagpipes often provide beautiful background music as the cemetery pays tribute to veterans. (Palko.)

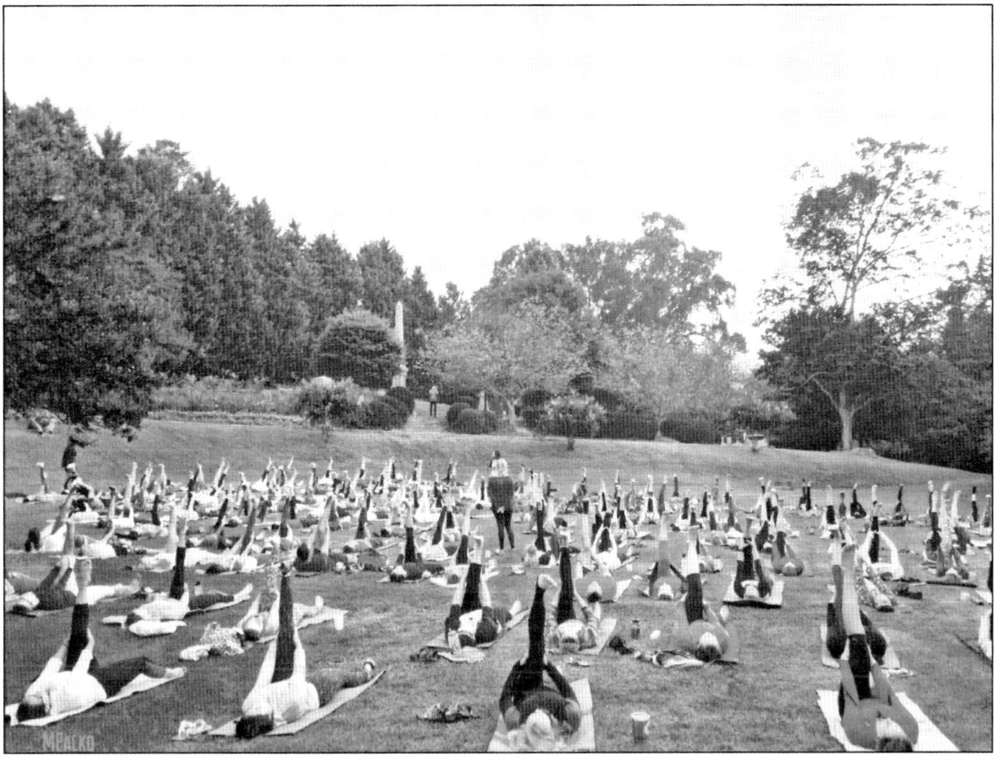

As a social center, Oakwood hosts many nontraditional community events. In 2015, over 150 individuals participated in yoga in the early morning hours in the green field (the old "horse pasture") at the cemetery entrance. Participants ranged from people who had never been to Oakwood to those who have loved ones interred here. (Palko.)

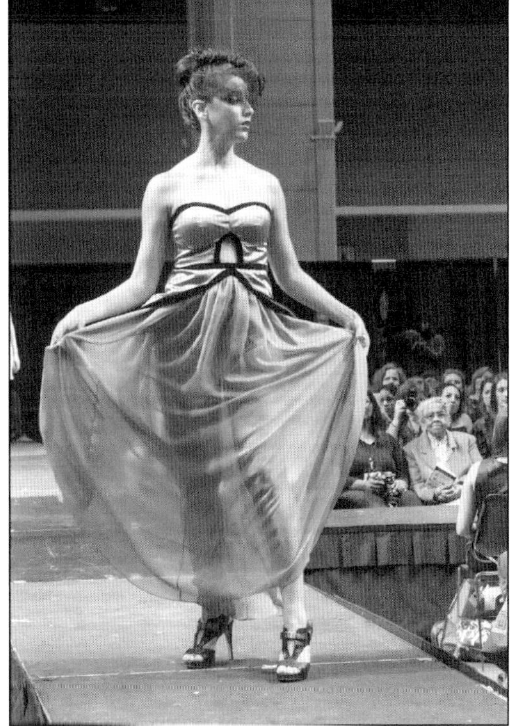

Oakwood Cemetery also participates in activities off-site. Activate Good hosts an annual fashion fundraiser, "Couture for a Cause," which highlights local nonprofits. Designers are partnered with nonprofits, and their creations on the runway echo the missions of the organizations. Cemetery fashion has proven to be a creative way to show an Oakwood "full of life." (Activate Good.)

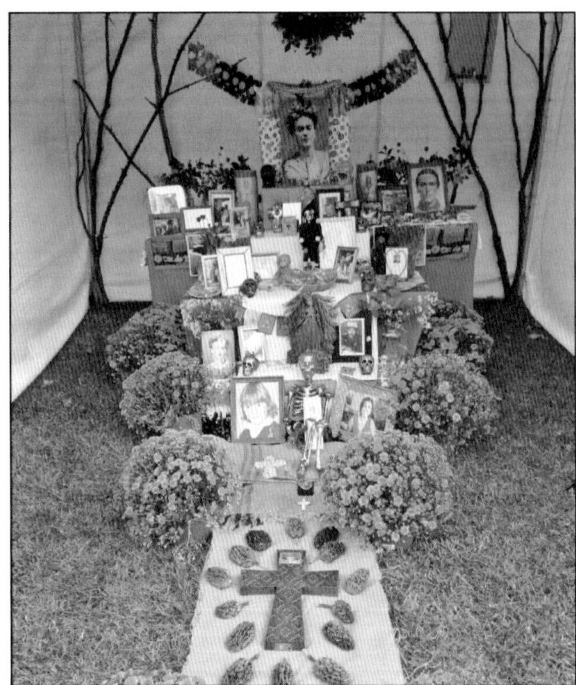

The Day of the Dead (Día de los Muertos) is a colorful Mexican holiday that honors the lives of those who have gone before. With an "altar of remembrance" near the front gate, visitors are invited to place photographs or trinkets; runners of all ages compete in a 5K race on cemetery roads to benefit the Brentwood Boys and Girls Club of Raleigh. The cemetery truly comes to life on the Day of the Dead. (Palko.)

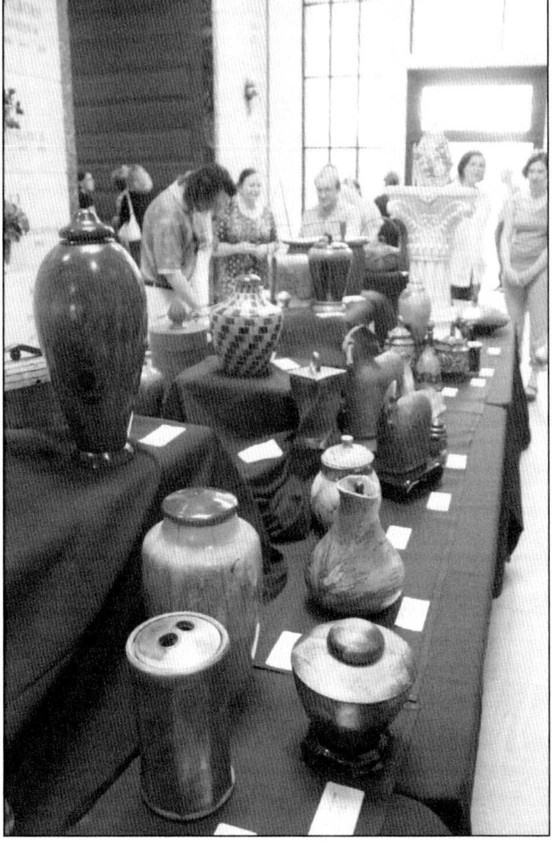

In 2014, Oakwood Cemetery hosted its first Urn Art & Garden Faire, a national competition with 92 urns from 17 states entered. Entries ranged from carved wooden pieces to benches made of concrete mixed with cremation remains. The event was organized by the Friends of Oakwood, with live music and over 300 guests on-site. The story was picked up by the Associated Press and ran in over 100 newspapers around the world. (Tim Blaisdell.)

In 2016, to take full advantage of Oakwood's garden setting, the cemetery opened Mordecai's Meadow, Raleigh's first natural burial ground. Interments must be unembalmed and in a biodegradable coffin or shroud with no outer burial container. Adjacent to the meadow are the cemetery's four beehives, maintained by the cemetery staff and Wake Monument Company. (Palko.)

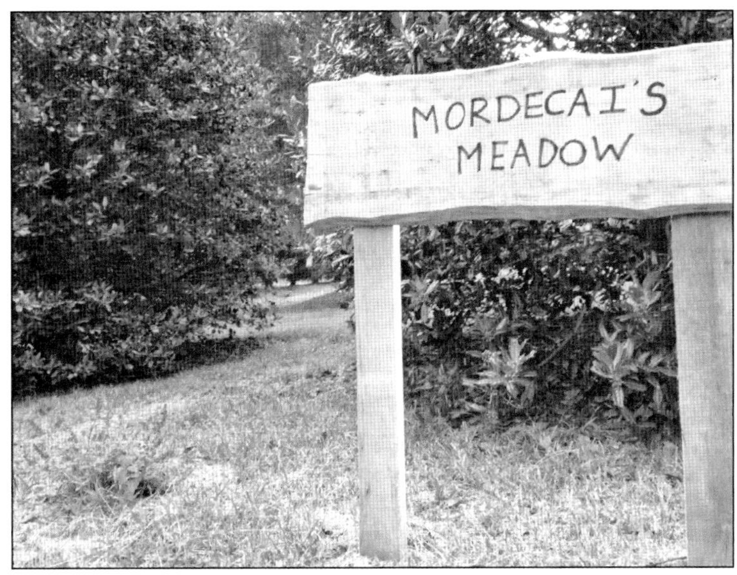

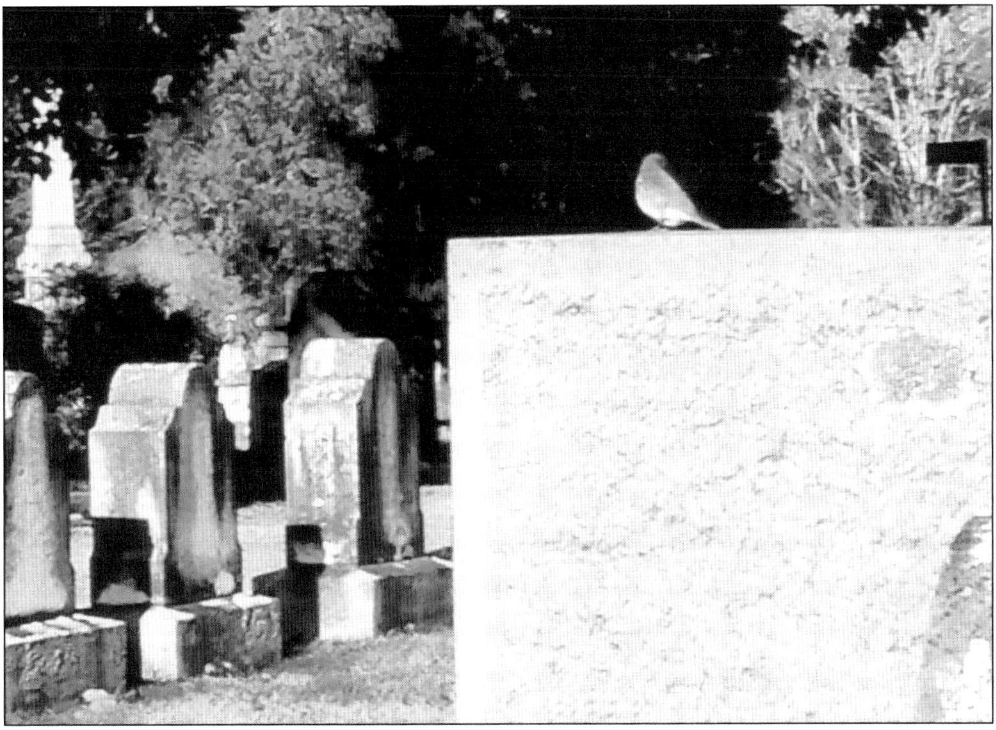

Oakwood Cemetery is a friend not only to the community but also to the creatures that call it home. The cemetery is a Certified Wildlife Habitat and, in 2013, became an official North Carolina Bluebird Society trail. Sixteen bluebird houses are scattered around the grounds and are checked weekly during the bluebird season by a volunteer. The cemetery grounds crew changes mowing patterns to protect fledglings. (Palko.)

Index

Key to section abbreviations:

AND: Anderson; **BAT**: Battle; **BEE**: Beechwood; **BRI**: Briggs; **CED**: Cedar Hill; **CHC**: Chapel Circle; **CHR**: Christ Church; **CRK**: Creekside; **CON**: Confederate Cemetery; **EAS**: East Branch; **FOR**: Forrest; **HEB**: Hebrew Cem; **HECK**: Heck; **HILN**: Hillside North; **HILS**: Hillside South; **JOH**: Johnson; **LIN**: Linden Lawn; **MAG**: Magnolia Hill; **MAU**: Mausoleum; **MOR**: Mordecai; **PES**: Pescud; **POLK**: Polk; **PUL**: Pullen; **SECA/B/C/etc.**: Section A/B/C/etc.; **SGR**: Single Graves; **SPR**: Spring; **TUC**: Tucker; **VET**: Veteran Section/Field of Honor; **WES**: West Branch.

Allen, Martha J. POLK 111
Anderson, George Burgwyn AND, 22
Anderson, William Edward AND, 22
Andrews, Alexander Boyd, Jr. MOR, 88
Andrews, Helen Sharples MOR, 88
Ashe, Thomas Martin JOH, 117
Atkins, Eleanor Hope Swain JOH, 81
Aycock, Charles Brantley BEE, 51
Badger, George Edmund MAG, 54
Baggett, Curtis Franklin SGR, 45
Bagley, Worth CHR, 39
Bailey, Edith Walker Pou MAG, 55
Bailey, Josiah William MAG, 55
Bailey, Kincheon Hubert Jr. MAG, 44
Bailey, Tommye Lou MAG, 44
Barefoot, Virginia Lee EAS, 112
Battle, Kemp Plummer BAT, 69
Battle, William Horn BAT, 69
Bauer, Adolphus Gustavus WES, 80
Bauer, Rachel Blythe WES, 80
Bragg, Thomas BAT, 48
Bradsher, Billy Ray SECC, 114
Briggs, Everitt Edward Jr. BRI, 41
Briggs, Thomas Henry BRI, 21, 23
Brimley, Clement Samuel JOH, 94
Brimley, Herbert Hutchinson SECA, 94
Broughton, Carrie Lougee MAG, 53
Broughton, Needham Bryant MAG, 77
Brown, Henry Jerome MAG, 61
Broyles, Jesse Littleton SECA, 105
Bryan, Frederick Outlaw BAT, 102
Bryan, John Heritage III BAT, 102
Bryan, Minnie Speight BEE, 102
Bseiso, Farouk A. SECJ, 116
Burgwyn, "Harry" King CON, 17, 79
Capps, James Lee Jr. SECF, 103
Carroll, Elizabeth Delia Dixon AND, 75
Cathey, George L. CON, 19
Charles, Lorenzo Emile CED, 72
Clark, Walter McKenzie MAG, 57
Conn, Emma Dowell MAG, 77
Cox, William Ruffin BAT, 37
Cresimore, James Leonard SECA, 116
Crocker, Robert Lafar AND, 42
Daniels, Josephus SECA, 39, 51, 60
Deitrick, William Henley AND, 100
Devereux, Annie Lane MOR, 17, 79
Devereux, John MOR, 12
Devereux, Margaret Lane MOR, 12
Dewey, Charles BRI, 110
Dinwiddie, James AND, 74
Dolson, John O. CON, 16
Edwards, Lucius Wade FOR, 91
Edwards, Mary Eliz Anania FOR, 91
Erwin, William Allen BEE, 108
Eure, Thaddeus Armie, Sr. and Jr. HILN, 58
Farmer, Charles D. BEE, 97
Field of Honor, 46, 122
Forrest, Asa B. BEE, 31
Fowle, Daniel Gould BAT, 50
God's Acre, 113
Harper, Derward Blake EAS, 41
Harrison, William Henry LIN, 34
Hawkins, Alexander Boyd JOH, 99
Hawkins, Martha Bailey JOH, 99
Hawkins, William Joseph MOR, 99
Haynes, Louise E. Bunker AND, 87
Haynes, Zacharias W. AND, 87
Haywood, Ernest HECK, 84
Haywood, Edmund Burke HECK, 26
Haywood, John HECK, 26, 59
Haywood, Marshall DeLancey CHR, 98
Hebrew Cemetery, 13
Heck, Jonathan McGee HECK, 28
Helms, Dorothy Jane Coble CRK, 56
Helms, Jesse Alexander Jr. CRK, 56

Henderson, Raymond Sr. SECG, 103
Henry, Jane Eliz Massenburg TUC, 78
Hilton, Myrtle Mills BEE, 43
Hinton, John SECA, 33
Hogg, Gavin HECK, 115
Hoke, Lydia Ann VanWyck PUL, 82
Hoke, Michael PUL, 82
Hoke, Robert Frederick PUL, 82
Holden, William Woods BAT, 48,49
Holladay, Alexander Quarles LIN, 71
Honeycutt, James D. SECC, 92
Hood, Mattie J. AND, 110
Hood, Ouida Estelle Emery FOR, 85
House of Memory CON, 20
Hudson, Karl Grier Jr. CHC, 65
Hudson, Karl Grier Sr. SECA, 65
Hudson, Mary White SECA, 65
Hunter, Aaron Burtis BAT, 73
Hunter, Sarah Lothrop BAT, 73
Johnson, Albert AND, 62
Johnson, Charles Earl JOH, 64
Johnson, Kate Burr BEE, 53
Joyner, James Yadkin SECA, 75
Lewis, John Davis Jr. SECG, 95
Little, Mollie POLK, 109
McKimmon, Jane Simpson HECK, 96
McGehee, Robert Burton SPR, 64
Maglenn, James AND, 16
Manly, Basil Charles MAG, 34
Mason, Charles Winder MAG, 38
Mason, Mary Ann Bryan BAT, 78
Mason, Richard Sharp(e) BAT, 78
Mausoleum HILN, 118
Moore, Bartholomew Figures BAT, 25
Moore, Daniel Killian CRK, 52
Moore, Jeanelle Coulter CRK, 52
Mordecai family, 13
Mordecai, Geo Washington MOR, 27
Mordecai, Henry MOR, 11, 12, 27
Mordecai, Marg Cameron MOR, 27
Mordecai, Martha Hinton MOR, 11
Mordecai, Moses MOR, 13, 27
Morson, Hugh WES, 76
Olds. Frederick Augustus PES, 105
O'Quinn, Jesse Lee BEE, 66
Park, John Alsey EAS, 106
Partridge, Sophia HECK, 10
Patton, Frances Gray CHR, 90
Pearson, Richmond Mumford PES, 108
Peele, William Joseph BEE, 70
Pfeiffer, Jacob CON, 16
Pittenger, Isaac McKendree BEE, 114
Polk, Leonidas Lafayette POLK, 70
Pou, James Hinton MAG, 66
Privette, Lori Anne VET, 45
Procter, Madeline Jane Jones TUC, 98
Pullen, Richard Stanhope PUL, 24
Purser, Charles Everett Jr. AND, 20
Ragsdale, George Young BEE, 69
Raleigh Cemetery Association (RCA), 21, 23, 118
Raney, Kate Whiting Denson MAG, 83
Raney, Olivia Blount Cowper MOR, 83
Raney, Richard Beverly MAG, 83
Receiving Vault POLK, 117
Royster, Arkansas Delaware BRI, 36
Royster, Iowa Michigan BRI, 36
Royster, Vermont Connecticut AND, 93
Shepherd, Sylvester Brown AND, 109
Shotwell, Randolph CON, 35
Silver, Henry Sprague TUC, 40
Skinner, John Ludlow POLK, 84
Smedes, Aldert BAT, 74
Smedes, Bennett BAT, 74
Smith, Gilbert Graves HILN, 115
Smith, Jacob Brinton BAT, 73
Smith, Willis SECA, 56
Swain, David Lowry JOH, 68, 81
Swepson, George William MAG, 30
Tarlton, William Samuel CEH, 107
Taylor, John Louis PES, 57
Upshaw, Berrien Kinnard SECA, 86
Valvano, James Thomas CED, 72
Vass, William Worrell HECK, 29
Walsh, "Lieutenant" CON, 14
Ward, William Charles BAT, 92
Watson, Thomas Harry BEE, 40
White, William McClanahan BEE, 65
Wilkerson, Annie Louise MAG, 101
Williams, Miriam C. White HECK, 62
Williamson, William Holt BEE, 63, 111
Winston, Robert Watson BEE, 104
Wise, Andrew J. CON, 19
Woodruff, Carle Augustus MAG, 38
Worth, Jonathan CHR, 47
Wynne, William Andrew PUL, 97

Consistent with our mission to preserve history on a local level, this book was printed in South Carolina on American-made paper and manufactured entirely in the United States. Products carrying the accredited Forest Stewardship Council (FSC) label are printed on 100 percent FSC-certified paper.

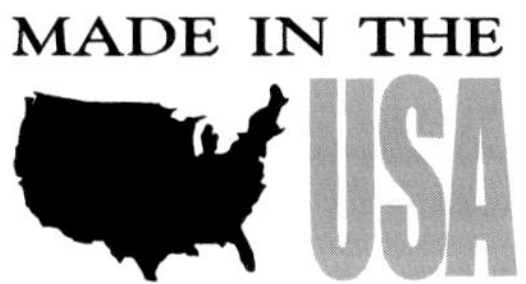